LATTER-DAY
PROPHETS
☆ ☆ AND THE ☆ ☆
UNITED STATES
CONSTITUTION

RELIGIOUS STUDIES CENTER PUBLICATIONS

BOOK OF MORMON SYMPOSIUM SERIES

The Book of Mormon: The
Keystone Scripture
The Book of Mormon: First
Nephi, the Doctrinal
Foundation

The Book of Mormon: Second
Nephi, the Doctrinal Structure
The Book of Mormon: Jacob
Through Words of Mormon,
To Learn with Joy

MONOGRAPH SERIES

Nibley on the Timely and the
Timeless
Deity and Death
The Glory of God Is
Intelligence
Reflections on Mormonism
Literature of Belief
The Words of Joseph Smith
Book of Mormon Authorship
Mormons and Muslims
The Temple in Antiquity

Isaiah and the Prophets
Scriptures for the Modern World
The Joseph Smith Translation:
The Restoration of Plain and
Precious Things
Apocryphal Writings and the
Latter-day Saints
The Pearl of Great Price:
Revelations From God
The Lectures on Faith in
Historical Perspective

SPECIALIZED MONOGRAPH SERIES

Supporting Saints: Life Stories
of Nineteenth-Century
Mormons
The Call of Zion: The Story of
the First Welsh Mormon
Emigration
The Religion and Family
Connection: Social Science
Perspectives

Welsh Mormon Writings
from 1844 to 1862: A
Historical Bibliography
Peter and the Popes
John Lyon: The Life of a
Pioneer Poet
Latter-day Prophets
and the United States
Constitution

OCCASIONAL PAPERS SERIES

Excavations at Seila, Egypt

LATTER-DAY PROPHETS
☆ ☆ AND THE ☆ ☆
UNITED STATES
CONSTITUTION

Edited with an Introduction by
DONALD Q. CANNON

Volume Seven
in the Religious Studies Center
Specialized Monograph Series

Religious Studies Center
Brigham Young University
Provo, Utah

Copyright © 1991 by
Religious Studies Center
Brigham Young University

Library of Congress Catalog Card Number: 90-63820

ISBN 0-88494-783-1

First Printing, 1991

Distributed by BOOKCRAFT, INC.
Salt Lake City, Utah

Printed in the United States of America

Contents

Abbreviations of Titles Cited

CF	Ezra Taft Benson, *Cross Fire: The Eight Years with Eisenhower*
CHB	Ezra Taft Benson, *The Constitution: A Heavenly Banner*
CR	*Conference Report*
Enemy	Ezra Taft Benson, *An Enemy Hath Done This*
GFC	Ezra Taft Benson, *God, Family, Country: Our Three Great Loyalties*
HC	*History of the Church*
JD	*Journal of Discourses*
JH	*Journal History of the Church*
JT Papers	Samuel W. Taylor and Raymond W. Taylor, *The John Taylor Papers: Records of the Last Utah Pioneer*
LJT	B. H. Roberts, *The Life of John Taylor*
MFP	James R. Clark, *Messages of the First Presidency of The Church of Jesus Christ of Latter-day Saints*
PWJS	*The Personal Writings of Joseph Smith*
RC	Ezra Taft Benson, *The Red Carpet*
TETB	*The Teachings of Ezra Taft Benson*
TL	Ezra Taft Benson, *Title of Liberty*
TPJS	*Teachings of the Prophet Joseph Smith*
TSWK	*Teachings of Spencer W. Kimball*
WJS	*The Words of Joseph Smith*
WW	*Wilford Woodruff's Journal*

Introduction

In his opening address at the 157th semiannual general conference of The Church of Jesus Christ of Latter-day Saints, President Ezra Taft Benson spoke about the U.S. Constitution. In the course of his remarks that Saturday morning, October 3, 1987, President Benson asked this important question: "Do we know what the prophets have said about the Constitution and the threats to it?" ("Our Divine Constitution" 7).

I knew that President Benson had talked hundreds of times about the Constitution and that he had a strong interest in that inspired document, having read many of his books and statements. However, nothing he had said before had such an impact on my mind as that brief question asked in general conference. It struck me that I didn't know all the things the latter-day prophets have said about the U.S. Constitution and that probably very few others did. So I decided to find out what they have said about it.

With my research assistant, Duane Knowles, I began a systematic search of what the prophets and Presidents of the Church in this dispensation have said specifically about the U.S. Constitution. We found that they had said a lot about it, and in several months we had quite a large selection of quotations from the thirteen men who have presided over the Church since it was organized in 1830.

At first, we thought to organize the quotations according to topic so we could see what all the prophets had said on a specific topic. But when we looked at the manuscript following the topical format, we saw that we had split the different prophets up and so scattered their ideas throughout the book that without a photographic memory we could not really see what each individual prophet's ideas had been or how those ideas had developed in his lifetime.

It was suggested that presenting all the statements made by each prophet about the U. S. Constitution in the chronological order of his making them would not only show the development of his ideas, but also how his ideas and emphases fit into U.S. history. Then we could place the topics we had thought to include in our original organizational scheme in a topical index. This way our readers would have access to the topics the prophets had spoken on, the historical development of each prophet's ideas, and each prophet's relationship with the U.S. government and Constitution.

Consequently, this book is divided into thirteen chapters, one for each prophet of this dispensation. Each chapter begins with a photograph of the prophet followed by a brief biographical sketch of his life and a statement about his relationship with the U.S. government. This is then followed by his statements about the U.S. Constitution, listed in chronological order. We have also noted which statements each man made first as an Apostle and then as the prophet. The quotes are also numbered for ease of reference.

We have listed the source for each quotation in a parenthetical reference following the quotation. When we found quotations that appeared in more than one source, we listed most or all of these sources, with the original source listed first. Knowing that many of these original sources would not be readily available to most readers, we have checked the accuracy of each quotation against what we believed to be the most accessible rather than the original source. When we could not locate the original source we listed whatever information we had in the parenthetical reference to give readers the context of the original quotation. All of the sources are listed in full in the bibliography. As we have not used every quotation made by the prophets on the U.S. Constitution, we hope that readers will use this bibliography to pursue their own individual study of the latter-day prophets and the U.S. Constitution.

The topical index incorporates not only the fifteen topics from the first organizational scheme, but many additional topics as well. Some of these topics provide information which has not been readily available. An example of this kind of material is the topic identified as "Hanging by a Thread." The idea that the Constitution would one day hang by a thread, first put forth by

Joseph Smith, is one of the most interesting and controversial subjects related to LDS teachings about the U.S. Constitution. Although frequently quoted, it has been subject to careful scrutiny and even skepticism.

As late as 1948, articles have appeared which state that there was no direct evidence that Joseph Smith had even made such a statement (Nibley 24). In recent years we have been able to verify that Joseph Smith did, indeed, make such a statement. New compilations of original documents from the Joseph Smith period, such as *The Words of Joseph Smith* and *The Papers of Joseph Smith*, have made such evidence readily available.

Our study shows that eight modern prophets have made statements about the Constitution's hanging by a thread, and that all eight of them quoted Joseph Smith as well as adding ideas of their own. However, Joseph Smith and the other twelve prophets of this dispensation have all said that at some time in the future the Constitution would be in jeopardy, and it would be rescued by the Elders of Israel. This book should help us understand this subject more fully.

Although we collected many of each President's quotations on the Constitution, we have not been able to include all of them here. Instead, we have used a selection process to eliminate peripheral, extraneous, and repetitious quotations.

An example of the selection process is included here, using Brigham Young as an example. The following quotation was not included in the book because it refers to the Constitution only in passing rather than makes a pointed statement about it:

> What law have we transgressed? I have tried to find out. We have examined the Constitution of the United States and the laws pertaining to these matters; and if anybody here or elsewhere can point out any law that we have transgressed as American citizens, they know more about it than I have been able to learn; and I should like such a person to put me in possession of the information. (*JD* 6:2)

The following quotation was included because it does make a specific statement about the Constitution and the views of the President of the Church concerning it:

> We are in the midst of these mountains, and we have good and salutary laws to govern us. We have our Constitutional laws and our

Territorial laws; we are subject to these laws; and always expect to be, for we love to be. If there is any man among us who has violated any constitutional law, try the law upon him, and let us see whether there is any virtue in it, before we try the strong arm of despotism and tyranny. I stand for Constitutional law, and if any transgress, let them be tried by it, and, if guilty, suffer its penalty. (*JD* 10:109)

We have also included a number of quotations that do not mention the Constitution specifically, but which refer to the Founding Fathers and other topics closely related to the Constitution. Even though we have used a selection process, a large majority of the quotations from each President of the Church do appear in this book.

It is our hope that the teachings of LDS Church Presidents concerning the Constitution will be helpful and meaningful to all who read them. Perhaps, in a small way, these readers can become sufficiently informed about the Constitution to warrant the approval of the Church Presidents whose ideas they are studying. Hopefully our readers will increase in both knowledge and appreciation of the Constitution of the United States.

Several people have assisted me in making this book a reality. My research assistant, Duane Knowles, did the major research and should be recognized for his excellent work. My secretary, Janiel A. Lind, has spent time examining the quotations, working with the manuscript, and has been most helpful in other ways. The Religious Studies Center Publications Office has been a tremendous help: Charles D. Tate, Jr., Charlotte A. Pollard, Rebecca H. Christensen, and Brian Osmond Call have contributed much to the success of the project. Several of my colleagues have taken time to read the manuscript and to offer suggestions. Reed A. Benson has been especially willing to assist in this work. Finally, President Ezra Taft Benson should be acknowledged for his inspiration and direction.

Donald Q. Cannon

Joseph Smith   1

Biographical Information

Born: 23 December 1805
Ordained an Apostle: May – June 1829
First Elder: 6 April 1830
President of the Church: 25 January 1832 – 27 June 1844
Murdered by a Mob: 27 June 1844

* * * * * * * * *

Relationship with the Constitution and U.S. Government

Joseph Smith had a very positive relationship with the U.S. Constitution, having inherited a strong love for it from his patriotic ancestors. The Prophet's relationship with the U.S. Government, however, was not a positive one. Joseph Smith and the Saints he led had serious problems and conflicts with several state governments and with the federal government. These conflicts developed from persecution which arose against the Saints, most heavily in Missouri.

The Saints believed their constitutional rights had been violated because they had been deprived of their right to worship as they believed. The Constitution gave them these rights, but the government failed to enforce the provisions of the Constitution.

In an effort to plead this case, Joseph Smith and others traveled to Washington, D.C. in 1839, carrying with them petitions from the Saints outlining their losses and grievances. Although they met with several government leaders, their pleas for redress and help fell on deaf ears, as when President Martin Van Buren told them, "Gentlemen, your cause is just, but I can do nothing for you" (TPJS 302, compare 327).

Themes Discussed in the Quotations

Main theme: The Constitution assures rights.
Minor themes:
  1. The Constitution will hang by a thread.
  2. All should obey the law of the land.
  3. What the Constitution is and how it operates.

Quotations

As the President of the Church

1.1. Let no man break the laws of the land, for he that keepeth the laws of God hath no need to break the laws of the land. (D&C 58:21)

1.2. And that law of the land which is constitutional, supporting that principle of freedom in maintaining rights and privileges, belongs to all mankind, and is justifiable before me. Therefore, I, the Lord, justify you, and your brethren of my church, in befriending that law which is the constitutional law of the land. (D&C 98:5-6)

1.3. We think it would be wise in you to try to git [*sic*] influence by offering to print a paper in favor of the government as you know we are all friends to the Constitution yea true friends to that Country for which our fathers bled. (*PWJS* 287)

1.4. And again I say unto you, those who have been scattered by their enemies, it is my will that they should continue to importune for redress, and redemption, by the hands of those who are placed as rulers and are in authority over you—
  According to the laws and constitution of the people, which I [the Lord] have suffered to be established, and should be

maintained for the rights and protection of all flesh, according to just and holy principles. (D&C 101:76-77)

1.5. Have mercy, O Lord, upon all the nations of the earth; have mercy upon the rulers of our land; may those principles, which were so honorably and nobly defended, namely, the Constitution of our land, by our fathers, be established forever. (D&C 109:54)

1.6. Be wise; let prudence dictate all your counsels; preserve peace with all men, if possible; stand by the Constitution of your country; observe its principles; and above all, show yourselves men of God, worthy citizens. (*MFP* 1:74-75)

1.7. While other men were peacefully following their vocations and extending their interests they [the Saints in Clay County] have been deprived of the right of citizenship, prevented from enjoying their own, charged with violating the sacred principles of our Constitution and laws. (*MFP* 1:78)

1.8. By their complying with your request to leave they [the Saints in Clay County] are surrendering some of the dearest rights guaranteed in the Constitution of our country; and that human nature can be driven to a certain extent when it will yield no further. (*MFP* 1:80)

1.9. The Constitution of our country [was] formed by the Fathers of liberty. . . . Exalt the standard of Democracy! Down with that of priestcraft, and let all the people say Amen! that the blood of our fathers may not cry from the ground against us. Sacred is the memory of that blood which bought for us our liberty. (*HC 3:9*)

1.10. Blessed be the memory of those few brethren who contended so strenuously for their constitutional rights and religious freedom, against such an overwhelming force of desperadoes! (*HC* 3:59)

1.11. Having an opportunity of speaking to General Wilson, I inquired of him why I was thus treated. I told him I was not aware of having done anything worthy of such treatment; that I had always been a supporter of the Constitution and of democracy. His answer was, "I know it, and that is the reason why I want to kill you, or have you killed." (*HC* 3:191)

1.12. Where has the genius of the pedistal [*sic*] of the laws and constitution of our boasted country fled? (*PWJS* 419)

1.13. Hence we say, that the Constitution of the United States is a glorious standard; it is founded in the wisdom of God. It is a heavenly banner; it is to all those who are privileged with the sweets of liberty, like the cooling shades and refreshing waters of a great rock in a thirsty and weary land. It is like a great tree under whose branches men from every clime can be shielded from the burning rays of the sun. . . .

We say that God is true; that the Constitution of the United States is true; that the Bible is true. (*TPJS* 147-48)

1.14. I ask the citizens of this Republic whether such a state of things is to be suffered to pass unnoticed, and the hearts of widows, orphans, and patriots to be broken, and their wrongs left without redress? No! I invoke the genius of our Constitution. I appeal to the patriotism of Americans to stop this unlawful and unholy procedure; and pray that God may defend this nation from the dreadful effects of such outrages. (*HC* 3:332)

1.15. Your constitution guarantees to every citizen, even the humblest, the enjoyment of life, liberty, and property. It promises to all, religious freedom, the right to all to worship God beneath their own vine and fig tree, according to the dictates of their conscience. It guarantees to all the citizens of the several states the right to become citizens of any one of the states, and to enjoy all the rights and immunities of the citizens of the state of his adoption. (*HC* 4:37)

1.16. Even this Nation will be on the very verge of crumbling to peices [*sic*] and tumbling to the ground and when the constitution is upon the brink of ruin this people will be the Staff up[on] which the Nation shall lean and they shall bear the constitution away from the very verge of destruction. (*WJS* 416)

1.17. This people will be the staff upon which the nation shall lean and they shall bear the Constitution away from the very verge of destruction.—Then shall the Lord say: Go tell my servants who are the strength of mine house, my young men and middle-aged, etc., Come to the land of my vineyard and fight the battle of the Lord. Then the Kings and Queens shall come, yea the foreign saints shall come to fight for the land of my vineyard, for in this thing shall be their safety and they will have no power to choose but will come as a man fleeth from a sudden destruction. I know these things by the visions of the Almighty. (Joseph Smith Collection; from an address given 19 Jul 1840)

1.18. The Mayor, Aldermen and Councilors [of the City of Nauvoo, IL], before entering upon the duties of their office, shall take and subscribe an oath or affirmation that they will support the Constitution of the United States, and of this State and that they will well and truly perform the duties of their offices to the best of their skill and abilities. (*HC* 4:240)

1.19. We may continue to expect the enjoyment of all the blessings of civil and religious liberty, guaranteed by the Constitution. The citizens of Illinois have done themselves honor, in throwing the mantle of the Constitution over a persecuted and afflicted people. (*TPJS* 185)

1.20. I am tired of the misrepresentation, calumny and detraction, heaped upon me by wicked men; and desire and claim, only those principles guaranteed to all men by the Constitution and laws of the United States and of Illinois. (*HC* 5:15)

1.21. The Constitution is not a law, but it empowers the people to make laws. . . . The Constitution tells us what shall not be a lawful tender. . . . The legislature has ceded up to us the privilege of enacting such laws as are not inconsistent with the Constitution of the United States. . . . The different states, and even Congress itself, have passed many laws diametrically contrary to the Constitution of the United States.

... Shall we be such fools as to be governed by its laws, which are unconstitutional? No! ... The Constitution acknowledges that the people have all power not reserved to itself. I am a lawyer; I am a big lawyer and comprehend heaven, earth and hell, to bring forth knowledge that shall cover up all lawyers, doctors and other big bodies. This is the doctrine of the Constitution, so help me God. The Constitution is not law to us, but it makes provision for us whereby we can make laws. Where it provides that no one shall be hindered from worshipping God according to his own conscience, is a law. No legislature can enact a law to prohibit it. The Constitution provides to regulate bodies of men and not individuals. (*HC* 5:289-90; also in *TPJS* 278)

1.22. In the month of May 1843. Several miles east of Nauvoo. The Nauvoo Legion was on parade and review. At the close of which Joseph Smith made some remarks upon our condition as a people and upon our future prospects contrasting our present condition with our past trials and persecutions by the hands of our enemies. Also upon the constitution and government of the United States stating that the time would come when the Constitution and Government would hand [*sic*] by a brittle thread and would be ready to fall into other hands but this people the Latter-day Saints will step forth and save it.

General Scott and part of his staff on the American Army was [*sic*] present on the occasion.

I James Burgess was present and testify to the above. (*WJS* 279; from James Burgess Notebook, LDS Church Archives)

1.23. I prophesy in the name of the Lord God of Israel, unless the United States redress the wrongs committed upon the Saints in the state of Missouri and punish the crimes committed by her officers that in a few years the government will be utterly overthrown and wasted, and there will not be so much as a potsherd left, for their wickedness in permitting the murder of men, women and children, and the wholesale plunder and extermination of thousands of her citizens to go unpunished, thereby perpetrating a foul and corroding blot upon the fair fame of this great republic, the very thought of which would have caused the high-minded and patriotic framers of the Constitution of the United States to hide their faces with shame. (*TPJS* 302-03)

1.24. I want you to hear and learn, O Israel, this day, what is for the happiness and peace of this city and people. If our enemies are determined to oppress us and deprive us of our constitutional rights and privileges as they have done, and if the authorities that are on the earth will not sustain us in our rights, nor give us that protection which the laws and constitution of the United States and of this state guarantee unto us, then we will claim them from a higher power—from heaven—yea, from God Almighty. (*Discourses Delivered by Presidents Joseph Smith and Brigham Young* 1; also in *HC* 5:466; *WJS* 217)

1.25. If we have to give up our chartered rights, privileges, and freedom, which our fathers fought, bled, and died for, and which the constitution of the United States and of this state guarantee unto us, we will do it only at the point of the sword and bayonet. (*Discourses Delivered by Presidents Joseph Smith and Brigham Young* 4; also in *HC* 5:468; *WJS* 218-19)

1.26. We have not enjoyed unmolested those rights which the constitution of the U.S.A. and our Charters grant. (*Discourses Delivered by Presidents Joseph Smith and Brigham Young* 4; also in *HC* 5:469; *WJS* 219)

1.27. Shall we longer bear these cruelties which have been heaped upon us for the last ten years in the face of heaven, and in open violation of the constitution and law of these United States and of this state? God forbid! I will not bear it. If they take away my rights, I will fight for them manfully and righteously until I am used up. We have done nothing against the rights of others. (*Discourses Delivered by Presidents Joseph Smith and Brigham Young* 5; also in *HC* 5:471; *WJS* 220)

1.28. The benefits of the constitution and laws are alike for all; and the great Eloheim has given me the privilege of having the benefits of the constitution and the writ of habeas corpus. *(Discourses Delivered by Presidents Joseph Smith and Brigham Young* 5; also in *HC* 5:471; *WJS* 221)

1.29. [Governor Ford] is sworn to support the Constitution of the United States and also of this State [Illinois], and these constitutions guarantee religious as well as civil liberty to all religious societies whatever. *(TPJS* 317)

1.30. I am the greatest advocate of the Constitution of the United States there is on the earth. In my feelings I am always ready to die for the protection of the weak and oppressed in their just rights. The only fault I find with the Constitution is, it is not broad enough to cover the whole ground.

Although it provides that all men shall enjoy religious freedom, yet it does not provide the manner by which that freedom can be preserved, nor for the punishment of Government officers who refuse to protect the people in their religious rights, or punish those mobs, states, or communities who interfere with the rights of the people on account of their religion. Its sentiments are good, but it provides no means of enforcing them. It has but this one fault. Under its provision, a man or a people who are able to protect themselves can get along well enough; but those who have the misfortune to be weak or unpopular are left to the merciless rage of popular fury.

The Constitution should contain a provision that every officer of the Government who should neglect or refuse to extend the protection guaranteed in the Constitution should be subject to capital punishment; and then the president of the United States would not say, "Your cause is just, but I can do nothing for you." (*HC* 6:56-57; also in *TPJS* 326-27)

1.31. We believe in enjoying the constitutional privilege and right of worshiping Almighty God according to the dictates of our own consciences. (*HC* 6:92)

1.32. I would admonish you, . . . to read in the 8th section and 1st article of the Constitution of the United States, the *first*, *fourteenth* and *seventeenth* "specific" and not very "limited powers" of the Federal Government, what can be done to protect the lives, property, and rights of a virtuous people, when the administrators of the law and law-makers are unbought by bribes. . . . And God, who cooled the heat of a Nebuchadnezzar's furnace or shut the mouths of lions for the honor of a Daniel, will raise your mind above the narrow notion that the General Government has no power, to the sublime idea that Congress, with the President as Executor, is as almighty in its sphere as Jehovah is in his. (*HC* 6:160)

1.33. The Constitution, when it says, "We, the people of the United States, in order to form a more perfect union, establish justice, ensure domestic tranquility, provide for the common defense, promote the general welfare, and secure the blessings of liberty to ourselves and our posterity, do ordain and establish this Constitution for the United States of America," meant just what it said without reference to color or condition, *ad infinitum*. (*HC* 6:198)

1.34. The aspirations and expectations of a virtuous people, environed with so wise, so liberal, so deep, so broad, and so high a charter of *equal rights* as appears in said Constitution, ought to be treated by those to whom the administration of the laws is entrusted with as much sanctity as the prayers of the Saints are treated in heaven, that love, confidence, and union, like the sun, moon, and stars, should bear witness,

"For ever singing as they shine,
The hand that made us is Divine!" . . .

I will adopt in part the language of Mr. Madison's inaugural address: ". . . to hold the union of the States as the basis of their peace and happiness; to support the Constitution, which is the cement of the Union, as well in its limitations as in its authorities." (*Powers and Policy of the Government* 6, 10-11; also in *HC* 6:198, 201)

1.35. I would not have suffered my name to have been used by my friends on anywise as President of the United States, or candidate for that office, if I and my friends could have had the privilege of enjoying our religious and civil rights as American citizens, even those rights which the Constitution guarantees unto all her citizens alike. (*HC* 6:210)

1.36. If I lose my life in a good cause I am willing to be sacrificed on the altar of virtue, righteousness and truth, in maintaining the laws and Constitution of the United States, if need be, for the general good of mankind. (*HC* 6:211; also in *TPJS* 332; *WJS* 320)

1.37. The constitution expects every man to do his duty; and when he fails the law urges him; or should he do too much, the same master rebukes him. (*HC* 6:220)

1.38. Joseph commenced the organization of a Council for the purpose of taking into consideration the necessary steps to obtain redress for the wrongs which had been inflicted upon us by our persecutors, and also the best manner to settle our people in some distant and unoccupied territory; where we could enjoy our civil and religious rights, without being subject to constant oppression and mobocracy, under the protection of our own laws, subject to the Constitution. (Young, "History of Brigham Young" 328)

1.39. *To the Honorable the Senate and House of Representatives of the United States of America, in Congress Assembled*:
    Your memorialist, a free-born citizen of these United States, respectfully showeth that from his infancy his soul has been filled with the most intense and philanthropic interest for the welfare of his native country; and being fired with an ardor which floods cannot quench, crowns cannot conquer, nor diplomatic intrigue corrupt, to see those principles which emanated from the bosoms of the fathers of seventy-six, and which cost the noblest talents and richest blood of the nation, maintained inviolate and perpetuated to future generations; and the proud eagle of American freedom soar triumphant over every party prejudice and local

sinistry, and spread her golden pinions over every member of the human family, who shall stretch forth their hands for succor from the lion's paw or the oppressor's grasp; and firmly trusting in the God of liberty, that He has designed universal peace and good-will, union, and brotherly love to all the great family of man, your memorialist asks your honorable body to pass the following . . . Ordinance for the Protection of the Citizens of the United States Emigrating to the Territories, and for the Extension of the Principles of Universal Liberty. (*HC* 6:275)

1.40. Joseph Smith has offered and does hereby offer these United States, to show his loyalty to our Confederate Union and the Constitution of our Republic. (*HC* 6:276)

1.41. Judge Thomas has been here and given his advice in the case, which I shall strictly follow until I hear from your Excellency, and in all cases shall adhere to the Constitution and laws. (*HC* 6:480)

1.42. We have never violated the laws of our country. (*HC* 6:498)

1.43. Come, all ye lovers of liberty, break the oppressor's rod, loose the iron grasp of mobocracy, and bring to condign punishment all those who trample under foot the glorious Constitution and the people's rights. (*HC* 6:499)

1.44. Genl. J. Smith . . . briefly explained the object of the mob and showed that they waged a war of extermination upon us because of our religion. He called upon all the volunteers who felt to support the constitution from the Rocky Mountains to the Atlantic Ocean to come with their arms, ammunition & defend the constitution. (*WJS* 383-84)

1.45. We have ever held ourselves amenable to the law. . . . I am ever ready to conform to and support the laws and Constitution, even at the expense of my life. I have never in the least offered any resistance to law or lawful process, which is a well-known fact to the general public. (*HC* 6:526)

1.46. We have never gone contrary to constitutional law, so far as we have been able to learn it. (*HC* 6:539)

1.47. If there is trouble in the country, neither I nor my people made it, and all that we have ever done, after much endurance on our part, is to maintain and uphold the constitution and institutions of our country, and to protect an injured, innocent, and persecuted people against misrule and mob violence. (*TPJS* 385-86)

1.48. Will the Constitution be destroyed? No: it will be held inviolate by this people; and, as Joseph Smith said, "The time will come when the destiny of the nation will hang upon a single thread. At that critical juncture, this people will step forth and save it from the threatened destruction." It will be so. (*JD* 7:15; quoted by Brigham Young)

1.49. We are friendly to our country, and when we speak of the flag of our Union, we love it, and we love the rights the Constitution guarantees to every citizen. What did the Prophet Joseph say? When the Constitution shall be tottering we shall be the people to save it from the hand of the foe. (Tyler 350; quoted by Jedediah M. Grant)

1.50. It is said that brother Joseph in his lifetime declared that the Elders of this Church should step forth at a particular time when the Constitution should be in danger, and rescue it, and save it. This may be so; but I do not recollect that he said exactly so. I believe he [Joseph] said something like this—that the time would come when the Constitution and the country would be in danger of an overthrow; and said he, If the Constitution be saved at all, it will be by the Elders of this Church. I believe this is about the language, as nearly as I can recollect it. (*JD* 6:152; quoted by Orson Hyde)

1.51. My sisters, My remarks in conclusion will be brief. I heard the prophet Joseph Smith say if the people rose up and mobbed us and the authorities countenanced it, they would have mobs to their hearts' content. I heard him say that the time would come when this nation would so far depart from its original purity, its glory, and its love for freedom and its protection of civil rights and religious rights, that the Constitution of our country would hang as it were by a thread. He said, also, that this people, the sons of Zion, would rise up and save the Constitution and bear it off triumphantly. (Snow, Eliza R. 556)

1.52. And then you would have *"further truths from the teachings of the Prophet* [Joseph Smith]." . . . And he taught us relating to the Kingdom of God, as it would become organized upon the earth through "all nations learning war no more," and all adopting the God-given constitution of the United States as a Paladium [*sic*] of Liberty and Equal Rights. (Johnson 5-6)

Brigham Young 2

Biographical Information

Born: 1 June 1801
Ordained an Apostle: 14 February 1835
President of the Twelve: 14 April 1840
President of the Church: 27 December 1847 – 29 August 1877
Died: 29 August 1877

* * * * * * * * *

Relationship with the Constitution and U.S. Government

As a fellow New Englander, Brigham Young shared Joseph Smith's reverence for the Constitution. He also experienced the same kind of conflict with the government. During his administration he faced conflicts on two fronts:
1. The issue of statehood
2. The principle of polygamy
As Governor of the Utah Territory, Brigham Young pushed for the admission of Utah as a state, sending dozens of representatives to the nation's capitol to urge that action. These many attempts were frustrated, largely because of polygamy. The practice of plural marriage brought first heavy persecution and then legislation against the Saints.

Themes Discussed in the Quotations

Main theme: The laws created under the Constitution are good, but they are frequently violated by our lawmakers.

Minor themes:
  1. The Constitution should be altered.
  2. The government should be sustained.

Quotations

As an Apostle

2.1. Our fathers, nay some of us, have fought and bled for our country, and we love her Constitution dearly. (*HC* 7:403)

2.2. I find no fault with the Constitution or laws of our country, they are good enough. It is the abuse of those laws which I despise, and which God, good men and angels abhor. (*HC* 7:573)

2.3. Pres Young met with Col. Kane in Elder Woodruff's carriage and conversed about the state of the nations. The President told Col. Kane the time would come when the Saints would support the government of the U. S. or it would crumble to atoms. (*JH* [13 Jul 1846] 1)

2.4. Council adjourned at twenty eight minutes after ten a.m. to G D Grant's tent, i.e. the Twelve, Bishop Newell K. Whitney, John D Lee and Col Thomas L. Kane who wished to know the intentions of the brethren.
     President Young informed the Col. they intended settling in the great Basin or Bear River Valley, and those who went round by water would settle at San Francisco. They would be glad to raise the American flag, said the President: "We love the Constitution of our country, but are opposed to mobocracy; and will not live under such oppression as we have done. We are willing to have the banner of the U.S. constitution float over us. If the government of the U.S. is disposed to do us good; we can do them as much good as they can us." (*JH* [7 Aug 1846] 2)

As the President of the Church

2.5. There never was a better constitution on the face of the earth than the constitution of the United States. There is nothing but the people of God could enjoy under it. But the Federal constitution is trodden under foot. All that I am afraid of is that the Elders of Israel will forget their God. (*JH* [8 Jul 1849] 3)

2.6. I arose and spoke substantially as follows: . . . I love the government and the constitution of the United States, but I do not love the damned rascals who administer the government. (*JH* [8 Sep 1851] 3-4)

2.7. Sustain the government of the nation wherever you are, and speak well of it, for this is right, and the government has a right to expect it of you, so long as that government sustains you in your civil and religious liberty, in those rights which inherently belong to every person born on the earth and if you are persecuted in your native land, and denied the privilege of worshipping the true God in spirit and in truth, flee to the land of Zion, to America—to the United States, where constitutional rights and freedoms are not surpassed by any nation—where God saw fit, in these last days, to renew the dispensation of salvation, by revelations from the heavens, and where all, by the constitution and laws of the land, when executed in righteousness, are protected in all the civil and religious freedom that man is capable of enjoying on earth; and our national institutions will never fail, unless it be through the wickedness of the people, and the designs of evil men in brief authority; for those rights were ordained of God on this land, for the establishment of the principles of truth on the earth; and our national organization originated in the heavens. (*MFP* 2:98)

2.8. The revolutions made by the Government of the United States, with regard to real progression generally, are small indeed; so small that it is impossible to perceive any advancement. It is true the Constitution has been revised by the voice of the people; but wherein is it bettered? Some say it is bettered; but as to the light and knowledge that now exist with regard to the true spirit of republicanism, the revolution is on the retrograde motion. No one will question for a moment that many revolutions in the United States have become in a great degree popular, notwithstanding they have been in many instances unconstitutional and in open violation of the statute laws, and have been winked at by the most influential officers of the Government. (*JD* 7:9)

2.9. Let us look at it in another point of view. Suppose this people inhabiting these mountains are broken off entirely from the nations of the world, rendering no allegiance to any earthly power combined or isolated; free to make laws, to obey them, or to break them; free to act, to choose, and to refuse, and, in every sense of the word, to do as they please, without any fixed order of government whatever; and they wish a Constitution—a system of government for mutual protection and advancement in the principles of right, to be framed according to the best wisdom that can be found in this community;—I say, let them govern themselves by a Republican system of government, selecting a man from their midst to preside over them. And whom should they select to fill so important a station? The best man they can find. Should they keep him in office only four years? Should they make a clause in their Constitution that a President shall serve at most for only two terms without a vacation in his services? That is an item that should not be found in the Constitution of the United States, nor in the constitution made by this or any other people. We should select the best man we could find, and centre our feelings upon him, and sustain him as our President, dictator, lawgiver, controller, and guide in a national capacity, and in every other capacity wherein he is a righteous example. Though we find as good a man as there is in the nation, yet we should not lay facilities before him to become evil, were he so disposed. Great care should be exercised to guard against placing such a power at the command of any mortal. (*JD* 7:11)

2.10. It is yet in the power of the people of the United States to lay a foundation to redeem themselves from the growing consequences of past errors. What would be the result, were the United

States to take this course—viz., to strike out that clause in the Constitution that limits the services of a President to four years, or the term of service of any good man, and continue to revise the Constitution and laws as they become familiar with their defects; then reduce the salaries of all officers in all the departments? . . .

The General Constitution of our country is good, and a wholesome government could be framed upon it, for it was dictated by the invisible operations of the Almighty; he moved upon Columbus to launch forth upon the trackless deep to discover the American Continent; he moved upon the signers of the Declaration of Independence; and he moved upon Washington to fight and conquer, in the same way as he moved upon ancient and modern Prophets, each being inspired to accomplish the particular work he was called to perform in the times, seasons, and dispensations of the Almighty. God's purpose, in raising up these men and inspiring them with daring sufficient to surmount every opposing power, was to prepare the way for the formation of a true Republican government. They laid its foundation; but when others came to build upon it, they reared a superstructure far short of their privileges, if they had walked uprightly as they should have done. (*JD* 7:13)

2.11. Can the Constitution be altered? It can; and when we get a President that answers our wishes to occupy the executive chair, there let him sit to the day of his death, and pray that he may live as long as Methuselah; and, whenever we have good officers, strive to retain them, and to fill up vacancies with good men, until there are none who would let the nation sink for a can of oysters and a lewd woman.

The signers of the Declaration of Independence and the framers of the Constitution were inspired from on high to do that work. But was that which was given to them perfect, not admitting of any addition whatever? No; for if men know anything, they must know that the Almighty has never yet found a man in mortality that was capable, at the first intimation, at the first impulse, to receive anything in a state of entire perfection. They laid the foundation, and it was for after generations to rear the superstructure upon it. It is a progressive—a gradual work. If the framers of the Constitution and the inhabitants of the United States had walked humbly before God, who defended them and fought their battles when Washington was on the stage of action, the nation would now have been free from a multitude of place-hunters who live upon its vitals. The country would not have been overrun with murderers and thieves, and our cities filled with houses of ill-fame, as now; and men could have walked the streets of cities, or travelled on conveyances through the country, without being insulted, plundered, and perhaps murdered; and an honest, sober, industrious, enterprising, and righteous people would now have been found from one end of the United States to the other. (*JD* 7:14)

2.12. The progress of revolution is quite considerable in every government of the world. But is the revolution for the constitutional rights of the people in progress? No: it is on the retrograde. I know how they can be brought back to the people, and the Government be redeemed and become one of the most powerful and best on the earth. It was instituted in the beginning by the Almighty. He operated upon the hearts of the Revolutionary Fathers to rebel against the English King and his Parliament, as he does upon me to preach "Mormonism." Both are inspired by him; but the work unto which they are called is dissimilar. The one was inspired to fight, and the other to preach the peaceable things of the kingdom of God. He operated upon that pusillanimous king to excite the colonists to rebellion; and he is still operating with this nation, and taking away their wisdom, until by-and-by they will get mad and rush to certain destruction.

Will the Constitution be destroyed? No: it will be held inviolate by this people; and, as Joseph Smith said, "The time will come when the destiny of the nation will hang upon a single thread. At that critical juncture, this people will step forth and save it from the threatened destruction." It will be so.

With regard to the doings of our fathers and the Constitution of the United States, I have to say, they present to us a glorious prospect in the future, but one we cannot attain to until the present abuses in the Government are corrected. (*JD* 7:14-15)

2.13. In these secluded vales we gather the Saints that we may enjoy the rights and privileges of the Constitution, denied to us elsewhere; that we may have the privilege of worshipping God according to the dictates of our own consciences. (*MFP* 2:136)

2.14. In this view we consider that the men of the Revolution were inspired by the Almighty, to throw off the shackles of the mother government, with her established religion. For this cause were Adams, Jefferson, Franklin, Washington, and a host of others inspired to deeds of resistance to the acts of the King of Great Britain, who might also have been led to those aggressive acts, for aught we know, to bring to pass the purposes of God in this establishing a new government upon a principle of greater freedom, a basis of self-government allowing the free exercise of religious worship.

It was the voice of the Lord inspiring all those worthy men who bore influence in those trying times, not only to go forth in battle, but to exercise wisdom in council, fortitude, courage, and endurance in the tented field, as well as subsequently to form and adopt those wise and efficient measures which secured to themselves, and suceeding [*sic*] generations, the blessing of a free, and *independent government.* This government, so formed, has been blessed by the Almighty until she spreads her sails in every sea, and her power is felt in every land.

The American Government is second to none in the world in influence, and power, and far before all others in liberal, and free institutions. Under its benign influence the poor, down trodden masses of the old world can find an asylum where they can enjoy the blessings of peace, and freedom, no matter to what caste or religious sect they belong, or are disposed to favor, or whether they are disposed to favor any, or none at all. It was in this government, formed by men inspired of God, although at the time they knew it not, after it was firmly established in the seat of power and influence, where liberty of conscience, and the free exercise of religious worship were a fundamental principle guaranteed in the Constitution, and interwoven with all the feelings, traditions, and sympathies of the people, that the Lord sent forth His angel to reveal the truths of heaven as in times past, even as in ancient days. This should have been hailed as the greatest blessing which could have been bestowed upon any nation, kindred, tongue, or people. It should have been received with hearts of gratitude and gladness, praise and thanksgiving. . . .

. . . No! Whenever the iron hand of oppression, and persecution has fallen upon this people, our opposers have broken their own laws, set at defiance, and trampled under foot every principle of equal rights, justice, and liberty found written in that rich legacy of our fathers, THE CONSTITUTION OF THE UNITED STATES. . . .

. . . And should it not be the duty, as well as the pride, of every American citizen to extend that provision of the CONSTITUTION to us which he claims for himself? And is not that sacred instrument invaded, and broken as much in debarring, and excluding this people from its privileges, rights, and blessings, as it would be if your rights, and privileges were thus invaded? No, gentlemen, we have broken no laws, our Glorious CONSTITUTION guarantees unto us, all that we claim. Under its broad folds, in its obvious meaning, and intents, we are safe, and can always rejoice in peace. All that we have ever claimed, or wish to, on the part of the government, is the just administration of the powers, and privileges of the National Compact. (*Discourses Delivered by Presidents Joseph Smith and Brigham Young* 6-7; also in *JD* 2:170-72)

2.15. To accuse us of being unfriendly to the Government, is to accuse us of hostility to our religion, for no item of inspiration is held more sacred with us than the Constitution under which she acts. As a religious society, we, in common with all other denominations, claim its protection; whether our people are located in the other states or territories, as thousands of them are, or in this territory, it is held as a shield to protect the dearest boon of which man is susceptible—his religious views and sentiments.

. . . She [the government] has calmly looked on and permitted one of the fundamental and dearest provisions of the Constitution to be broken; she has permitted us to be driven and trampled under foot with impunity. Under these circumstances what course is left for us to pursue? I answer that, instead of seeking to destroy the very best government in the world, as seems to be the fears of some, we, like all other good citizens, should seek to place these men in power who will feel the obligations and responsibilities they are under to a mighty people; who would feel, and realize the important trusts reposed in them by the voice of the people who call them to administer law under the solemn sanction of an oath of fidelity to that heaven inspired instrument, to the inviolate preservation of which we look for the perpetuity of our free institutions. (*Discourses Delivered by Presidents Joseph Smith and Brigham Young* 8-9; also in *JD* 2:175)

2.16. It is incumbent upon us to use our influence for the preservation of ourselves, our wives, our children, our brethren, our sisters, and all of our society from the contaminating influence of vice, sin, immorality, and iniquity, let it emanate from where it will. If it exists in high places, so much the more need of rebuking it, for from thence it will do the most harm.

I claim this as a right, as a Constitutional right; I believe it is legal to exercise all the power and influence which God has given me for the preservation of virtue, truth, and holiness; and because we feel sensitive upon points such as these, should it be construed that we are enemies to the Federal Government? . . . In this view of the case the Government should also be our friends. . . .

This then is our position towards the Government of the United States, and towards the world, to put down iniquity, and exalt virtue; to declare the word of God which He revealed unto us, and build up His Kingdom upon the earth. . . . To serve God, and keep His commandments are first and foremost with me. If this is higher law, so be it. As it is with me, so should it be with every department of the Government; for this doctrine is based upon the principles of virtue, and integrity; with it the Government, her Constitution, and free institutions are safe; without it no power can avert their speedy destruction. It is the life giving power to the government; it is the vital element on which she exists and prospers; in its absence she sinks to rise no more.

We now proceed to discuss the question, does our faith and practice,—our holy religion, as we hold and believe it, come within the purview of the Constitution; or in other words, is it a religious question over which the Constitution throws its protecting shield? (*Discourses Delivered by Presidents Joseph Smith and Brigham Young* 9; also in *JD* 2:176)

2.17. Brethren and sisters, our friends wish to know our feelings towards the Government. I answer, they are first-rate, and we will prove it too, as you will see if you only live long enough, for that we shall live to prove it is certain; and when the Constitution of the United States hangs, as it were, upon a single thread, they will have to call for the "Mormon" Elders to save it from utter destruction; and they will step forth and do it.

We love the Constitution of our country; it is all we could ask; though in some few instances there might be some amendments made which would better it. We love the Federal Government, and the laws of Congress. There is nothing in those laws that in the least militates against us, not even to our excluding common law from this Territory. I can inform our lawyers who plead at the bar here, that the congress of the United States [has] passed laws giving us the privilege of excluding common law at our pleasure, and that too without any violation of the Constitution, or general statutes. They have also given us privilege to stop drunkenness, swearing, and gambling, and to prevent horse-racing, and to punish men for hurting and robbing each other. The Constitution of the United States, and the whole Federal Government, in their acts, have given us this privilege. . . .

Corrupt men cannot walk these streets with impunity, and if that is alienism to the Government, amen to it. The Constitution of the United States we sustain all the day long, and it will sustain and shield us, while the men who say we are aliens, and cry out "Mormon disturbance," will go to hell. . . .

But to proceed; the principal evil is in the rulers, or those who profess to be rulers, and in the dispensers of the law, and not the Constitution, it is pure. (*Discourses Delivered by Presidents Joseph Smith and Brigham Young* 12-13; also in *JD* 2:182-84)

2.18. If they wish to send a Governor here, and he is a gentleman, like the one I have referred to, every heart would say "Thank God, we have a man to stand at our head in a gubernatorial capacity; a man who has got a good heart, and is willing that we should enjoy the federal rights of the Constitution as well as himself." I am with all such men, heart and hand. . . .

Have I any feelings against the man who has a true heart for Constitutional rights? I have nothing but love and good feelings for all such. (*Discourses Delivered by Presidents Joseph Smith and Brigham Young* 15; also in *JD* 2:188)

2.19. It was observed this morning that the government of the United States was the best or most wholesome one on the earth, and the best adapted to our condition. That is very true. And if the constitution of the United States, and the laws of the United States, and of the several States, were honored by the officers, by those who sit in judgment and dispense the laws to the people, yes, had even the letter of the law been honored, to say nothing of the spirit of it, of the spirit of right, it would have hung Governors, Judges, Generals, Magistrates, &c., for they violated the laws of their own States. . . .

I say again that the constitution, and laws of the United States, and the laws of the different States, as a general thing, are just as good as we want, provided they were honored. But we find Judges who do not honor the laws, yes, officers of the law dishonor the law. Legislators and law makers are frequently the first violators of the laws they make. "When the wicked rule the people mourn" [D&C 98:9], and when the corruption of a people bears down the scale in favor of wickedness, that people is nigh unto destruction. (*JD* 2:310-11)

2.20. When the day comes in which the Kingdom of God will bear rule, the flag of the United States will proudly flutter unsullied on the flag staff of liberty and equal rights, without a spot to sully its fair surface; the glorious flag our fathers have bequeathed to us will then be unfurled to the breeze by those who have power to hoist it aloft and defend its sanctity. (*JD* 2:317)

2.21. We as a people have more reason to respect, honor, love and cherish the Government of the United States, and her Constitution and free institutions than any other people upon the face of the earth. ("Oration by His Excellency Governor Young" 4; also in Vetterli 378)

2.22. The Constitution of the United States forbids making an *ex post facto* law. The presenting of the resolution alluded to shows their feelings, they wish the Constitution out of existence, and there is no question but that they will get rid of it as quickly as they can, and that would be by *ex post facto* law, which the Constitution of the United States strictly forbids. (*JD* 4:39)

2.23. There is not a Territory in the Union that is looked upon with so suspicious an eye as is Utah, and yet it is the only part of the nation that cares anything about the Constitution. (*JD* 4:40)

2.24. We are more indifferent in regard to this subject in a religious than in a political sense, for, whether we are organized in a Territorial or State capacity, Government is bound to protect us in the rights of conscience, or over-ride plain Constitutional guarantees. And no intelligent person holds in very high estimation that union which is hourly endangered by the frenzied zeal of rampant, misguided, and fanatical demagogues, who trample that heaven-inspired instrument—the Constitution—into the dust, and regard neither their fathers' legacy nor their children's inheritance. (*MFP* 2:203)

2.25. There is no statute law in the United States, in neither the constitution nor the statutes at large, but what allows the Latter-day Saints every prerogative they could ask for. There is no right or privilege that we could ask to enjoy—none that any other people could reasonably ask to enjoy, but what is guaranteed unto us by the constitution and laws of the United States. Officials who feel to traduce the name and character of the Latter-day Saints, whether they be judges, marshals, Indian agents, or holding any other office under the United States' Government in this Territory, have to violate and trample under their feet their oaths to be loyal to the Government and laws by which they profess to be governed, in order to intrude in the least on the rights of this or any other peaceful, law-abiding community. To the honour of a few of those officials that have come here, we can say that they have honoured the law under which they came, while others have trampled it under their feet. . . . If men will only observe the laws of the United States—will only honour the laws they are sworn to honour, we are safe. (*JD* 4:347)

2.26. It is a pretty bold stand for this people to take, to say that they will not be controlled by the corrupt administrators of our General Government. We will be controlled by them, if they will be controlled by the Constitution and laws; but they will not. Many of them do not care any more about the constitution and the laws that they make than they do about the laws of another nation. That class tramples the rights of the people under their feet, while there are also many who would like to honour them. All we have ever asked for is our constitutional rights. We wish the laws of our Government honoured, and we have ever honoured them; but they are trampled under foot by administrators.

   I do not lift my voice against the great and glorious Government guaranteed to every citizen by our Constitution, but against those corrupt administrators who trample the Constitution and just laws under their feet. They care no more about them than they do about the Government of France; but they walk them under their feet with impunity. And the most of the characters they have sent here as officers cared no more about the laws of our country and of this Territory than they did about the laws of China, but walked them under their feet with all the recklessness of despots. (*JD* 5:231-32)

2.27. Every man is allowed by the Constitution to have what religion he pleases and to profess what religion he pleases. That liberty is guaranteed by the Constitution. (*JD* 5:235)

2.28. The Constitution and laws of the United States resemble a theocracy more closely than any government now on the earth, or that ever has been, so far as we know, except the government of the children of Israel to the time when they elected a king. (*JD* 6:342)

2.29. It is alleged and reiterated that we do not love the institutions of our country. I say, and have so said for many years, that the Constitution and laws of the United States combine the best form of Government in force upon the earth. But does it follow that each officer of the Government administers with justice? No; for it is well known throughout our nation that very many of our public officers are as degraded, debased, corrupt, and regardless of right as men well can be.

I repeat that the Constitution, laws, and institutions of our Government are as good as can be, with the intelligence now possessed by the people. But they, as also the laws of other nations, are too often administered in unrighteousness; and we do not and cannot love and respect the acts of the administrators of our laws, unless they act justly in their offices. (*JD* 6:344)

2.30. The kingdom of God will be extended over the earth; and it is written, "I will make thine officers peace, and thine exactors righteousness" [Isa 60:17]. Is that day ever coming? It is; and the doctrine we preach leads to that point. Even now the form of the Government of the United States differs but little from that of the kingdom of God.

In our Government a President is elected for four years, and can be re-elected but once, thus limiting the time of any one person to but eight years at most. Would it not be better to extend that period during life or good behaviour; and when the people have elected the best man to that office, continue him in it as long as he will serve them? . . .

When the best man is elected President, let him select the best men he can find for his counsellors or cabinet. . . . Our Father in heaven does not visit every place in person to guide and administer the law to the people, and to do this, that, and the other: he never did and never will; but he has officers, whom he sends when and where he pleases, giving to them their credentials and missions, as does our Government to our fellow-men here. (*JD* 6:345)

2.31. The administrators of the Government of the United States violated every principle of the Constitution in the very act of making a war upon their own subjects; and if the laws of Congress were carried out, they would be treated as traitors to the Government. I was in Missouri through the troubles. Did this people transgress the law of that State or of the United States? Did they do anything to justly bring the wrath of that State or of the Government upon them? No. This people observed the laws of Missouri and the law of God more strictly than any other class. (*JD* 8:224)

2.32. Is the form of the Government ruined? Has its form become evil? No; but the administrators of the Government are evil. As we have said many times, it is the best form of human government man ever lived under; but it has as corrupt a set to administer it as God ever permitted to disgrace his footstool. (*JD* 8:321)

2.33. If our present happy form of government is sustained, which I believe it will be, it will be done by the people I am now looking upon, in connection with their brethren and their off-spring. The present Constitution, with a few alterations of a trifling nature, is just as good as we want; and if it is sustained on this land of Joseph, it will be done by us and our posterity. Our national brethren do not know how to do it. They are not capable of controlling their own passions, to say nothing of ruling a nation. What is the reign of a king who cannot control his passions? Will not his subjects sorrow? Yes, they will feel the weight of his wrath, and their backs will ache, and their heads will ache, and they will receive the lash from a heavy hand. (*JD* 8:324)

2.34. I can tell all the world that we mean to sustain the Constitution of the United States and all righteous laws. (*JD* 9:157)

2.35. According to the Constitution of our Government, we have rights in common with our fellow-countrymen. We have a right to settle in any unoccupied and unclaimed part of the public domain owned by our Government, where the machinery of the Government has not extended, and there govern and control ourselves according to republican principles; and the Congress of the United States is not authorized in the least, by the Constitution that governs it, to make laws for the new settlement, and appoint adjudicators and administrators of the law for it. . . . In "Amendments to the Constitution of the United States," articles nine and ten, it is definitely stated that "The enumeration in the Constitution of certain rights, shall not be construed to deny or disparage others retained by the people." . . ."The powers not delegated to the United States by the Constitution, nor prohibited by it to the States, are reserved to the States respectively, or to the people." . . .

We will cling to the Constitution of our country, and to the Government that reveres that sacred charter of freemen's rights; and, if necessary, pour out our best blood for the defence of every good and righteous principle.

. . . The spirit and letter of our Constitution and laws will always give us our rights. . . .

If we do not do this [form a state government], we are living beneath those rights set forth in the Declaration of Independence, and the privileges granted to us in the Constitution of the United States which our fathers bought so dearly for us. Let us unfurl the stars and stripes—the flag of our country; let us sustain the Constitution that our fathers have bequeathed to us in letters of blood; and those who violate it will have to meet the crushing and damning penalties that will bury them in the mire of everlasting disgrace. If we sustain it, it will be sustained; otherwise it will not. (*JD* 10:39-41)

2.36. If there is a people within the pales of this nation that is worthy of the constitution, good laws and institutions of the American Government, it is this people called Latter-day Saints. It is the best earthly Government that ever was framed by man, and the true and righteous are alone worthy of it. It cannot long be administered by wicked hands. "When the wicked rule, the people mourn" [D&C 98:9]. (*JD* 9:368)

2.37. Five hundred of our able-bodied men had been taken from us by the call of the Government, and went to fight the battles of their country. There are women and children sitting here to-day, whose husbands, sons and fathers went on that campaign to prove to our Government that we were loyal, who became widows and orphans in consequence of that requisition.

. . . We were accused of disloyalty, alienation, and apostacy [*sic*] from the Constitution of our country. We were accused of being secessionists. I am, so help me God, and ever expect to be a secessionist from their wickedness, unrighteousness, dishonesty and unhallowed principles in a religious point of view; but am I or this people secessionists with regard to the glorious Constitution of our country? No. Were we secessionists when we so promptly responded to the call of the General Government, when we were houseless and friendless on the wild prairies of Pottawattamie? I think not. We there told the brethren to enlist, and they obeyed without a murmur. . . .

. . . I knew then as well as I do now that the Government would call for a battalion of men out of that part of Israel, to test our loyalty to the Government. . . .

. . . Have we not shown to the world that we love the Constitution of our country and its institutions better than do those who have been and are now distracting the nation? You cannot find a community, placed under the circumstances that we were, that would have done as we did on the occasion of furnishing the Mormon Battalion, after our leading men had been slain and we had been compelled to leave our farms, gardens, homes and firesides, while, at the same time, the general Government was called upon in vain to put a stop to such a series of abuses against an innocent people. . . .

After all this, to prove our loyalty to the Constitution and not to their infernal meanness, we went to fight the battles of a free country to give it power and influence, and to extend our happy institutions in others parts of this widely extended republic. In this way we have proved our loyalty. We have done everything that has been required of us. Can there anything reasonable and constitutional be asked that we would not perform? No. . . .

. . . The outside pressure now is that this people, called the Latter-day Saints, are secessionists in their feelings, and alien to the Constitution and institutions of our country. This is entirely false. There is not another people upon the face of the earth that could have borne what we have, and still remain as loyal to our brethren as we have been and are. They might be displeased with some of the acts of the administrators of the law, but not with the Constitutional laws and institutions of the Government. (*JD* 10:105-08)

2.38. We are in the midst of these mountains, and we have good and salutary laws to govern us. We have our Constitutional laws and our Territorial laws; we are subject to these laws; and always expect to be, for we love to be. If there is any man among us who has violated any constitutional law, try the law upon him, and let us see whether there is any virtue in it, before we try the strong arm of despotism and tyranny. I stand for Constitutional law, and if any transgress, let them be tried by it, and, if guilty, suffer its penalty. (*JD* 10:109)

2.39. Had the rulers of our nation known how to sustain the Union to an everlasting continuance, this knowledge would have been beyond all price. Had they possessed wisdom to have maintained the nation in its true character, in all its liberal institutions built upon the Constitution and Declaration of Rights, the Government would have continued inviolate in truth and purity and power, and would have continued to increase in power, importance and extent. (*JD* 10:189)

2.40. The seeds of sin which are in them are sufficient to accomplish their destruction. Every government of the world has the seeds of its own destruction in itself.

I hope and trust and pray that the government of our country may remain, because it is so good; but if they cut off this, and cast out that, and institute another thing, they may destroy all the good it contains. This, I hope, they will not do; they cannot do it. I expect to see the day when the Elders of Israel will protect and sustain civil and religious liberty and every constitutional right bequeathed to us by our fathers, and spread those rights abroad in connection with the Gospel for the salvation of all nations. (*JD* 11:262-63)

2.41. I told General Thomas L. Kane, that friend to humanity, when he visited us in 1857, that the coming of that army was the entering wedge to split the Government of the United States in pieces, and that soon. He, of course, could not see how this could ever be. They then were in great prosperity, and were going to annex the whole continent and neighboring islands, and so continue to annex until the whole world should take shelter under our national banner. He only saw this from a political stand point, basing his expectations of such grand results upon the goodness of the Constitution and laws. I acknowledged to him that we have the best system of government in existence, but queried if the people of this nation were righteous enough to sustain its institutions. I say they are not, but will trample them under their feet. I told General Kane that the Government of the United States would be shivered to pieces. Will this Government ever be restored to its former peace and tranquility, and the institutions thereof ever be maintained and honored? If they are, it will be by this people. (*JD* 12:119-20)

2.42. Every organization of our government, the best government in the world, is crumbling to pieces. Those who have it in their hands are the ones who are destroying it. How long will it be before the words of the prophet Joseph will be fulfilled? He said if the Constitution of the United States were saved at all it must be done by this people. It will not be many years before these words come to pass. (*JD* 12:204)

2.43. The first telegram that was ever sent over the transcontinental wire was by . . . President Brigham Young, . . . "Utah has not seceded, but is firm for the constitution and laws of our once happy country." (*JH* [30 Apr 1889] 10; quoted by Heber J. Grant)

2.44. I want to say to every man, the Constitution of the United States, as formed by our fathers, was dictated, was revealed, was put into their hearts by the Almighty, who sits enthroned in the midst of the heavens; although unknown to them, it was dictated by the revelations of Jesus Christ, and I tell you in the name of Jesus Christ, it is as good as I could ask for. (Henry 678; also in Roberts, *Mormonism* 27-28)

2.45. That people [the Latter-day Saints], whom the very great majority have striven to obliterate, will step forward and continue to honor the Heaven-inspired Constitution bequeathed to us so rich a legacy by our forefathers. (Hansen 166; from the Brigham Young Papers, Coe Collection, Yale University Library)

John Taylor   3

Biographical Information

Born: 1 November 1808
Ordained an Apostle: 19 December 1838
President of the Twelve: 6 October 1877
President of the Church: 10 October 1880 – 25 July 1887
Died: 25 July 1887

* * * * * * * *

Relationship with the Constitution and U.S. Government

John Taylor, third President of the Church, was born in Milnthrop, Westmoreland, England, making him the only foreign-born President of the Church. He was, however, intensely interested in the U.S. Constitution. In fact, he commented more on the Constitution than any other President except President Ezra Taft Benson.

John Taylor's relationship with the government centered on the continuing struggle over polygamy. This battle became so intense that he and other Church leaders were forced into hiding. He lived in a form of exile with various Latter-day Saint families for most of his term as President of the Church.

Themes Discussed in the Quotations

Main theme: The Saints have ever honored and upheld constitutional law.
Minor themes:
1. The nation abounds with traitors.

2. We believe all legislative assemblies should confine themselves to constitutional principles.
3. We ought to pray for those in authority, that they may lead in the right way.

Quotations

As an Apostle

3.1. Gentlemen, I now stand among men whose fathers fought for and obtained one of the greatest blessings ever conferred upon the human family—the right to think, to speak, to write; the right to say who shall govern them, and the right to worship God according to the dictates of their own consciences—all of them sacred, human rights, and now guaranteed by the American Constitution. I see around me the sons of those noble sires, who, rather than bow to the behests of a tyrant, pledged their lives, fortunes and sacred honors to burst those fetters, enjoy freedom themselves, bequeath it to their posterity, or die in the attempt. (*LJT* 53-54)

3.2. We believe that our fathers were inspired to write the Constitution of the United States, and that it is an instrument, full, lucid, and comprehensive; that it was dictated by a wise and foreseeing policy, and does honor to the heads and hearts of its framers; that it is the great bulwark of American liberty; and that the strict and implicit observance of which is the only safeguard of this mighty nation. We therefore rest ourselves under its ample folds. (*The Gospel Kingdom* 309-10)

3.3. We believe that all legislative assemblies should confine themselves to constitutional principles; and that all such laws should be implicitly obeyed by every American. ("Introductory Address" 2)

3.4. She [the U.S.] has, out of the chaotic, confused mass of material associated with corrupt governments, organized a system of government and framed a constitution that . . . guarantees to all, to the fullest extent, "Liberte, Egalite, Fraternite. . . ." Here man is free to speak, free to think, free to write, free to act, free to do good. The very genius of our Constitution and institutions is freedom. If there is fault, it is the fault of party, sectional strife, or narrow bigotry; it is not in our institutions. (*JT Papers* 1:195)

3.5. Would I, as a citizen of the United States, come out in rebellion against the United States, and act contrary to my conscience? Verily no. Would brother Young? Verily no. Would brother Kimball, or brother Wells? Verily no.

Are they not true patriots—true Americans? Do they not feel the fire of '76 burning in their bosoms? Assuredly they do. Would they do a thing that is wrong? No; and they will also see that others do not do it. That is the feeling, the spirit, and principle that actuate them.

There are thousands of you who are Americans, who have been born in this land, whose fathers fought for the liberties we used to enjoy, but have not enjoyed for some years past. There are thousands of such men here who feel the same spirit that used to burn in their fathers' bosoms—the spirit of liberty and equal rights—the spirit of according to every man that which belongs to him, and of robbing no man of his rights.

Your fathers and grandfathers have met the tyrant when he sought to put a yoke on your necks; as men and true patriots, they came forward and fought for their rights and in defence of that liberty which we, their children, ought to enjoy. You feel the same spirit that inspired them; the same blood that coursed in their veins flows in yours; you feel true patriotism and a strong attachment to the Constitution and institutions bought by the blood of your fathers, and bequeathed to you by them as your richest patrimony. (*JD* 5:148-49)

3.6. Right on the back of all the insults, robbery and fraud which we had endured, we still went Constitutionally to work. . . . Is there any step that we have taken that is contrary to law? There is not. (*JD* 5:152; revised in *LJT* 275)

3.7. I declare it before you and the world, that this people are the most peaceable, law-abiding, and patriotic people that can be found in the United States. (*JD* 5:152)

3.8. We are citizens of the United States, and profess to support the Constitution of the United States; and wherein that binds us, we are bound; wherein it does not, we are not bound. . . .

. . . If there is any man in this congregation, or anywhere else, that will show me any principle or authority in the Constitution of the United States that authorizes the President of the United States to send out governors and judges to this Territory, I would like to see it. (*JD* 5:154; revised in *LJT* 275)

3.9. There was not virtue enough either in state or general government to protect an innocent, helpless people in the enjoyment of their Constitutional rights. (*LJT* 274)

3.10. I wish to quote to you one little thing. If I had the Constitution here, I would read it to you. It is to the effect, "That the powers not delegated to the United States by the Constitution, nor prohibited by it to the States, are reserved to the States respectively, or to the people" [US Const. Amend. X]. (*JD* 5:155)

3.11. What was the great cause of complaint at the time the Constitution was framed? In the Declaration of Independence, it was stated that the people had rulers placed over them, and they had no voice in their election. Read that instrument. It describes our wrongs as plainly as it did the wrongs the people then laboured under and discarded.

As American citizens and patriots, and as sons of those venerable sires, can we, without disgracing ourselves, our fathers and our nation, submit to these insults and tamely bow to such tyranny? We cannot do it, and we will not do it. We will rally round the Constitution, and declare our rights as American citizens and we will sustain them in the face of high heaven and the world.

No man need have any qualms of conscience that he is doing wrong. You are patriots, standing by your rights and opposing the wrong which affects all lovers of freedom as well as you; for those acts of aggression have a withering, deadly effect, and are gnawing, like a canker-worm, at the very vitals of religious and civil liberty. You are standing by the Declaration of Independence, and sustaining the Constitution which was given by the inspiration of God; and you are the only people in the United States [at] this time that are doing it—that have the manhood to do it. . . .

According to the genius and spirit of the Constitution of the United States, we are pursuing the course that would be approved of by all high-minded, honourable men; and no man but a poor, miserable sneak would have any other feeling.

. . . I have watched with no little anxiety the encroachments of Government and the manifest desire to trample upon your rights. It is for you, however, to maintain them; and if those men that are traitors to the spirit and genius of the Constitution of the United States have a mind to trample under foot those principles that ought to guarantee protection to every American citizen, we will rally around the standard, and bid them defiance in the name of the Lord God of Israel.

In doing this, we neither forget our duties as citizens of the United States, nor as subjects of the kingdom and cause of God; but as the Lord has said, if we will keep His commandments, we need not transgress the laws of the land. We have not done it; we have maintained them all the time.

When we talk about the Constitution of the United States, we are sometimes apt to quote—"Vox populi, vox Dei;" that is, The voice of the people is the voice of God. But in some places they ought to say, VOX POPULI, VOX DIABOLI; that is, the voice of the people is the voice of the Devil.

We are moved by a higher law. . . .

We are not taking any steps contrary to the laws and the Constitution of the United States, but in everything we are upholding and sustaining them. (*JD* 5:156-57; also in Melville 27; revised in *LJT* 278)

3.12. In speaking upon this subject once before, I showed you that, by the Constitution and the very genius of our Government, they had no right to interfere with us. (*JD* 5:185)

3.13. We are not rebelling against the United States, neither are we resisting the Constitution of the United States; but it is wicked and corrupt usurpers that are oppressing us and that would take our rights from us. (*JD* 5:187)

3.14. Will you endeavour to disannul the Government? No; but we will rally round the Constitution that was purchased by the blood of our fathers, and will support it. . . .

These are our views; and while we do not trample under foot the Constitution, we will take care that others do not do it. . . .

Shall we still bless the human family? Yes. Shall we rally around the Constitution of the United States and protect it in its purity? Yes; we will save it when others forsake it. (*JD* 5:246-47)

3.15. In regard to our religion, it is perhaps unnecessary to say much, yet whatever others' feelings may be about it, with us it is honestly a matter of conscience. This is a right guaranteed unto us by the Constitution of our country, yet it is on this ground, and this alone, that we have suffered a continued series of persecutions. (*LJT* 287)

3.16. They have, however, discovered the difference between a blind submission to the caprices of political demagogues, and obedience to the Constitution, laws, and institutions of the United States; nor can they in the present instance be hood-winked by the cry of "treason." If it be treason to stand up for our Constitutional rights; if it be treason to resist the unconstitutional acts of a vitiated and corrupt administration, who by a mercenary armed force would seek to rob us of the rights of franchise, cut our throats to subserve their own party, and seek to force upon us their corrupt tools, and violently invade the rights of American citizens; if it be treason to maintain inviolate our homes, our firesides, our wives, and our honor, from the corrupting, and withering blight of a debauched soldiery; if it be treason to maintain inviolate the Constitution and institutions of the United States, when nearly all the states are seeking to trample them under their feet—then indeed are we guilty of treason.

It is not as some suppose the "voice of Brigham" only, but the universal, deep settled feeling of the whole community. Their cry is "Give us our Constitutional rights; give us liberty or death." (*LJT* 288; also in *JT Papers* 1:213)

3.17. We have at all times been subject to and supported the constitution of the United States, and the laws of this State. Had the authorities of government sent out a committee to have counselled with us, and investigate the matter, they would have been treated with respect, and their counsel adhered to, as we never had any quarrel with our country, and if we or any of us had broken the laws, we were willing to be tried by and adhere to those laws, and that Constitution which the blood of our Fathers still endears to our memory. (*A Short Account of the Murders, Roberies, . . .* 6)

3.18. The origin for the unprecedented prosperity of the United States will be found in a free and liberal constitution. (*JT Papers* 1:224)

3.19. The Constitution of the United States has ever been respected and honored by us. We consider it one of the best national instruments ever formed. Nay, further, Joseph Smith in his day said it was given by inspiration of God. We have ever stood by it, and we expect when the fanaticism of false, blatant friends shall have torn it shred from shred, to stand by the shattered ruins and uphold the broken, desecrated remnants of our country's institutions in all their primitive purity and pristine glory. (*JT Papers* 1:228)

3.20. Well, but do you not hold allegiance to the government of the United States also? Do you not believe in the laws and institutions thereof? Yes, we have always sustained and upheld them; and although we have had many very heavy provocations to make us feel rebellious and opposed to that government, yet we have always sustained it under all circumstances and in every position. When they tried to cut our throats, we rather objected to that, you know. We had some slight objection to have our heads cut off and be trampled under foot; we did not think it was either constitutional or legal. But when they took their swords away from our necks and said that we might enjoy the rights of American citizens, that was all we wanted.

There is, however, a kind of political heresy that we have always adopted. We have always maintained that we had a right to worship God as we thought proper under the constitution of the United States, and that we would vote as we pleased. But some people took a notion to say "they would be damned if we should." We told them, however, that was a matter of their own taste; that we would seek to be saved and yet we would do it. It has always been a principle with us, and in fact is given in one of our revelations, "that he who will observe the laws of God need not transgress the laws of the land" [D&C 58:21]. . . . I am prepared to say that, as a population, as a people, as a Territory, we have always been loyal to the institutions of our government, and I am at the defiance of the world to prove anything to the contrary. When we left—I was going to say the United States— what did we leave for? Why did we leave that country? Was it because its institutions were not good? No. Was it because its constitution was not one of the best that was ever framed? No. Was it because the laws of the United States, or of the States where we sojourned, were not good? No. Why was it? It was because there was not sufficient virtue found in the Executive to sustain their own laws. That was the reason, gentlemen. Is this anything to be proud of? It is a thing that should make every honorable American hide his head in shame; and all reflecting, intelligent, and honorable men feel thus. . . .

But did we rebel? No, we did not act as the Southern States have done. We came here; and, in the absence of any other government, we organized a provisional state government, just the same as Oregon did before us. Thus, in the midst of this abuse heaped upon us, we showed our adherence to the institutions and constitution of our country. If bad men bore rule, if corrupt men held sway—men who had neither the virtue nor the fortitude to maintain the right and protect the institutions and constitution of this, shall I say, our once glorious country,—if men could not be found who possessed sufficient integrity to maintain their oaths and their own institutions, there was a people here found of sufficient integrity to the constitution and institutions of the United States not to abandon them. . . . Still we have been true to our trust, to our integrity, and to the institutions and constitution of our country all the time in the midst of these things.

. . . Sometimes people think we are acting almost hypocritically when we talk of loyalty to the constitution of the United States. We will stand by that constitution and uphold the flag of our country when everybody else forsakes it. We cannot shut our eyes to things transpiring around us. We have our reason, and God has revealed unto us many things; but never has he revealed anything in opposition to those institutions and that Constitution, no, never; and, another thing, he never will. (*JD* 11:90-92)

3.21. As we have progressed the mist has been removed, and in relation to these matters, the Elders of Israel begin to understand that they have something to do with the world politically as well as religiously, that it is as much their duty to study correct political principles as well as religious, and to seek to know and comprehend the social and political interests of man, and to learn and be able to teach that which would be best calculated to promote the interests of the world. (*JD* 9:340)

3.22. We do not expect that Congress is acquainted with our religious faith; but . . . we do claim the guarantees of the Constitution and immunity from persecution on merely religious grounds. (*JD* 11:223; revised in *JT Papers* 1:233)

3.23. Then do you profess to ignore the laws of the land? No; not unless they are unconstitutional, then I would do it all the time. Whenever the Congress of the United States, for instance, pass[es] a law interfering with my religion, or with my religious rights, I will read a small portion of that instrument called the Constitution of the United States, now almost obsolete, which says—"Congress shall pass no law interfering with religion or the free exercise thereof" [US Const. Amend. I]; and I would say, gentlemen, you may go to Gibraltar with your law, and I will live my religion. When you become violators of the Constitution you have sworn before high heaven to uphold, and perjure yourselves before God, then I will maintain the right, and leave you to take the wrong just as you please. (*JD* 11:343; revised in *JT Papers* 1:232)

3.24. There have been attempts made here to interfere with the trial by jury, a right guaranteed by the Constitution of the United States as well as by the Magna Charta of England. . . .

No man should make a scapegoat of me; if he wished to violate constitutional rights he should do it on his own responsibility. Some men will endure a great deal in matters of this kind, and they will call it humility; but I desire no such humility. I want a principle that will maintain, uphold, and stand by the rights of man, giving to all men everywhere equal rights, and that will preserve inviolate the fundamental principles of the Constitution of our country. (*JD* 11:343)

3.25. And why should we feel ashamed to acknowledge that those patriots and statesmen who framed the Constitution of the United States were led by inspiration? It is an honor to any man or group of men to seek the inspiration of the Almighty. It is a greater honor to receive it. (*JT Papers* 1:269)

3.26. Under a government just and equitable . . . this country flourished, following the arts of industry and peace, as no nation ever did before. . . . She prospered under the direction, the guidance and protection of the Constitution. Well might Joseph Smith exclaim, "It was given by inspiration of God." In such a condition, surrounded by so many blessings, what might have been her destiny? (*JT Papers* 1:271)

3.27. As part of the common brotherhood of the nation, we will perform the part of a good citizen; rally round the cause of right;

maintain inviolate the Constitution of the United States. (*JT Papers* 1:272)

3.28. The honorable framers of the Constitution of the United States were no less alive to these matters, and while they threw safeguards around the civil power, [they] were very anxious to protect the people in their individual, social, religious and political rights. (*JT Papers* 1:279)

3.29. The worst wish we have for the human family is that the principles enunciated in our Constitution may reverberate over the wide earth, and spread from shore to shore, until all mankind shall be free. (*JD* 14:267)

3.30. I may be here met with the statement that we are only a territory; but we are American citizens, and have never abjured our citizenship nor relinquished our Constitutional guarantees. . . .

The facts are the people, one hundred thousand American citizens, living in the Territory of Utah, with the full rights of free men, and the protecting guarantees of a written constitution, find in the persons of federal officers "another government" not of the people, and in violation of Constitutional guarantees and authority; claiming to come from the United States, "*imperium in imperio.*" (*LJT* 314-15)

3.31. It may be asked why the framers of the Constitution did not carry out the views enunciated by the declarers of independence, in regard to the inalienable rights of man? . . .

It may be asked, if this instrument was imperfect, why do you sustain it? Simply that, with this one fault, it was the best instrument in existence, and it was all and more than the nation has ever lived up to. (*JT Papers* 1:282)

3.32. We are told, however, that "eternal vigilance is the price of liberty;" and as we possess the best Constitution and the best government in the world, let us preserve it, and transmit it intact, pure and unadulterated to our children. (*JT Papers* 1:285)

3.33. I have taken the oath of allegiance to the United States government, not being American born, and I have always admired its institutions; and I have been very desirous to see the practice and carrying out of these fundamental principles of our government; I have been anxious to see public affairs conducted in an honorable, intelligent, correct, philosophic, patriotic and statesmanlike form in all things. These have been my sentiments. (Hollister 5)

3.34. Mr. T[aylor]—For instance, referring to the government of the United States; do you believe that its Constitution is binding upon Congress and upon the Supreme Court?

Mr. H[ollister]—Yes, sir.

Mr. T[aylor]—Then, although I am sorry to say it, yet I believe that both of these exalted branches of the government have violated their most sacred obligations to sustain that instrument. (Hollister 6)

3.35. Mr. T[aylor]—However we may respect the government and its institutions I would respectfully say we are not the parties who produce this antagonism. It is men who place themselves in antagonism to the Constitution of the United States. We are governed by the law of God, which is not in violation of that Constitution. (Hollister 6)

3.36. Again in regard to political matters, where is there a nation to-day, under the face of the whole heavens that is under the guidance and direction of the Lord in the management of their public affairs? You cannot find one. It is true that the founders of this nation, as a preliminary step for the introduction of more correct principles and that liberty and the rights of man might be recognized, and that all men might become equal before the law of the land, had that great palladium of liberty, the Constitution of the United States, framed. This was the entering wedge for the introduction of a new era, and in it were introduced principles for the birth and organization of a new world. The Prophet Joseph Smith said that "The Constitution of the United States was given by the inspiration of God." But good, virtuous and holy principles may be perverted by corrupt and wicked men. The Lord was opposed by Satan, Jesus had his Judas, and this nation abounds with traitors who ignore that sacred palladium of liberty and seek to trample it under foot. Joseph Smith said they would do so, and that when deserted by all, the elders of Israel would rally around its shattered fragments and save and preserve it inviolate. But even this, good as it was, was not a perfect instrument; it was one of those stepping stones to a future development in the progress of a man to the intelligence and light, the power and union that God alone can impart to the human family. And while we acknowledge, as citizens of the United States, the laws and institutions thereof (which by the way are very easily complied with), we have a higher law, more noble principles, ideas that are more elevated and expansive; principles that reach to the whole human family, and which he will continue to reveal to us. Does that prevent us from obeying the laws of the land? Certainly not. But then, is that a perfect system? I do not think that many of you will say it is, nor do I think that the people of the United States of any political party will tell you it is. ... We are united, then, as a body politic, as an integral part of this Government, and it becomes our duty to submit to the laws and institutions of that Government—to all that are constitutional, framed and based upon correct principles, and not in violation of what the fathers of the country instituted. (*JD* 21:31-32)

3.37. When the people shall have torn to shreds the Constitution of the United States the Elders of Israel will be found holding it up to the nations of the earth and proclaiming liberty and equal rights to all men, and extending the hand of fellowship to the oppressed of all nations. This is part of the programme, and as long as we do what is right and fear God, he will help us and stand by us under all circumstances. (*JD* 21:8)

3.38. But if they think we cannot stand up for our rights under God and the Constitution, they will find they are egregiously mistaken. (*JT Papers* 2:65)

3.39. Need we be surprised that they should trample under foot the Constitution of the United States? No; Joseph Smith told us that they would do it. Many around me here knew long ago that they would do this thing and further knew that the last people that should be found to rally around the sacred instrument and save it from the grasp of unrighteous men would be the Elders of Israel! When, therefore, we see these things progressing need we be astonished? I do not think we need be. (*JD* 20:318)

3.40. And they will tear away one plank of liberty after another, until the whole fabric will totter and fall; and many other nations will be cast down and empires destroyed; and this nation will have to suffer as others will. And it will be as Joseph Smith once said, "When all others forsake the Constitution, the Elders of this Church will rally around the standard and save its tattered shreds." We will come to its rescue and proclaim liberty to all men. (*JD* 20:357)

3.41. We are under the United States, but the United States is not the kingdom of God. It does not profess to be under his rule, nor his government, nor his authority. Yet we are expected as citizens of the United States to keep the laws of the United States, and hence we are, as I said before, an integral part of the government, [*sic*] Very well, what is expected of us? That we observe its laws, that we conform to its usages, that we are governed by good and wholesome principles, that we maintain the laws in their integrity and that we sustain the government, and we ought to do it. But there is a principle here that I wish to speak about. God dictates in a great measure the affairs of the nations of the earth, their kingdoms and governments and rulers and those that hold dominion. He sets up one and pulls down another, according to his will. That is an old doctrine, but it is true to-day. Have we governors? Have we a president of the United States? Have we men in authority? Yes. Is it right to traduce their characters? No, it is not. Is it right for us to oppose them? No, it is not. Is it right for them to traduce us? No, it is not. Is it right for them to oppress us in any way? No, it is not. We ought to pray for these people, for those that are in authority, that they may be lead [*sic*] in the right way, that they may be preserved from evil, that they may administer the government in righteousness, and that they may pursue a course that will receive the approbation of heaven. . . .

. . . Well, shall we be governed by them? Yes. Shall we obey the law? Yes. Shall I as a citizen of this city obey the laws of this city? Yes. . . . Shall I cause trouble or speak evil of the mayor or city council or any of the administrators of the law? No, I ought to pray for them that they may lead aright and administer justice equitably and act for the welfare and interest of the community wherein they live and for whom they operate. Am I a citizen of the United States? Yes, and I ought to feel the same toward them. (*JD* 21:69)

3.42. We will sustain the government in its administration, and be true to it, and maintain this position right along. And when division, strife, trouble and contention arise, we will try to still the troubled waters, and act in all honesty as true friends to the government; and when war shall exist among them, and there is no one found to sustain the remnants of liberty that may be left, the Elders of Israel will rally round the standard of freedom and proclaim liberty to all the world. (*CR* [Apr 1880] 102)

As the President of the Church

3.43. Will we oppose the principles of this government? No. We will sustain them. But if people will act foolishly we cannot help it. If this nation can stand the results of the violation of constitutional principles, we can. If they tear down the bulwarks of freedom and with impunity trample underfoot the rights of men we cannot help it. If it is our turn, to-day, to suffer wrong, it will be somebody else's to-morrow, national retrogressions are not often arrested. It behooves statesmen to pause in their career. The floodgates once opened who shall stay the torrent? We of all men would save the ship of state and would say to these national patricides avaunt [go away]! But if they will act foolishly and continue to do so until they subvert the principles of liberty, and thus destroy one of the best governments ever instituted on earth, then if forsaken by all else, the elders of this Church will rally round the Constitution, lift up the standard of freedom, which is being trodden under foot and bedrabbled by demagogues, and proclaim liberty to the world; equal rights, liberty and equality; freedom of conscience and of worship to all men everywhere. That is not a prophecy of mine; it is a prophecy of Joseph Smith's, and I believe it very strongly. (*JD* 21:349-50)

3.44. But should this nation persist in violating their Constitutional guarantees, tear away the bulwarks of liberty, and trample upon the principles of freedom and human rights, that are sacred to all men, and by which all men should be governed, by and by the whole fabric will fall, and who will sustain it? We will, in the name of Israel's God. Of this the Prophet Joseph Smith prophesied long, long ago. (*JD* 22:229)

3.45. But all honorable men, all men who do right and maintain the laws and the Constitution of the United States, we are their friends and will sustain them to the last. . . .

We see many signs of weakness which we lament, and we would to God that our rulers would be men of righteousness, and that those who aspire to position would be guided by honorable feelings—to maintain inviolate the Constitution and operate in the interest, happiness, well-being, and protection of the whole community. But we see signs of weakness and vacillation. We see a policy being introduced to listen to the clamor of mobs and of unprincipled men who know not of what they speak, nor whereof they affirm, and when men begin to tear away with impunity one plank after another from our Constitution by and by we shall find that we are struggling with the wreck and ruin of the system which the forefathers of this nation sought to establish in the interests of humanity. But it is for us still to sustain these glorious principles of liberty bequeathed by the founders of this nation, still to rally round the flag of the Union, still to maintain all correct principles, granting the utmost extent of liberty to all people of all grades and of all nations. (*JD* 22:143)

3.46. There is one thing I wish to speak about here politically. "What do you think about the government of the United States," so the people say. "What are your opinions?" I will tell you what I think about the Constitution. I have just the same opinion of it that Joseph Smith had, and he said it was given by inspiration of God. The men did not know this who wrote it; the men did not know it who adopted it; nevertheless it is true. There is an embodiment of principles contained therein that are calculated to bless and benefit mankind. "What do you think about the government of the United States as a government? I think it is a good deal ahead of most governments, but I think the administrators are apostatizing very fast from the principles that the fathers of this nation instituted." It has become quite a question now-a-days, whether men can be preserved in their rights or not, whether men can worship God according to the dictates of their conscience or not, or whether we are living in a land of freedom or not. What is the matter? Why, they are like the religionist. How is it with them? They profess to believe in the Bible. They do believe it shut, but when you open it they deny it. The people of this nation profess to believe in the Constitution. They do until it comes to be applied to the people and then they do not. That is perhaps too broad a saying; but I will say there are many who feel like this—not all by a long way. There are thousands and tens of thousands who are imbued with the same principles as were the framers of the Constitution and who desire to see human freedom perpetuated. The principles of freedom and the love of human liberty have not quite died out of the hearts of all men in these United States. There is a respectable balance in favor of liberty and freedom and equal rights. . . . We would say to men who profess so much loyalty and patriotism to the government, be true to your institutions, be true to the Constitution of the United States, as we say to all our people to be true to the same. We expect the Latter-day Saints to be so, and to be subject to law, to avoid lawlessness of every kind and the interference with men's rights in any shape. (*JD* 22:295-96)

3.47. It is for us to maintain those sacred principles enunciated in our Constitution, and not only preserve our own liberties, so far as we can, but also those of our nation and of the world. (*JT Papers* 2:202)

3.48. But if the professed friends of the nation—those who boast so much about human liberty and Constitutional rights—can afford to root up, override and destroy the principles of that very liberty about which they talk, and trample underfoot the sacred barriers of the Constitution, we can afford to have them do it. (*JT Papers* 2:203)

3.49. If the rulers of this nation can afford to tamper with the sacred rights of the people guaranteed by the constitution of this great nation, and ruthlessly tear down the temple of freedom erected at the cost of so much blood and treasure, instead of anticipated glory, they will bring destruction upon the nation and ruin and infamy upon themselves. The sacred bulwarks of freedom once tampered with, the floodgates of anarchy and confusion will be thrown open and dissolution and ruin will follow in their train in rapid succession. It is for us to sustain and maintain the principles guaranteed in that sacred palladium of human rights—the Constitution of the United States, and to contend inch by inch in every legal and constitutional manner for our own rights and human freedom, leaving misrule, anarchy, violations of law and the trampling under foot of the rights of man and constitutional guarantees to religious fanatics and clamoring demagogues; and if they can afford to tamper with those sacred guarantees, we certainly can afford to have them do it. It is for us to seek more exalted ideas, to abide by constitutional law, to maintain inviolate the principles of human freedom, and to contend with unwavering firmness for those inalienable rights of all men—life, liberty and the pursuit of happiness; and to seek continually to our God for wisdom to accomplish so great, noble and patriotic a purpose. (*JD* 23:36)

3.50. Upon passage of the Edmunds' law, President Taylor declared: "When the Constitution of the United States was framed and adopted, those high contracting parties did positively agree that they would not interfere with religious affairs. Now, if our marital relations are not religious, what is? This ordinance of marriage was a direct revelation to us, through Joseph Smith, the prophet. . . . This is a revelation from God and a command to his people, and therefore it is my religion. I do not believe that the Supreme Court of the United States has any right to interfere with my religious views, and in doing it they are violating their most sacred obligations." (Smith and Stewart 45)

3.51. Have we been opposed to the United States? No! no! no! We never have and we are at the defiance of all men to prove anything of the kind. There are falsehoods set afoot by low, degraded, unprincipled men. We believe that the Constitution of the United States was given by inspiration of God. And why? Because it is one of those instruments which proclaims liberty throughout the land, and to all the inhabitants thereof [Lev 25:10]. And it was because of those noble sentiments, and the promulgation of those principles which were given by God to man, we believe that it was given by the inspiration of the Almighty. We have always esteemed it in this light, and it was so declared by Joseph Smith. Did we do any wrong in coming here in the way we did? I think not. Did we transgress any of the laws of the nations we left? I think not. We gathered together simply because we were told there was a Zion to be built up. (*JD* 23:53)

3.52. The young people asserted that it had been taught to them by their parents from their youth up, and that the principles of purity, virtue, integrity and loyalty to the government of the United States had been instilled into their minds and hearts since their earliest childhood. (*JD* 23:60)

3.53. Truth ultimately will triumph, as according to the old adage, "Truth, crushed to earth, will rise again." And what will you do? Contend for constitutional principles, or lie down and let the vicious, the mendacious and unprincipled run over and overslaugh you? (*JD* 23:61)

3.54. Congress will soon have something else to do than to prescribe and persecute an innocent, law-abiding and patriotic people. Of all bodies in the world, they [Congress] can least afford to remove the bulwarks that bind society together in this nation, to recklessly trample upon human freedom and rights, and to rend and destroy that great Palladium of human rights—the Constitution of the United States. Ere long they will need all its protecting influence to save this nation from misrule, anarchy and mobocratic influence. They can ill afford to be the foremost in tampering with human rights and human freedom, or in tearing down the bulwarks of safety and protection which that sacred instrument has guaranteed. It is lamentable to see the various disordered and disorganized elements seeking to overthrow the greatest and best government in existence on the earth. Congress can ill afford to set a pattern of violation of that Constitution which it has sworn to support. The internal fires of revolution are already smoldering in this nation, and they need but a spark to set them in a flame. Already are agencies at work in the land calculated to subvert and overthrow every principle of rule and government; already is corruption of every kind prevailing in high places and permeating all society; already are we, as a nation, departing from our God, and corrupting ourselves with malfeasance, dishonor, and a lack of public integrity and good faith; already are licentiousness and debauchery corrupting, undermining and destroying society; already are we interfering with the laws of nature and stopping the functions of life, and have become the slayers of our own offspring, and employ human butchers in the shape of physicians to assist in this diabolical and murderous work. (*JD* 23:62)

3.55. Besides the preaching of the Gospel, we have another mission, namely, the perpetuation of the free agency of man and the maintenance of liberty, freedom, and the rights of man. There are certain principles that belong to humanity outside of the Constitution, outside of the laws, outside of all the enactments and plans of man, among which is the right to live; God gave us the right and not man; no government gave it to us, and no government has a right to take it away from us. We have a right to liberty—that was a right that God gave to all men; and if there has been oppression, fraud or tyranny in the earth, it has been the result of the wickedness and corruptions of men and has always been opposed to God and the principles of truth, righteousness, virtue, and all principles that are calculated to elevate mankind. The Declaration of Independence states that men are in possession of certain inalienable rights, among which are life, liberty and the pursuit of happiness. This belongs to us; it belongs to all humanity. I wish, and the worst wish I have for the United States, is, that they could have liberality enough to give to all men equal rights. (*JD* 23:63)

3.56. But what I admired in those Senators and Members was their fealty to the government, to the Constitution and the maintenance of the freedom and the inalienable rights of man, of every color, creed and profession.

We have no fault to find with our government. We deem it the best in the world. But we have reason to deplore its maladministration, and I call upon our legislators, our governors and president to pause in their career and not to tamper with the rights and liberties of American citizens, nor wantonly tear down the bulwarks of American and human liberty. God has given to us glorious institutions; let us preserve them intact and not pander to the vices, passions and fanaticism of a depraved public opinion. . . .

We do not wish to place ourselves in a state of antagonism, nor act defiantly towards this government. We will fulfill the letter, so far as practicable, of that unjust, inhuman, oppressive and unconstitutional law, so far as we can without violating principle; but we cannot sacrifice every principle of human right at the behest of corrupt, unreasoning and unprincipled men; we cannot violate the highest and noblest principles of human nature and make pariahs and outcasts of high-minded, virtuous and honorable women, nor sacrifice at the shrine of popular clamor the highest and noblest principles of humanity!

We shall abide all constitutional law, as we always have done; but while we are God-fearing and law-abiding, and respect all honorable men and officers, we are no craven serfs, and have not learned to lick the feet of oppressors, nor to bow in base submission to unreasoning clamor. We will contend inch by inch, legally and constitutionally, for our rights as American citizens. . . . We stand proudly erect in the consciousness of our rights as American citizens, and plant ourselves firmly on the sacred guarantees of the Constitution; and that instrument, while it defines the powers and privileges of the President, Congress and the judiciary, also directly provides that "the powers not delegated to the United States by the Constitution, nor prohibited by it to the States, are reserved to the States, respectively or to the people" [US Const. Amend. X].

We need have no fears, no trembling in our knees about these attempts to deprive us of our God-given and constitutional liberties. God will take care of His people, if we will only do right. (*JD* 23:64-67; revised in *LJT* 364-65)

3.57. We will stand by our covenants, and the Constitution will bear us out in it. Among other things, that instrument says that Congress shall make no law impairing the validity of contracts. You have contracted to be united with your wives in time and in eternity, and it would not do for us to break a constitutional law, would it?

Now, what will we do in our relations with the United States? We will observe the law as we have done, and be as faithful as we have been. We will maintain our principles and live our religion and keep the commandments of God, and obey every constitutional law, pursuing that course that shall direct us in all things. (*JD* 23:68)

3.58. Concerning the course taken by the United States, they have a right to reject this law [law of Celestial Marriage] themselves, as they have a right to reject the Gospel; but it is contrary to the provisions of the constitution, which is the supreme law of the land, for them to prohibit you from obeying it.

Therefore, abide in my law which I have revealed unto you, saith the Lord God, and contend for your rights by every legal and constitutional method and in accordance with the institutions, laws, and Constitution of the United States. (*JT Papers* 2:243)

3.59. If other people can afford to trample under foot the sacred institutions of this country, we cannot. And if other people trample upon the Constitution and pull it to pieces, we will gather together the pieces and rally around the old flag, or what is left of it, and proclaim liberty to the world, as Joseph Smith said we would. Is that treason? I do not know; no matter, it is true. Are we going to hurt anybody? No. (*JD* 23:239)

3.60. What course shall we pursue? We purpose to contend for human rights, for the Constitution of the United States, and for the rights and privileges of man and the freedom of humanity. We will try to live our religion and keep the commandments of God. We will put in a word for the liberty of man, equal rights and constitutional principles, and these we will maintain so far as God gives us power. When we have done that we will live our religion; we will cleave unto God and unto truth, maintain virtue, purity and righteousness, and seek for the Spirit of the Lord; we will be humble, faithful and diligent, and we will pray for our enemies and for all men. (*JD* 23:240)

3.61. Our counsel, then, is to the Latter-day Saints who can truthfully take this oath, there is no reason that we know of in the Gospel, or in any of the revelations of God, which prevents you from doing so. You owe it to yourselves; you owe it to your posterity; you owe it to those of your co religionists who, by this law, are robbed worse than even many of yourselves, of their rights under the Constitution; you owe it to humanity everywhere; you owe it to that free and constitutional form of government, which has been bequeathed to you through the precious sacrifices of many of your forefathers—to do all in your power to maintain religious liberty and free, republican government in these mountains, and to preserve every constitutional right intact, and not to allow, either through supineness or indifference, or any feeling of resentment or indignation because of wrongs inflicted upon you, any right or privilege to be wrested from you. . . . Then having done this, and everything else in your power to preserve constitutional government and full religious freedom in the land, you can safely trust the Lord for the rest. He has promised to fight your battles. . . .

Let us guard well our franchise, and in one unbroken phalanx, maintain and sustain our political status, and, as patriots and the freemen, operate together, in the defence of what few liberties are left us, in the defence of the Constitution, and in the defence of the inalienable rights of man; which rights always exist and are before and above all constitutions, and thus perpetuate to posterity the inestimable blessings of freedom, including the right to live, the right to be free, and the right to pursue happiness, unmolested by any influence, power, or combination. (*An Address to the Members of the Church of Jesus Christ of Latter-day Saints* 5-6; also in *MFP* 2:346)

3.62. They are described in the Declaration of Independence as inalienable rights, one of which is that men have a right to live; another is that they have a right to pursue happiness; and another is that they have a right to be free and no man has authority to deprive them of those God-given rights, and none but tyrants would do it. These principles I say, are inalienable in man; they belong to him; they existed before any constitutions were framed or any laws made. Men have in various ages striven to strip their fellowmen of these rights, and dispossess them of them. And hence the wars, the bloodshed and carnage that have spread over the earth. We therefore are not indebted to the United States for these rights; we were free as men born into the world, having the right to do as we please, to act as we please, as long as we do not transgress constitutional law nor violate the rights of others.

As politicians or statesmen they must at least give us the benefit of the Constitution and laws. (*JD* 23:263-64)

3.63. It may not be among the improbabilities, that the prophecies of Joseph Smith may be fulfilled and that the calumniated and despised Mormons may yet become the protectors of the Constitution and the guardians of religious liberty and human freedom in these United States. (*JD* 23:266)

3.64. [The wicked] are laying the axe at the root of this government, and unless they speedily turn round and repent and follow the principles they have sworn to sustain—the principles contained in the Constitution of the United States—they will be overthrown, they will be split up and divided, be disintegrated and become weak as water; for the Lord will handle them in his own way. I say these things in sorrow; but as sure as God lives unless there is a change of policy these things will most assuredly take place. (*JD* 23:270)

3.65. We are charged with being a menace to the United States, with being inimical to the Constitution and Government, simply because we have undertaken to legitimately and legally test in the courts, as we have the most perfect right to do, the legality and constitutionality of the law and the commissioners' rulings. ("Ecclesiastical Control in Utah" 4)

3.66. If our Constitution, our laws, and the fundamental principles of our Government are to be trampled underfoot, it would seem to be high time that all honorable men should stand up in defense of liberty and the rights of man. ("Ecclesiastical Control in Utah" 5; revised in *JT Papers* 2:300)

3.67. Many persons suppose that there is some provision in the United States Constitution touching this subject. This is an error. The Constitution leaves all matters relating to marriage to be regulated by the people of the various States; and hence it is that so many diversified marriage and divorce codes exist throughout the country. ("Ecclesiastical Control in Utah" 5)

3.68. They came to Utah not, as alleged, to erect an establishment of religion contrary to the Constitution and laws, but to found a State where all sects would have equal rights to worship God according to the dictates of the consciences of their members, which right the Latter-day Saints had been denied in Missouri and Illinois. ("Ecclesiastical Control in Utah" 9)

3.69. In our government, whether in a National, State, or Territorial form, all officers, of every grade, are requested to take a solemn oath to sustain and maintain the constitution of the United States, and of the State, or if a Territory, the organic act of the Territory as the case may be. If these things are not a fiction all these officers and authorities throughout the land in every department of Nation, State or Territorial government, are as much bound by their obligations and oaths as the people are bound to be subject to all constitutional laws, and the people are not one whit more bound to the observance of the law than these men are bound to the observance of the sacred and solemn covenants which they have entered into. And if the people have given up to governors, legislatures, the judiciary and to the officers of the law certain powers, rights and privileges, this authority coming of or from the people, it is expected that they shall act for and in the interests of the people; and furthermore, that while they possess those rights ceded to them by the people, whatever is not thus ceded and placed in the hands of their rulers is emphatically stated to be reserved to the several States or to the people. . . . But it must be understood here in matters pertaining to our government, that no charters or grants of any kind can be given by any parties, in excess of the rights which they themselves possess, and that the same obligations which vest in regard to constitutional rights and guarantees must be observed in all those municipal regulations by the recipients as of the grantees of those charters.

These rights and privileges in our government are formulated upon the idea that our government is "of the people, by the people and for the people." (*JD* 26:348-49)

3.70. It is said in the Doctrine and Covenants, that he that keepeth the laws of God, hath no need to break the laws of the land [58:21]. It is further explained in section 98, what is meant in relation to this. That all laws which are constitutional must be obeyed, as follows:

"And now, verily I say unto you concerning the laws of the land, it is my will that my people should observe to do all things whatsoever I command them.

"And that the law of the land which is constitutional, supporting that principle of freedom in maintaining rights and privileges, belongs to all mankind, and is justifiable before me;

"Therefore I the Lord justify you and your brethren of the Church in befriending that law which is the constitutional law of the land. And as pertaining to laws of man, whatsoever is more or less than these cometh of evil" [D&C 98:4-7].

That is taking this nation as an example, all laws that are proper and correct, and all obligations entered into which are not violative of the constitution should be kept inviolate. But if they are violative of the constitution, then the compact between the rulers and the ruled is broken and the obligation ceases to be binding. Just as a person agreeing to purchase anything and to pay a certain amount for it, if he receives the article bargained for, and does not pay its price, he violates his contract; but if he does not receive the article he is not required to pay for it. (*JD* 26:350)

3.71. If we have got farms, or city lots, or inheritances of any kind, we have paid for them according to the laws of the United States. We have complied with all the requisitions of the United States that are constitutional, and mean to do that all the time. (*JD* 26:325)

3.72. We Latter-day Saints—what are we? Professors of religion. Are we? Yes. There are laws being enacted in order to deprive us of our religious rights, whereas the Constitution of the United States says that Congress shall make no law respecting an establishment of religion, or prohibiting the free exercise thereof [US Const. Amend. I]. Is that true? Read it for yourselves in the Constitution. This is what we profess as Americans. We have men in our midst who have introduced test oaths, whereas the Constitution says, that "no religious test shall ever be required" [US Const. Art. VI]; yet they have introduced test-oaths, and people are obliged to swear certain things that the Constitution says shall not be permitted. Are we American citizens here? I think so. Have we any rights? I think we ought to have. Are they being trampled upon? Yes, they are; and these things are being done with impunity. How is it? Why, the Constitution is treated by the politicians of to-day as the Bible is treated by professors of religion. . . . As I have said, the Constitution provides that Congress shall make no law respecting an establishment of religion, or prohibiting the free exercise thereof. . . .

. . . At the time when the Edmunds law was passed I was living in what is known as the Gardo House. I had most of my wives living with me there, and after looking carefully over the Edmunds law I thought to myself, why Congress is growing very wild; this Government is getting very, very foolish; they are trampling upon Constitutional rights. No matter, I said, I will obey this law. . . . "[W]e shall stand up for our rights and protect ourselves in every proper way, legally and constitutionally, and dispute inch by inch every step that is taken to deprive us of our rights and liberties." And we will do this in the way that I speak of. We are doing it to-day; and as you have heard it expressed on other occasions, it looks very much like as though the time was drawing near when this country will tumble to pieces; for if the people of this nation are so blind and infatuated as to trample under foot the Constitution and other safeguards provided for the liberties of man, we do not propose to assist them in their suicidal and traitorous enterprises; for we have been told by Joseph Smith that when the people of this nation would trample upon the Constitution, the Elders of this Church would rally round the flag and defend it. And it may come to that; we may be nearer to it than some of us think, for the people are not very zealous in the protection of human rights. And when legislators, governors and judges unite in seeking to tear down the temple of liberty and destroy the bulwarks of human freedom, it will be seen by all lovers of liberty, that they are playing a hazardous game and endangering the perpetuity of human rights. For it will not take long for the unthinking to follow their lead, and they may let loose an element that they never can bind again. (*JD* 25:348-50)

3.73. We will do right, we will treat all men right, and we will maintain every institution of our country that is according to the Constitution of the United States, and the laws thereof, and we will sustain them. (*JD* 26:38)

3.74. By and by, you will find they will tear the Constitution to shreads, as they have begun now; they won't have to begin; they have started long ago to rend the Constitution of our country in pieces; and in doing so they are letting loose and encouraging a principle which will re-act upon themselves with terrible consequences; for if law-makers and administrators can afford to trample upon justice, equity, and the Constitution of this country, they will find thousands and tens of thousands who are willing to follow in their wake in the demolition of the rights of man, and the destruction of all principles of justice, and the safeguards of the nation; but we will stand by and maintain its principles and the rights of all men of every color, and every clime; we will cleave to the truth, live our religion and keep the commandments of God, and God will bless us in time and throughout the eternities that are to come. (*JD* 26:39)

3.75. Am I to disobey the law of God? Has any man a right to control my conscience, or your conscience, or to tell me I shall believe this or believe the other, or reject this or reject the other? No man has a right to do it. These principles are sacred, and the forefathers of this nation felt so and so proclaimed it in the Constitution of the United States, and said "Congress shall make no law respecting an establishment of religion, or prohibiting the free exercise thereof" [US Const. Amend. I]. (*JD* 26:152)

3.76. The Constitution expressly says that no law shall be passed impairing the obligation of contracts. But we have entered into covenants and contracts in our most sacred places. . . . I have never broken any law of these United States. . . .

Well, what will you do? I will obey every Constitutional law so far as God gives me ability. (*JD* 26:153)

3.77. When this infamous Edmunds law was passed, I saw that there were features in that which were contrary to law, violative of the Constitution, contrary to justice and the rights and the freedom of men. (*JD* 26:153)

3.78. But we now have test oaths introduced, which is another violation of the Constitution and by which an attempt is being made to hold all men guilty until they prove themselves innocent.

... Another portion of the Constitution must be broken to introduce a test oath without any authority [US Const. Art. VI]. ...

Well, what would you do? Observe the laws as much as you can. Bear with these indignities as much as you can. (*JD* 26:154-55)

3.79. And while other men are seeking to trample the Constitution under foot, we will try to maintain it. We have prophecies something like this somewhere; that the time would come when this nation would do as they are now doing—that is, they would trample under foot the constitution and institutions of the nation, and the Elders of this Church would rally around the standard and maintain those principles which were introduced for the freedom and protection of men. We expect to do that, and to maintain all correct principle. I will tell you what you will see by and by. You will see trouble, trouble, trouble enough in these United States. ... But let us be on the side of human liberty and human rights, and the protection of all correct principles and laws and government, and maintain every principle that is upright and virtuous and honorable, and let the world take the balance if they want, we don't want it. We will cleave to the truth, God being our helper, and try to introduce principles whereby the will of God will be done on earth as it is in heaven. And we will obey every institution of man for the Lord's sake so far as we can without violating our consciences and doing things that are wrong and improper. (*JD* 26:156-57)

3.80. Do not permit any of these abuses with which we have to cope, to tempt you to retaliate in kind, or to violate any Constitutional law of the land. You will remember that Joseph Smith has said that that sacred instrument was given by inspiration of God, and it becomes our bounden duty to sustain it in all its provisions. ...

During the lifetime of the Prophet Joseph Smith he predicted that the time would come when it would devolve upon the Latter-day Saints to uplift, defend and maintain the Constitution of the United States. Recent events in our Territory have given great significance to this prediction, and have brought it forcibly to the minds of all who have heard concerning it. These events appear to be forcing us into the exact position so plainly described by the Prophet through the spirit of prophecy. Attempts are now being made to destroy our rights under the Constitution, and to effect this, that instrument—which the Prophet Joseph Smith said was given by inspiration of God—is being trampled upon by those who should be its administrators and guardians. This compels us to contend for constitutional principles. We must uphold them to the best of our ability. An attack has been made upon our religion, and it appears to be determined that we shall either abandon it or be visited with the most severe pains and penalties. Under the cover of this attack upon the principle of patriarchal marriage, we are denied the most of the rights which belong to freemen, and which our ancestors enjoyed for ages before even they were enunciated in writing in the Constitution of the United States. For proof of this we need but refer to our right to be tried only by a jury of our peers—a right which men of our race have enjoyed from the most remote times. Our religion is made the pretext for this deprivation of rights, and for bitter threats against the few remaining liberties which we possess. To preserve these liberties, and to regain the rights of which we are already unjustly deprived, we must contend earnestly, manfully, legally and constitutionally.

. . . We have rights under the Constitution, and however much these may be denied to us, it is still our bounden duty to contend for them, not only in behalf of ourselves, but for all our fellow citizens and for our posterity, and for humanity generally throughout the world. Were we to do less than this, we would fail in performing the mission assigned to us, and be recreant to the high trust which God has reposed in us. . . .

. . . And while we at present are in circumstances that are painful, and that have been brought about by the action of inconsiderate, unreflecting and, in many instances, wicked and unscrupulous men, some of whom are officials, yet we have never felt like wavering in our fidelity to our government, nor like ignoring the principles of equal rights guaranteed by that sacred palladium of human liberty—the Constitution of the United States. . . .

We repeat, that we desire that all men should be aware of the fact that we have been the upholders of the Constitution and laws enacted in pursuance of that sacred instrument. We still entertain the same patriotic disposition, and propose to continue acting in conformity with it to the last. Neither have we any desire to come in active conflict even with statutes that we deem opposed to the Constitution both in letter and spirit. . . . Were we to make such a surrender, our conduct in that respect would not be in harmony with the guaranties [*sic*] of the Constitution, which we are in duty bound to uphold. (*MFP* 3:12-14, 16, 19, 30)

3.81. Completely enveloping it [the question of polygamy], has been the design to destroy our rights as citizens, to take away from us our liberties under the Constitution and the laws, and to obtain the political control of our country. (*MFP* 3:51)

3.82. The preamble of the Constitution of the United States assigns as reasons why it was framed: "To form a more perfect union, establish justice, insure domestic tranquility, provide for the common defense, promote the general welfare, and secure the blessings of liberty to ourselves and our posterity." Most excellent reasons for framing such a charter of liberty, and every officer who acts under it should keep these objects in view. But many of the officers sent here have acted as though they were determined that none of these blessings for which the Constitution was framed should reach us. (*MFP* 3:52)

3.83. It would appear that we have reached that era in our history, so long foretold, when the Constitution of the United States would hang by a single thread, and the Elders of Israel alone would contend for its preservation. (*JT Papers* 2:464)

3.84. We will rally around the flag of our country and maintain the glorious Constitution for weal or woe. (*JT Papers* 2:446)

3.85. We wish it fully understood by the Saints and by all the world that we have a profound respect for all wholesome and constitutional laws. (*MFP* 3:80)

3.86. The powers of the government and the rights and privileges of the citizen are regulated and plainly defined by the Constitution itself, and when a Territory becomes a part of the United States, the Federal Government enters into possession in the character impressed upon it by those who created it. It enters upon it with its powers over the citizen strictly defined and limited by the Constitution from which it derives its own existence, and by virtue of which alone it continues to exist as a government and sovereignty. It has no power of any kind beyond it, and it cannot when it enters a Territory of the United States put off its character, and assume discretionary or despotic powers which the Constitution has denied to it. It cannot create for itself a new character separate from the citizens of the United States, and the duties it owes to them under the provisions of the Constitution. (*MFP* 3:116-17)

3.87. It was through and by the power of God, that the fathers of this country framed the Declaration of Independence, and also that great palladium of human rights, the Constitution of the United States. There is nothing of a bigoted, narrow-contracted feeling about that instrument; it is broad and comprehensive. ("The Constitution Is an Inspired Document" 644)

Wilford Woodruff   4

Biographical Information

Born: 1 March 1807
Ordained an Apostle: 26 April 1839
President of the Twelve: 10 October 1880
President of the Church: 7 April 1889 – 2 September 1898
Died: 2 September 1898

*   *   *   *   *   *   *   *   *

Relationship with the Constitution and U.S. Government

Born at Avon, Hartford, Connecticut, Wilford Woodruff developed a love for the U.S. Constitution that rivaled that of Joseph Smith and Brigham Young. During his tenure as Church President he continued the struggle with the U.S. Government over the issue of polygamy. He realized that this struggle would probably destroy the Church, and consequently he inquired of the Lord about the problem. In 1890 President Woodruff issued the Manifesto (Official Declaration—1), thus bringing to a close the practice of polygamy, or at least signaling the beginning of its end. This move made statehood and a flourishing two-party system possible for Utah.

Themes Discussed in the Quotations

Main theme: The Constitution ensures freedom of worship.
Minor themes:
    1. The framing of the Constitution was inspired.
    2. The benefits of the Constitution are for all.
    3. The Saints will rescue the Constitution.

4. Members are under divine commandment to revere the Constitution.

Quotations

As an Apostle

4.1. But O!! America America!! whose land is choice above that of all the footstool of God, whose constitution was framed by the Spirit of inspiration & whose Government was established by the hand of Omnipotent power. (*WW* 2:42)

4.2. The Saints feel dispose [*sic*] to exercise those rights which the Constitution & Laws of the United States guarrentee [*sic*] unto us equal with all other citizens in attending the elections & voting for whom we please. (*WW* 2:182)

4.3. But says the mob what dangerous powers. But the constitution of the United States nor of this state is not dangerous against good men but bad men, the breakers of the law.

Shall we longer bear these cruelties which have been bearing upon us for the last ten years in the face of heaven & in open violation of the constitution & laws of these United States & of this State? May God forbid. I will not bear it. (*WW* 2:253)

4.4. The benefits of the constitution & law is [*sic*] for all alike & the great [E]loheem [*sic*] God has given me the privilege of having the benefits of the constitution. (*WW* 2:253-54)

4.5. I am glad and my soul rejoices in these things, and I believe that the people are ready to shoulder their guns and walk into these kanyons [*sic*] and line them from here to Fort Bridger in defence of the Constitution of the United States and the rights which both the laws of God and man guarentee [*sic*] to us. (*JH*

[27 Sep 1857] 4; also in "Remarks" 246; from an address given at the Bowery, Salt Lake City, UT, 27 Sep 1857)

4.6. The Lord . . . has spoken concerning our Government and Constitution, and he has said—"Ye are justified in maintaining the Constitution and laws of the land, for they make you free, and the Gospel maketh you free; and you shall seek to sustain good and wise men for rulers, and whatsoever is more or less than this cometh of evil." . . . The laws of Heaven command us not to uphold and sustain men, except they are good men, who will sustain the Constitution of our country; and we are fulfilling the revelations in this respect as in many others, and we are carrying out the requirements of the Constitution of the United States. (*JD* 7:104)

4.7. A great deal has been said about the form of government, and the constitution under which we live. They have been the praise of all Americans, and perhaps of people living in other portions of the earth. We consider that we have been blessed as a nation in possessing the freedom and privileges guaranteed by the Constitution of the United States. They have been a rich legacy from our fathers. We consider our form of government superior to any other on the earth. It guarantees to us "life, liberty and the pursuit of happiness." And while the inhabitants of many other governments have been tyrannically bound up, and their minds controlled in certain channels, and they have been deprived of the right of liberty of speech and of many other rights valued by freemen, ours has guaranteed unto us all the liberty that can be enjoyed by man. Still, I have many times thought that we, as American Citizens, have not prized the gifts and blessings guaranteed to us by the Constitution of our country. For the last few years, especially, the Constitution at times, has been looked upon as a matter of the smallest consequence. In some respects, however, it has been a blessing to us as a people, and it is to the whole nation, as far as it is carried out. But in order to fully receive its blessings we have to honor its precepts. (*JD* 12:275)

4.8. We live in a land and under a constitution which guarantees the right to worship God according to the dictates of conscience to every sect, party, name and denomination under heaven, then why should we be so narrow-minded as to hate or seek to persecute or kill our neighbor because he differs from us in religion? (*JD* 17:194)

4.9. Give every inhabitant of the earth the right to worship God according to the dictates of their [*sic*] own conscience. This is a principle which we believe in as Latter-day Saints, we ever have believed in it, and it is a principle which even the laws of our country, the constitution of our government holds out to all of its citizens.

We say to all men, "Enjoy your religion, worship God according to the dictates of your own conscience." We ask the same right as the children of God. We claim this by the Constitution and laws of our country, and upon this principle we have embraced the fulness of the everlasting Gospel of Jesus Christ. (*JD* 22:341-42)

4.10. We live in a government raised up by the God of heaven. We have a constitution that was given by inspiration from God to man. I believe it is the best human form of government that was ever given to the human family. Now, I say if our rulers and governors become corrupt and attempt to trample those principles under their feet; though the nation itself might go to pieces, yet it is beyond the power of man to destroy the principles of the constitution. They may destroy one another, yet the principles contained in that instrument will live, and the God of heaven will maintain them until Jesus Christ comes in the clouds of heaven to set up His throne in Jerusalem, and to reign on the earth a thousand years. (*JD* 22:346)

4.11. The Prophet Joseph Smith had said the time would come when the principles of the Constitution would be forsaken and that instrument would be rent asunder, and this people would then step forward and rescue it from entire destruction. (*JH* [6 Apr 1882] 3)

4.12. The Lord inspired the men that framed the Constitution of our country, and has guarded the nation from its foundation, in order to prepare free people in which to establish his kingdom. Columbus was inspired of God to persevere as he did to discover this continent, and thus prepare the way for a class of people upon whom the Spirit of the Lord moved to follow; and when they were oppressed hard enough they declared themselves independent, and by the help of God they established and have maintained the government which God gave our forefathers, which is one of the best constitutional governments ever known among men. (*JD* 23:81; also in "The Constitution Is an Inspired Document" 644)

4.13. I have heard Joseph Smith say that if he were emperor of the whole world, holding the destinies of all men in his hands, he would defend the religious rights of every man, whether his religion was right or wrong. And especially ought this to be the case in this American nation, the constitution of which guarantees to all people the right to worship God according to the dictates of their own conscience. This is the broad platform upon which our government has been founded. I have looked upon the Constitution of the United States as one of the best instruments ever devised by man for the government of the inhabitants of the earth. (*JD* 24:237)

4.14. We have an anxiety to honor God and keep His commandments, and to honor our country and the Constitution of our Government. That Constitution we believe was given by revelation, and whatever laws are passed agreeable to it we desire to honor. It guarantees to all men the right to enjoy their religion, to worship God according to the dictates of their conscience. (*JD* 24:243)

4.15. I would to God that the rulers of our land—the President of the United States, the Congress of the United States, the Supreme Court of the United States—would learn the responsibility the God of heaven will hold them to in the administration of those glorious principles laid down in the Constitution of the government of this country. The God of heaven will hold this nation, as well as all other nations, responsible for the manner in which these principles are used. If they misuse them, it will be their loss. If they trample the Constitution under foot; if they undertake to deprive any portion of citizens of the rights the Constitution guarantees unto them, they will be held responsible, and will have to pay the bill. When innocent blood is shed, it costs something; and I would to God that our nation could understand the blessings they enjoy. There is no nation on the face of the earth that has the same liberty that is guaranteed to us by the Constitution of our country. (*JD* 25:11)

4.16. I feel to bear my testimony to these things. They are true. God is with this people. And we say to our nation—maintain the Constitution and we are satisfied. Give us the rights of that Constitution and we are satisfied. It is an instrument inspired by the power of God. Our forefathers were inspired when they framed it. Yet it is marvelous to reflect upon some principles that have been laid down—perhaps I ought not to allude to these things, but I am only expressing my own reflections—even by the supreme court of the United States. In effect it has said that we may think as we please, but must not act. I would ask, in the name of the Lord, was that all Thomas Jefferson, and others had in their minds when they framed the clause in reference to religious liberty? What about men acting? If it was only intended that men should think and not act, why not say so in the instrument? Why should it be stated that "Congress shall make no law respecting an establishment of religion, or prohibiting the free *exercise* thereof," [U.S. Constitution Amendment I] if men were not to be allowed to act? Why, in the exercise of their religion, men must act: and it is straining points, it is overstepping the bounds of the Constitution to pass laws taking away the rights and privileges of any people because of their religion—because they happen to differ from their neighbors. Where will such a course land our government? I will tell you what it will do. It will rend the government in twain like unto a potter's vessel. It will lay the nation in the dust. It will overthrow the government. When they get through with the Mormons there will be somebody else to deal with. The Constitution is good enough for anybody.

It is good enough for the Latter-day Saints. We have no principles but what are in accord with the Constitution of the United States and the laws of God. We are perfectly willing to trust ourselves and our interests in the hands of God, and to leave our nation in His hands also; for God will judge our nation; He will judge us; He will judge all the children of men and He will judge righteous judgment. What men sow they will reap. What measure they mete, it shall be measured to them again.

I pray God to bless this nation. I pray God to give our legislators wisdom, that they may maintain the Constitutional principles of the government, the only government on the face of God's earth where the Lord could have established His Church and Kingdom. (*JD* 25:210-11)

As the President of the Church

4.17. There is absolutely nothing in the Mormon's religion inconsistent with the most patriotic devotion to the government of the United States. Revelation and the commandments of the church require that the Constitution and the laws of the land be upheld. It is also part of our belief that the time will come when the country will be distracted and general lawlessness prevail. Then the Mormon people will step forward and take an active part in rescuing the nation from ruin. ("President Woodruff States the Facts" 788)

4.18. As far as constitutional liberty is concerned, I will say, the God of heaven has raised up our nation, as foretold by His Prophets generations ago. . . . It is also well known how our forefathers found a home and an asylum in this land from the hand of persecution, and how they planted here the tree of liberty and jealously guarded it from the attempt of the mother country to uproot and destroy it. The hand of God was in this; and it is through the intervention of His providence that we enjoy to-day the freest and most independent government the world ever saw. And what was the object of this? It was to prepare the way for the building up of the kingdom of God in this the last dispensation of the fullness of times; and as long as the principles of constitutional liberty shall be maintained upon this land, blessings will attend the nation. ("Discourse by President Wilford Woodruff" 801-02)

4.19. We declare that there is nothing in the ceremony of the Endowment, or in any doctrine, tenet, obligation or injunction of this Church, either private or public, which is hostile or intended to be hostile to the Government of the United States. On the contrary, its members are under divine commandment to revere the Constitution as a heaven-inspired instrument and obey as supreme all laws made in pursuance of its provisions. ("Official Declaration" 34; also in *MFP* 3:185)

4.20. We thank thee, O God of Israel, that thou didst raise up patriotic men to lay the foundation of this great American government. Thou didst inspire them to frame a good constitution and laws which guarantee to all of the inhabitants of the land equal rights and privileges to worship thee according to the dictates of their own consciences. Bless the officers, both judicial and executive. Confer abundant favors upon the President, his Cabinet, and Congress. Enlightened and guided by thy Spirit may they maintain and uphold the glorious principles of human liberty. . . .
　　Show unto them that we are their friends, that we love liberty, that we will join with them in upholding the rights of the people, the Constitution and laws of our country; and give unto us and our children an increased disposition to always be loyal, and to do everything in our power to maintain Constitutional rights and the freedom of all within the confines of this great Republic. (*Prayer Offered at the Dedication of the Temple of the Lord* 10-11)

4.21. Thou knowest all hearts and art our witness that in the misunderstandings and differences that have occurred, the people of these mountain vales have been loyal upholders of the constitution of our country and those republican institutions which Thou didst inspire the fathers of the nation to institute and establish. We desire, our Father, to maintain them inviolate. And now that we have acquired, through Thy blessing, the power to aid in their preservation, we pray Thee to bless us so to do and to secure that liberty to others which we prize for ourselves. *(Inaugural Address* 1)

4.22. I am going to bear my testimony to this assembly, if I never do it again in my life, that those men who laid the foundation of this American government and signed the Declaration of Independence were the best spirits the God of heaven could find on the face of the earth. They were choice spirits, not wicked men. General Washington and all the men that labored for the purpose were inspired of the Lord. Another thing I am going to say here, because I have a right to say it. Every one of those men that signed the Declaration of Independence, with General Washington, called upon me, as an Apostle of the Lord Jesus Christ, in the Temple at St. George, two consecutive nights, and demanded at my hands that I should go forth and attend to the ordinances of the House of God for them. Would those spirits have called upon me, as an elder in Israel, to perform that work if they had not been noble spirits before God? *(CR* [Apr 1898] 89-90)

Lorenzo Snow   5

Biographical Information

Born: 3 April 1814
Ordained an Apostle: 12 February 1849
Additional Counselor to Brigham Young: 8 April 1873
Assistant Counselor to Brigham Young: 9 May 1874
President of the Twelve: 7 April 1889
President of the Church: 13 September 1898 – 10 October 1901
Died: 10 October 1901

* * * * * * * * *

Relationship with the Constitution and U.S. Government

A native of Ohio with more formal education than earlier Presidents of The Church of Jesus Christ of Latter-day Saints, Lorenzo Snow had a deep affection for the Founding Fathers and the Constitution. He said relatively little about these subjects, but his feelings are nonetheless evident. Although his administration occurred after Wilford Woodruff issued the Manifesto, some conflict with the government over polygamy continued.

Theme Discussed in the Quotations

Main theme: The Constitution was founded by noble and inspired men.

Quotations

As an Apostle

5.1. We trace the hand of the Almighty in framing the constitution of our land, and believe that the Lord raised up men purposely for the accomplishment of this object, raised them up and inspired them to frame the constitution of the United States. (*JD* 14:301; also in Brown 359)

5.2. We look upon George Washington, the father of our country, as an inspired instrument of the Almighty; we can see the all-inspiring Spirit operating upon him. And upon his co-workers in resisting oppression, and in establishing the thirteen colonies as a confederacy; and then again the workings of the same Spirit upon those men who established the constitution of the United States. (*JD* 14:304)

5.3. Well, Governor, so far as I am concerned personally, I am not in conflict with any of the laws of the country. I have obeyed the laws as faithfully and conscientiously as I can thus far, and I am not here [Utah State Penitentiary] because of disobedience of any law. I am here wrongfully convicted and wrongfully sentenced.

   . . . We honor the law administered rightfully. ("Gov. West Is Baffled" 4)

As the President of the Church

5.4. They will sustain the constitution and laws and institutions of the United States, and be the champions of liberty and of that constitution when its integrity shall be threatened. (*JH* [15 Sep 1898] 3)

5.5. We thank thee for this opportunity to show our love for these heroes who have accomplished such wonders for the beloved

United States, which was founded by noble and inspired men. ("Mighty Demonstration of Joy and Rejoicing Greet the Heroes Everywhere" 1)

5.6. We thank thee for the opportunity of thus displaying our feelings and love for these magnificent heroes who have accomplished wonders in the interests of these United States, this great republic, the foundation of which was laid by the noble, generous men inspired of thee, and as thou hast been favorable to this republic even from the date of its foundation to the present time, and hast raised up men and boys willing to serve their country. ("Boys Are Welcomed Home by Patriotic Multitude" 1)

Joseph F. Smith 6

Biographical Information

Born: 13 November 1838
Ordained an Apostle and Counselor
to the First Presidency: 1 July 1866
Member of the Quorum of the Twelve: 8 October 1867
Second Counselor to John Taylor: 10 October 1880
Second Counselor to Wilford Woodruff: 7 April 1889
Second Counselor to Lorenzo Snow: 13 September 1898
First Counselor to Lorenzo Snow: 6 October 1901
President of the Church: 17 October 1901 – 19 November 1918
Died: 19 November 1918

* * * * * * * * *

Relationship with the Constitution and U.S. Government

Joseph F. Smith was the first second-generation LDS Church President, and he inherited a love for the Constitution from his forebears. His relationship with the federal government centered on the issue of polygamy. He testified at the Smoot Hearing in Washington, D.C. in support of Reed Smoot's being seated as a senator from Utah. (The government was trying to determine if the Church had really stopped practicing polygamy.) Smoot was eventually seated.

President Joseph F. Smith also presided over the Church during World War I, when thousands of Latter-day Saints served in the armed forces. This military service was generally regarded as a positive sign of Mormon loyalty and patriotism.

Themes Discussed in the Quotations

Main theme: We should be loyal to the Constitution.

Minor themes:
1. This government was established by the Lord in preparation for the restoration of the gospel.
2. The Constitution will hang by a thread, and the Latter-day Saints will come to the rescue.

Quotations

As an Apostle

6.1. The Lord Almighty has prepared the way for the coming forth of the kingdom of God in this dispensation by establishing the republican government of the United States; a government affording the widest liberty and the greatest freedom to man that has ever been known to exist among men, outside of those governed by the direct communication of heaven. It was part of the design of the Almighty when He influenced our fathers to leave the old world and come to this continent; He had a hand in the establishment of this government; He inspired the framers of the Constitution and the fathers of this nation to contend for their liberties; and he did this upon natural principles, that the way might be prepared, and that it might be possible for Him to establish His kingdom upon the earth, no more to be thrown down. (*JD* 22:44-45)

6.2. We are told . . . that no man need break the laws of the land who will keep the laws of God. . . . The law of the land, which all have no need to break, is that law which is the Constitutional law of the land, and that is as God himself has defined it. And whatsoever is more or less than this cometh of evil. Now it seems to me that this makes this matter so clear that it is not possible for any man who professes to be a member of the Church of Jesus Christ of Latter-day Saints to make any mistake, or to be in doubt as to the course he should pursue under the command of God in relation to the observance of the laws of the land. I maintain that the Church of Jesus Christ of Latter-day Saints has ever been faithful to the constitutional laws of our country. . . .

I ask myself, What law have you broken? What constitutional law have you not observed? I am bound not only by allegiance to the government of the United States, but by the actual command of God Almighty, to observe and obey every constitutional law of the land, and without hesitancy I declare to this congregation that I have never violated, nor transgressed any law, I am not amenable to any penalties of the law, because I have endeavored from my youth up to be a law-abiding citizen, and not only so, but to be a peacemaker, a preacher of righteousness, and not only to preach righteousness by word, but by example. . . . If lawmakers have a mind to violate their oath, break their covenants and their faith with the people, and depart from the provisions of the Constitution where is the law human or divine, which binds me, as an individual, to outwardly and openly proclaim my acceptance of their acts? (*JD* 23:70-71)

As the President of the Church

6.3. The legislation against polygamy by Congress, and the endeavors of the church to resist those enactments on the ground of their conflict with the first Amendment to the Constitution, are pretty well known to the American public. It is not so generally known that the final decision of the Supreme Court of the United States that the anti-polygamy laws were not in contravention of the Constitution was the chief reason for the change of attitude on the part of the church leaders. ("The 'Mormonism' of To-Day" 451)

6.4. By revelation to Joseph Smith, the Prophet, the Lord declared that he had established the Constitution of the United States through "wise men raised up unto this very purpose" [D&C 101:80]. It is also our belief that God has blessed and prospered this nation, and given unto it power to enforce the divine decrees concerning the land of Zion, that free institutions might not perish from the earth. Cherishing such convictions, we have no place in our hearts for disloyal sentiments. ("An Address" 489; also in *MFP* 4:150)

6.5. We love our country and pray for the perpetuity of its government, we support its institutions, we venerate the Constitution. ("Magazine Slanders Confuted" 724; also in *MFP* 4:229)

6.6. I hope with all my soul that the members of the Church of Jesus Christ of Latter-day Saints will be loyal in their very hearts and souls, to the principles of the Constitution of our country. From them we have derived the liberty that we enjoy. They have been the means of guaranteeing to the foreigner that has come within our gates, and to the native born, and to all the citizens of this country, the freedom and liberty that we possess. We cannot go back upon such principles as these. We may go back upon those who fail to execute the law as they should. We may be dissatisfied with the decision of judges, and may desire to have them removed out of their places. But the law provides ways and means for all these things to be done under the Constitution of our country, and it is better for us to abide the evils that we have than to fly to greater evils that we know not what the results will be. . . .

These principles that I propose to read to you are the foundation and basic principles of the Constitution of our country, and are eternal, enduring forevermore, and cannot be changed or ignored with impunity:

"And God spake all these words, saying, I am the Lord thy God which hath brought thee out of the land of Egypt, out of the house of bondage. Thou shalt have no other gods before me." . . .

"Thou shalt not make unto thee any graven image of any likeness of anything that is in heaven above or that is in the earth beneath, or that is in the water under the earth."

"Thou shalt not bow down thyself to them nor serve them." . . .

"Thou shalt not take the name of the Lord thy God in vain." . . .

"Six days shalt thou labor and do all thy work." . . .

"Honor thy father and thy mother." . . .

. . . "Thou shalt not kill." . . .

"Thou shalt not commit adultery." . . .

"Thou shalt not steal."

"Thou shalt not bear false witness against thy neighbor."

"Thou shalt not covet thy neighbor's house, thou shalt not covet thy neightbor's wife, nor his man-servant, nor his maid-servant, nor his ox, nor anything that is thy neighbor's" [Ex 20:1-6].

Now, these are the commandments of God, the principles contained in these commandments of the great Eternal are the principles that underlie the Constitution of our country and all just laws. ("The Mexican Trouble—Loyalty to the Constitution" 98-101)

6.7. Joseph Smith, the prophet, was inspired to affirm and ratify this truth, and he further predicted that the time would come, when the Constitution of our country would hang as it were by a thread, and that the Latter-day Saints above all other people in the world would come to the rescue of that great and glorious palladium of our liberty. We cannot brook the thought of it being torn into shreds, or destroyed, or trampled under foot and ignored by men. We cannot tolerate the sentiment, at one time expressed, by a man, high in authority in the nation. He said: "The Constitution be damned; the popular sentiment of the people is the Constitution!" That is the sentiment of anarchism that has spread to a certain extent, and is spreading over "the land of liberty and home of the brave." We do not tolerate it. Latter-day Saints cannot tolerate such a spirit as this. It is anarchy. It means destruction. It is the spirit of mobocracy, and the Lord knows we have suffered enough from mobocracy, and we do not want any more of it. Our people from Mexico are suffering from the effects of that same spirit. We do not want any more of it, and we cannot afford to yield to that spirit or contribute to it in the least degree. We should stand with a front like flint against every spirit or species of contempt or disrespect for the Constitution of our country and the constitutional laws of our land. ("The Mexican Trouble—Loyalty to the Constitution" 101-02)

6.8. I wish to say this, there isn't a feeling in my soul, nor in any fibre of my being that is disloyal to the government of the United States or to the desire that we have in our souls to maintain the principles of individual and National liberty, justice and freedom that have been established in the Constitution of our country. I believe in the Constitution of the United States. I believe in the principles which that instrument promulgates—the freedom of mankind to do right, to worship God according to the dictates of their own conscience, freedom to pursue their way in peace and to observe and maintain their rights, their freedom, their liberties, and justly recognize and equally preserve and defend their rights, freedom and liberty of their neighbors and of their fellow beings—and of all God's creatures. I believe that the Constitution of the United States was and still is an inspired instrument. The Lord God Almighty inspired the minds that framed it, and I believe it ought to be most sacredly preserved. It is worthy of the defense and should be upheld by all the people of our land. ("Thrift and Economy" 634-35)

6.9. It was part of the design of the Almighty when He influenced the fathers to leave the old world and come to this continent; He had a hand in the establishment of this government; He inspired the framers of the Constitution and the fathers of this nation to contend for their liberty. ("The Constitution Is an Inspired Document" 644)

Heber J. Grant　　7

Biographical Information

Born: 22 November 1856
Ordained an Apostle: 16 October 1882
President of the Twelve: 23 November 1916
President of the Church: 23 November 1918 – 14 May 1945
Died: 14 May 1945

*　*　*　*　*　*　*　*　*

Relationship with the Constitution and U.S. Government

Heber J. Grant served longer as President of the Church than any other Church President except Brigham Young. During this long term he consciously sought to develop strong ties with the U.S. Government. One of his counselors, J. Reuben Clark, Jr., had served in several State Department positions and as U.S. Ambassador to Mexico. Many of President Grant's friends also had close connections with Washington, D.C. President Grant's administration was an era of positive relationships with the Constitution and the government.

Themes Discussed in the Quotations

Main theme: The Constitution was inspired of God.
Minor themes:
1. We should obey the laws of the land.
2. We honor and must uphold the Constitution.

Quotations

As an Apostle

7.1. As a boy I was taught to love the institutions of my country and the liberty guaranteed under it. I then looked forward hopefully to the time when I should be a man and should enjoy the rights and assume the responsibilities of manhood. Now that I am a man I want every right that my country gives to other men. ("Speech of Hon. H. J. Grant" 1)

7.2. That man Joseph Smith, when he stood as the prophet and the leader of the people, proclaimed that the Constitution of our country was inspired by God. I ask if intelligent people are going to believe that the Latter-day Saints, guided by a prophet who proclaimed that the Constitution of our country was inspired, are in rebellion against the political system of our country? I say that the statement is absolutely false. (*JH* [30 Apr 1889] 10)

As the President of the Church

7.3. Our declaration to all the world, through the Prophet Joseph Smith, that the men who wrote the Constitution of this country were inspired of the living God . . . give[s] the lie to all the liars who are perpetually saying that we are opposed to this country. . . . We believe absolutely in the inspiration of God to the men who framed our Constitution. (*CR* [Oct 1919] 33)

7.4. President Grant said he was grateful for the Constitution and declared that no Latter-day Saint could live up to the teachings of his religion without being a good American. Latter-day Saints should so live that the world may know how they regard the Constitution and laws of this country. ("Constitution Topic of Tabernacle Sermons" 8)

7.5. Next Sunday, September 17, being Constitution Day, designated and set apart for commemoration of the great document which is the organic law and foundation of our glorious Republic, we earnestly desire that bishops and presidents of stakes arrange to have the speakers of their respective services on that day address themselves to the Constitution, its history, meaning and importance. (*JH* [16 Sep 1922] 1)

7.6. Perhaps there is nothing of greater importance, next to our spiritual growth, than a determination on the part of the Latter-day Saints to observe the laws of our country. . . .

One of the Articles of our Faith [no. 12] declares that we believe in sustaining the law and supporting the rulers. ("President Heber J. Grant's Conference Message" 677-78)

7.7. All Latter-day Saints believe absolutely that the Constitution of our Country was inspired of God, and that he used wise men, noble men, as instruments in his hands for establishing that Constitution, and when any law is enacted and becomes a constitutional law, no man who spends his money to help men break that law can truthfully say that he is a loyal citizen. (*CR* [Oct 1927] 5)

7.8. The "Mormons" have taught, from the days of the Prophet Joseph Smith, that the men who wrote the Constitution were raised up by God, and that it was adopted by inspired men. We believe in the inspiration of the living God, in the forming of our government. ("The Upholding of Constituted Law and Order" 509; from an address given at Salt Lake City, UT, 12 Feb 1928)

7.9. We are also told to obey constitutional law, and any man or woman in the Church of Christ that is breaking the prohibition law is also breaking the laws of God. ("The Upholding of Constituted Law and Order" 515; from an address given at Salt Lake City, UT, 12 Feb 1928)

7.10. The Latter-day Saints believe absolutely that the Constitution of our country was written by inspired men. We believe in upholding the laws of our country. We believe in being obedient to the laws. One of the Articles of our Faith [no. 12] says that it is our duty to do so. (*CR* [Oct 1928] 9)

7.11. The Latter-day Saints believe and have taught from the beginning that God raised up the men who wrote the Constitution of this country: that it was an inspired document, and that the Lord fought on the side of our revolutionary fathers. (*JH* [13 Apr 1930] 3-4)

7.12. Sustain the constitution of the United States. The Lord himself has said that he raised up the very men who prepared it to the end that it might be an example to all the world. Do you believe it? If you do then sustain it and don't let your voice be among those that shall deride and break down the things that are so important for us. This is our Father's work. We are his children, heirs to all blessings. (*CR* [Oct 1935] 122)

7.13. The Church does not interfere, and has no intention of trying to interfere, with the fullest and freest exercise of the political franchise of its members, under and within our Constitution which the Lord declared: "I established . . . by the hands of wise men whom I raised up unto this very purpose" [D&C 101:80], and which, as to the principles thereof, the Prophet, dedicating the Kirtland Temple, prayed should be "established forever" [D&C 109:54].

But Communism is not a political party nor a political plan under the Constitution; it is a system of government that is the opposite of our Constitutional government, and it would be necessary to destroy our government before Communism could be set up in the United States.

Since Communism, established, would destroy our American Constitutional government, to support Communism is treasonable to our free institutions, and no patriotic American citizen may become either a Communist or supporter of Communism. . . .

Furthermore, it is charged by universal report, which is not successfully contradicted or disproved, that Communism undertakes to control, if not indeed to proscribe the religious life of the people living within its jurisdiction, and that it even reaches its hand into the sanctity of the family circle itself, disrupting the normal relationship of parent and child, all in a manner unknown and unsanctioned under the Constitutional guarantees under which we in America live. Such interference would be contrary to the fundamental precepts of the Gospel and to the teachings and order of the Church.

Communism being thus hostile to loyal American citizenship and incompatible with true Church membership, of necessity no loyal American citizen and no faithful Church member can be a Communist.

We call upon all Church members completely to eschew Communism. The safety of our divinely inspired Constitutional government and the welfare of our Church imperatively demand that Communism shall have no place in America. ("Warning to Church Members" 488)

7.14. From my childhood days I have understood that we believe absolutely that the Constitution of our country was an inspired instrument, and that God directed those who created it and those who defended the independence of this nation. In other words, that He fought with Washington and others in the Revolutionary War. (*CR* [Oct 1936] 6)

7.15. Every Latter-day Saint believes that Abraham Lincoln was raised up and inspired of God, and that he reached the Presidency of the United States under the favor of our Heavenly Father. . . .

The following quotation from Lincoln with respect to the observance of law is . . . worth repeating often:

"Let every American, every lover of liberty, every well wisher to his posterity, swear by the blood of the revolution never to violate, in the least particular, the laws of the country, and never to tolerate their violation by others. As the patriots of seventy-six did to the support of the Declaration of Independence, so to the support of the Constitution and laws let every American pledge his life, his property, and his sacred honor. Let every man remember that to violate the law is to trample on the blood of his father, and to tear the charter of his own and his children's liberty. Let reverence for the law be breathed by every American mother to the lisping babe that prattles on her lap. Let it be taught in schools, in seminaries, and in colleges. Let it be written in primers, in spelling books, and in almanacs. Let it be preached from the pulpit, proclaimed in legislative halls, and enforced in courts of justice. In short, let it become the Political Religion of the Nation." . . .

From my childhood days I have understood that we believe absolutely that the Constitution of our country is an inspired instrument, and that God directed those who created it and those who defended the independence of this nation. Concerning this matter it is my frequent pleasure to quote the statement by Joseph Smith, regarding the Constitution:

"The Constitution of the United States is a glorious standard; it is founded in the wisdom of God. It is a heavenly banner; it is, to all those who are privileged with the sweets of liberty, like the cooling shades and refreshing waters of a great rock in a weary and thirsty land. It is like a great tree under whose branches men from every clime can be shielded from the burning rays of the sun" [*TPJS* 147].

And such the Constitution of the United States must be to every faithful Latter-day Saint who lives under its protection.

We honor the man that God honors. We honor Abraham Lincoln because we believe absolutely that God honored him and raised him up to be the instrument in His hands of saving the Constitution and the Union. ("Lincoln and Law" 73, 127)

7.16. The Constitutional Convention met and out from it came our God-inspired Constitution—"the most wonderful work," said Gladstone, "ever struck off at a given time by the brain and purpose of man."

The Lord Himself has declared as to this great document of human liberty, "I established the Constitution of this land by the hands of wise men whom I raised up unto this very purpose," and He added, referring to the war it cost to gain us our liberties: "and redeemed the land by the shedding of blood." (D&C 101:80.) . . .

Thus we had set up, under the guidance of God Himself, a government that made of this land the kind of land Lehi and Jacob had foreseen and prophesied—"a land of liberty." (*MFP* 6:105)

7.17. We again warn our people in America of the constantly increasing threat against our inspired Constitution and our free institutions set up under it. The same political tenets and philosophies that have brought war and terror in other parts of the world are at work amongst us in America. The proponents thereof are seeking to undermine our own form of government and to set up instead one of the forms of dictatorships now flourishing in other lands. . . .

. . . Communism and all other similar *isms* bear no relationship whatever to the United Order. They are merely the clumsy counterfeits which Satan always devises of the gospel plan. . . . Latter-day Saints cannot be true to their faith and lend aid, encouragement, or sympathy to any of these false philosophies. They will prove snares to their feet. (Grant and McKay 273, 343)

7.18. Every faithful Latter-day Saint believes that the Constitution of the United States was inspired of God, and that this choice land and this nation have been preserved until now in the principles of liberty under the protection of God. . . .

These principles are fundamental to our belief, fundamental to our protection. And in the providences of the Lord, the safeguards which have been incorporated into the basic structure of this nation are, if we preserve them, the guarantee of all men who dwell here against abuses, tyrannies, and usurpations. From my childhood days I have understood that we believe absolutely that the Constitution of our country is an inspired instrument, and that God directed those who created it and those who defended the independence of this nation. . . .

And such the Constitution of the United States must be to every faithful Latter-day Saint who lives under its protection. That the Lord may help him to think straight, and to pursue a straight course regardless of personal advantage, factional interest, or political persuasion, should be the daily prayer of every Latter-day Saint. I counsel you, I urge you, I plead with you, never, so far as you have voice or influence, permit any departure from the principles of government on which this nation was founded, or any disregard of the freedoms which, by the inspiration of God our Father, were written into the Constitution of the United States. ("Admonition and Blessing" 694-95)

George Albert Smith 8

Biographical Information

Born: 4 April 1870
Ordained an Apostle: 8 October 1903
President of the Twelve: 1 July 1943
President of the Church: 21 May 1945 – 4 April 1951
Died: 4 April 1951

* * * * * * * * *

Relationship with the Constitution and U.S. Government

George Albert Smith inherited a love of the U.S. Constitution from a long line of patriotic forebears. He cared deeply about the United States and its government. Serving as President of the Church at the end of World War II, he expressed gratitude for an inspired Constitution.

President Smith's relationship with the U.S. Government was very positive. When the Church sent food and supplies to war-ravaged Europe, he met with President Truman, who expressed his appreciation for the efforts of the Saints.

Themes Discussed in the Quotations

Main theme: We should sustain and support the Constitution.
Minor themes:
  1. The Constitution is a glorious standard.
  2. The Founding Fathers were inspired of God.

Quotations

As an Apostle

8.1. If I am disposed to sustain the Constitution of this great country that we live in; if there is a desire in my heart to uphold the great man whom God has honored to preside over the destinies of this nation; if there is within me love for my fellow-men and a desire to serve God and keep his commandments, these characteristics have come to me, my friends, as a result of the Gospel of Jesus Christ. (*Sharing the Gospel with Others* 19)

8.2. I feel that, as long as the people of this land obey, or strive to keep the commandments of God, this liberty will continue to flow unto us. . . . I say to you that our only hope, and the hope of the sons and daughters that God may bless us with, to enjoy peace and liberty in this land, is in standing by the Constitution that God has inspired to direct this government. . . . Let us stand by the law-makers, and encourage them in the making of just laws, and stand by the executive departments, and the judiciary in the administration of those laws. (*CR* [Oct 1911] 45)

8.3. We should be deeply concerned in the welfare of the nation, and sustain good and great men, as the Lord has commanded us, in order that we may continue to enjoy freedom. (*CR* [Apr 1914] 11)

8.4. So today in the midst of the difficulties that exist in the world, while there are transgressors of the laws of the land, and there are transgressors of the laws of God, in the midst of the conflict in which we are now engaged, this awful world war [WWI], it is a great joy and satisfaction to my soul that while there are those persons who are opposing this government set up by the power of God, there are no members of this Church in good standing but are sustaining the law and order and the government of the United States, so far as it lies in their power. There is one Church upon the continent of America that has been taught by God that this government has been raised up for the blessing of mankind. There is one Church whose members cannot remain in good fellowship in it if they criticize and find fault and tear down and oppose the legal action of the constituted authorities of the land, with reference to going into this war; and why? Because we have been trained by the gospel in a knowledge of the purpose of this government. We have been taught by inspired men, who have pointed the way, and all Israel, to a man, comes forward in the crucial hour and says: "If I am needed, Lord, here am I" [Abr 3:27]. If my country requires it, my all is on the altar, and my life if need be. God help us to be worthy of our heritage, help us to sustain the government that has been so good to us, that has made it possible for the establishment of this work. Let us sustain good men and great men everywhere, and pray for them as we are told to do in this same record. Pray for the chief executive of the Nation and his associates, asking God to inspire them to labor for the good of humanity and the liberty of mankind. (*CR* [Oct 1917] 45)

8.5. It is pleasing indeed, to me, that the Lord not only inspired men to prepare the Constitution but that he made record of the fact that he did raise them up for that purpose. In that particular we are peculiar as a people, for we believe that the Constitution was inspired by our heavenly Father. It is marvelous to contemplate what has occurred since that day . . . when wise men and great men gathered together and counseled with each other to bring about the document that is said to be the greatest palladium of human rights that the world has ever seen. . . . The Lord referred here [D&C 101] to the Constitution of the United States, and it is evident that he was looking down into the future; for he was preparing the way for the bringing forth of his own Church, and he called attention to the fact that in the preparation of the Constitution it was to be such an instrument that men would be required to observe it, if they observed his laws for he said, [D&C] Sec. 58, par. 21: "He that keepeth the laws of God hath no need to break the laws of the land." . . . We are loyal to this country and to its institutions—and have evidenced that by sending more than thirteen thousand of our sons to assist in this great conflict: and mothers, fathers, brothers and sisters who remain at home are giving of their substance. . . .

. . . The Constitution was so framed that every one might worship according to the dictates of their own conscience, and we see the result of it in the wonderful blessing that has been poured out upon this most favored of all lands.

. . . When our Father in heaven inspired men to write the Constitution, and give unto us the great charter that vouchsafed to us the liberty we enjoy, he did it in order that men might develop and be free, as the gospel of Jesus Christ intends that all men shall be. . . . They did not understand that underlying this apparent peacefulness, in this great land, there was a fixed determination that men should be free; that God himself had written it, as it were by his own finger, in the Constitution of our great government, . . . and then, when the time came, he inspired his sons to rally around Old Glory and, if need be, give their lives that liberty might be perpetuated in the earth.

. . . On this day, so near the anniversary of the birth of that great document, the Constitution of the United States, it is fitting that we should assemble ourselves together in commemoration of it. It is proper that the governors of the several states of this nation, and the mayors of cities, should call attention to it. On next Tuesday, in the city of Salt Lake, here in the valleys of the mountains, and I presume in other cities, but in this city in our public schools and high schools there will be delivered addresses to the children explaining to them the birth of the Constitution, and it will be brought to their attention in a more forceful way, perhaps, than it has ever been before.

These things are fundamental. The real purpose is that the children of men may learn to observe the laws of man, and observing those laws fulfill the requirement of our Heavenly Father to obey him and keep his commandments. So the government of the United States was begun under the direction of our Father in heaven, as declared by his own word of mouth to be an example unto the nations of the earth, and the liberties that we enjoy are pointed out in a most forceful way to the children of men. . . .

Today this wonderful land is not only a land of liberty and hope to us, but there goes out from these shores across the mighty ocean to other peoples encouragement in the struggle that they are making, that they may have something to do with the government that directs their destinies. *(JH* [15 Sep 1918] 4)

8.6. It is our duty to pray for good men and wise men, and to hold up their hands in their attempts to perpetuate peace and law and order among the nations of the earth. *(CR* [Oct 1921] 162)

8.7. There are those who would destroy the Constitution of this land; and there are some who would rejoice if they could overthrow this Nation, not realizing that our heavenly Father has given us the best government on earth. No loyal member of this great Church will raise his voice against the government, but he will be found upholding it; he will be found praying for those who have been exalted to the office of presidency and for those who make the laws, under the Constitution. *(CR* [Oct 1922] 94-95)

8.8. Our feet have been planted upon this sacred soil for a wise purpose. This land has been dedicated for the blessing of mankind. The Constitution and the laws that have been enacted under its provisions are calculated to insure liberty, not license, to all who dwell here. . . .

Upon you men of Israel—to whom the Priesthood of the Holy One has been given—there rests an obligation. You must serve the Lord and keep his commandments. It matters not what others may do, but for you there is only one course, and that is to be obedient to law, and to sustain the Constitution of this great land, and to sustain those influences and powers wherever they may be, that are calculated to uplift the human family. *(CR* [Oct 1922] 96)

8.9. That was the voice of him now stilled in death [Abraham Lincoln], who gave his life because of his desire for the perpetuation of the liberty that was guaranteed under the Constitution of the United States. He was unafraid. When the duty was placed upon him to battle for the liberties of mankind, he dedicated his life to that purpose, and in due time, our Father in heaven accepted his offering, and his name is emblazoned upon the pages of history as a great and noble man who dared to do right, and his praises will be sung and his virtues extolled throughout all time.

I am grateful that there is inherent in the Church of Jesus Christ of Latter-day Saints a determination to sustain the laws of the land. I am grateful for the government that our Heavenly Father gave to us, for he has said that he raised up wise men to prepare for us the Constitution of this great nation. ("Lincoln . . . and This Land" 77)

8.10. It is the duty of every man and every woman who is worthy of the name, Latter-day Saint, to give such information to the officers of the land as will enable them to enforce the law and put aside the wickedness that has developed so rapidly since the great World War [WWI]. We not only believe in honoring the law, we not only believe in obeying the law, but we believe in sustaining the law, and that can only [be] obtain[ed] by individual service. . . . This is our country, our heavenly Father gave it to us, and he expects each of us to show our appreciation of our birthright by helping in every possible way to purify society, and to develop those traits of character, and those virtues, that will enrich the community and prepare an environment for those who are now growing up and those who are yet unborn. . . .

. . . I do beg of you, my brethren and sisters, that you will appreciate, and sense fully the wonderful gifts of our heavenly Father, your mountain homes, your valley homes, your plain homes, your heritage, and the grand flag that represents the liberty of the greatest Nation upon the earth, and represents the combined wisdom of the very men whom our Father says he raised up to give to us the Constitution of this favored land. When we see that starry flag, men should uncover their heads in reverence, and our sisters should evidence their appreciation of it. Wherever we go, let us keep in our hearts this thought: this is the land of Zion, dedicated for the blessing and the uplift of mankind. ("Progress of the M.I.A.—Their Slogans" 902-04)

8.11. It is pleasing to me as a member of the Church to know that our heavenly Father is interested in us, and in our government. ...

In these days of confusion, when the Constitution of our country is assailed, by those who have no understanding of the purpose of God regarding this great country, it behooves those who do understand to consider seriously and faithfully, the benefits that will flow to us by honoring and sustaining the government that was reared under the direction of our heavenly Father.

We are a peculiar people in many ways, and in this particularly are we peculiar, in that we believe that the constitution of the United States was inspired by our heavenly Father, and he has told us that he raised up the very men who should frame the Constitution of the United States. Knowing that, we should not be led astray by the fallacies of individuals whose selfishness inclines them to attack that which our heavenly Father has prepared for the people of this land. (*CR* [Oct 1924] 44-46)

8.12. I felt that on this occasion, and at this time, when there is so much unrest in our land, that I would like to read to you what our people conceived to be their duty to the government under which they lived. We still believe that there is only one way whereby we may enjoy peace and happiness, and that is by observing the constitutional law of our land, and by sustaining that constitutional law that was inspired by our heavenly Father at the inception of this great government. There are those who are misguided in the belief that they may organize groups and take into their own hands the punishment of those who have differed from them in their ideas of religion or government. We may well understand that men who do that come in conflict with the orderly system that our heavenly Father has decreed should govern the children of men. ... I am grateful that I belong to a Church that has been directed by our heavenly Father to observe the constitutional law of the land. (*CR* [Oct 1924] 47-48)

8.13. Those men who framed the Constitution of the United States were not only wise in the things of this world, but they were inspired by our Heavenly Father who raised them up for that very purpose. This marvelous government that we enjoy in this favored land of liberty, was given to man that it might be a blessing to him. Here men and women are permitted to worship God according to the dictates of their conscience. (*CR* [Oct 1928] 92)

8.14. The Lord raised up mighty men to establish the United States of America, and we became a nation. He gave us a glorious Constitution for our guidance and protection. (*CR* [Oct 1936] 73-74)

8.15. Just think of the coming of the Pilgrim fathers to this land, and how the Lord preserved them and made it possible for them to extend their power when the United States was born. Think of how He blessed and raised up the very men who prepared the Constitution of the United States. (*CR* [Apr 1940] 85)

As the President of the Church

8.16. Since the God of this choice land is Jesus Christ, we know that his philosophy of free agency should prevail here. Thou didst amply demonstrate this great principle to us by raising up wise men for the very purpose of giving us our constitutional form of government, concerning which thou hast said:

> ... I have suffered to be established, and should be maintained for the rights and protection of all flesh, according to just and holy principles; That every man may act in doctrine and principle pertaining to futurity, according to the moral agency which I have given unto him, that every man may be accountable for his own sins in the day of judgment. Therefore, it is not right that any man should be in bondage one to another. And for this purpose have I established the Constitution of this land, by the hands of wise men whom I raised up unto this very purpose. ... (D&C 101:77-80.)

There are those, our Heavenly Father, both within and without our borders, who would destroy the constitutional form of government which thou hast so magnanimously given us, and would replace it with a form that would curtail, if not altogether deprive, man of his free agency. We pray thee, therefore, that in all these matters thou wilt help us to conform our lives to thy desires, and that thou wilt sustain us in our resolve so to do. We pray thee that thou wilt inspire good and just men everywhere to be willing to sacrifice for, support, and uphold the Constitution and the government set up under it and thereby preserve for man his agency.

We thank thee that thou hast revealed to us that those who gave us our constitutional form of government were men wise in thy sight and that thou didst raise them up for the very purpose of putting forth that sacred document.

Wilt thou, O our Father, bless the Chief Executive of this land that his heart and will may be to preserve to us and our posterity the free institutions thy Constitution has provided. Wilt thou too bless the legislative and judicial branches of our government as well as the executive, that all may function fully and courageously in their respective branches completely independent of each other to the preservation of our constitutional form of government forever.

We pray that kings and rulers and the peoples of all nations under heaven may be persuaded of the blessings enjoyed by the people of this land by reason of their freedom under thy guidance and be constrained to adopt similar governmental systems, thus to fulfil the ancient prophecy of Isaiah that ". . . out of Zion shall go forth the law, and the word of the Lord from Jerusalem." ("Dedicatory Prayer . . . Idaho Falls Temple" 564)

8.17. It is your duty and mine to remember in our prayers the President of the United States of America, to remember the men who represent us in the Congress of the United States, to remember the executives of the states of the nation, and to pray for them that they may have divine aid. They are God's sons, every one of them, and he wants them saved and exalted. (*Improvement Era* [Nov 1945] 721-22)

8.18. We have over three thousand missionaries in the world and many of them will be led to homes which before were closed but will now be open to hear their testimonies. It is our responsibility to carry the message of the gospel not only to the civilized world but also to those who are not considered to be so civilized. All this has been made possible because the Lord in his wisdom saw the necessity of giving us a nation in which we could thrive. In no other nation under heaven could the Church have been organized and gone forward as we have in this nation. The founding of the United States was not an accident. The giving to us of the Constitution of the United States was not an accident. Our Heavenly Father knew what would be needed, and so he paved the way to give us the Constitution. It came under the influence of prayer, and he guided those who framed that wonderful document.

I hope that the membership of this Church will not be deceived into thinking that other plans, other forms of government, other systems of direction whatsoever, are desirable. I want to say to you without any hesitation that no form of government in the world can be compared favorably with the government God gave to us. This is his plan. ("The Work of God" 267)

8.19. Again we pray, help us to love one another and to be worthy of our nation, the Constitution, and the men who gave their all in order that we might enjoy these blessings. ("Dedicatory Prayer: This Is the Place Monument" 12; also in *Sharing the Gospel with Others* 131)

8.20. Now, there are many things that I might talk about, tonight, but I want to raise my voice to you and say, our Heavenly Father raised up the very men that framed the Constitution of the United States. He said He did. He gave to us the greatest Palladium of human rights that the world knows anything about, the only system whereby people could worship God according to the dictates of their consciences without, in any way, being molested when the law, itself, was in effect. Now that is what the Lord gave to us. That is the Constitution of this country. Yet, we have people who would like to change that and bring some of those forms of government that have failed absolutely to make peace and happiness and comfort any other place in the world, and exchange what God has given to us—the fullness of the earth and the riches of liberty and happiness. Yet, there are those who go around whispering and talking and saying, "Let us change this thing." I am saying to you that to me the Constitution of the United States of America is just as much from my Heavenly Father as the Ten Commandments. When that is my feeling, I am not going to go very far away from the Constitution, and I am going to try to keep it where the Lord started it, and not let anti-Christs come into this country that began because people wanted to serve God. (*CR* [Apr 1948] 182)

8.21. He was ready to organize His Church, or would be soon, and so He raised up men that knew how to frame the Constitution of our great country and made it possible for an organization such as is in this house tonight to enjoy the blessings that we have enjoyed all these years, sometimes under difficulties, of course, but not the trials and distresses that other countries have had. So let us appreciate it and let us evidence to our Heavenly Father that we do appreciate it, not by talking about it but by letting our light so shine—the light of righteousness, the light of faith, the light of honesty, the light of generosity, the light of truthfulness, all those things that our Heavenly Father indicates that we should manifest to the world—let that light so shine that others seeing our good works will desire to be identified with an organization that seeks to live the commandments of God and honor Him. (*CR* [Apr 1948] 183)

8.22. During the great struggle for independence in the country under the leadership of George Washington, our Heavenly Father was preparing the way for the restoration of the gospel of Jesus Christ in its purity.

He gave to certain individuals the inspiration to frame the Constitution of the United States that has been referred to in this conference, the greatest palladium of human rights that we know anything about. Under such a Constitution the gospel of Jesus Christ was restored to the earth one hundred nineteen years ago....

Joseph Smith, the Prophet, and his brother Hyrum (the great-great-grandfather of the man who sits at my left here on the stand and grandfather of the man who sits behind me in this congregation) died as martyrs at the hands of a wicked mob. They were sacrificed not for any wrong they had done but because they had sought to teach the truth and call the people of the world to repent before it was too late. The work has gone on and under the Constitution of the United States we have been permitted to carry on in this great land. We have been permitted to teach the gospel of Jesus Christ. Our missionaries of course have gone all over the world, but I am speaking now of the United States of America. However, there are many people, many men and women in this land, some of whom may be friends or relatives who are misguided by the idea that the Constitution of the United States isn't as fine a system of government as they have in Russia or Germany or Italy or some other part of the world, notwithstanding the fact that the Lord himself said that he raised up the very men who framed the Constitution of the United States and directed that the membership of this Church should pray for and sustain those who represented the Constitution of this land. I hold in my hand the Bible and can read the Ten Commandments that were given to Moses for the guidance of the people wherein the Lord told Moses what the people should live for and do. If those Ten Commandments had been lived up to by the people of the world down to the present time, this earth could long ago have been celestialized. But the people refused.

You know, and I know, that the Ten Commandments contain the will of our Heavenly Father, and I am grateful, not only for the civil laws but also for the laws God has given to us. I feel bound to conform my life to the teachings of the Ten Commandments. I feel equally bound to sustain the Constitution of the United States which came from the same source as the Ten Commandments. Unless the people of this great nation can realize these things and repent, they may forfeit the liberty that they now enjoy, and the blessings that are so multiplied among us. I do hope and pray that they will discover before it is too late that God has spoken again. Your responsibility and mine is to let our light so shine that others seeing our good works will be constrained to glorify him who is the Author of our being. ("From a Prophet to His People" 303-04)

8.23. We believe that the Constitution of the United States was inspired by our Heavenly Father, and he has told us that he raised up the very men who should frame the Constitution of the United States. Knowing that, we should not be led astray by the fallacies of individuals whose selfishness inclines them to attack that which our Heavenly Father has prepared for the people of this land. ("Obedience to Law" 429)

8.24. The Lord raised up men to frame a Constitution for this nation because it was his nation. It was his desire that the people here would be blessed and there have been no people in all the world who have been more blessed than those who live in the United States of America.

We have every comfort that you can think of, every blessing that is enjoyed by people in any other nation, and then we have the privilege of worshiping Almighty God according to the dictates of our conscience because the Lord himself made that provision in the Constitution of the United States and in the framing of the laws that govern this nation. ("Welfare Program, A Wonderful Thing" 699)

8.25. I am grateful for the privilege that came to me of being reared in this part of the world under a government that God himself said was prepared by men that he raised up for that very purpose. I refer to the Constitution of the United States. ("Our Father's Work" 790)

8.26. When the Constitution of our country is assailed, openly or subtly, by those who have no understanding of the purpose of God regarding this great country, it behooves those who do understand to consider seriously and faithfully the benefits that will flow to us by honoring and sustaining the principles of government that were divinely established. . . .

There is only one way whereby we may enjoy peace and happiness, and that is by observing the law of our land, and by sustaining the principles embodied in the Constitution which was inspired by our Heavenly Father at the inception of this great government. So, as Latter-day Saints, we may know that no man is a faithful member of this Church who lends himself in any way to break down that organized system of laws that has been prepared for the good of all mankind. . . .

I say to you: Sustain the Constitution of the United States, and let not our voices be heard among those that deride or would violate the Constitution that is so important for us and for all men.

I am grateful to my Heavenly Father for his advice to us that we support the Constitution of the United States and maintain the liberty that we enjoy under it. ("Perpetuating Liberty" 93-94)

8.27. No nation in the world has a constitution that was given to it by our Heavenly Father except the United States of America. I wonder if we appreciate that. The Lord gave us a rule of life for this great nation, and as far as we have lived up to it and taken advantage of it, the nation has grown, and the people have been blessed. But there are many people who prefer, or at least they seem to prefer, something else.

As one man said to me, "Why not try what Russia has tried and Germany has tried?" And my answer to him was, "Why try something that has already failed? Why not hold on to what the Lord has given?" The Constitution of the United States was written, it is true, by men, George Washington, Benjamin Franklin, and others who were their associates, but we have in this book that I have in my hand, the book of Doctrine and Covenants, a revelation in which the Lord tells us that the Constitution of the United States was prepared by men raised up by him for this very purpose.

As Latter-day Saints we ought to know that there is nothing better anywhere else. And so we should cleave to the Constitution of the United States and in doing so, earn the blessings of our Heavenly Father. ("Liberty Under the Constitution" 964)

8.28. If there is any doubt in your minds about this being a blessed land in which you live, and that an all-powerful hand directs its destinies, remember that it was the Lord himself who raised up wise men to give to us our Constitution [D&C 101:80]—the greatest palladium of human rights that any people have ever known. . . .

. . . He [the Lord] watched over them [the Pilgrims] and safeguarded their descendants and those who followed them to America, and in due time, there came an opportunity to establish liberty such as humankind had not known before. The Lord raised up Washington, and with him that body of men who fought valiantly to establish for us in this land a government for which surely we are all grateful. . . .

The Lord has watched over his land: He directed Columbus to these shores: he led the Pilgrims here; he established the Constitution of the United States, and through the Prophet Joseph Smith restored the everlasting gospel to bless the children of men. If they will accept it and obey it, it will result in the salvation of the human family. ("For Law and Liberty—and Salvation" 869-70)

David O. McKay 9

Biographical Information

Born: 8 September 1873
Ordained an Apostle: 9 April 1906
Second Counselor to Heber J. Grant: 6 October 1934
Second Counselor to George Albert Smith: 21 May 1945
President of the Twelve: 30 September 1950
President of the Church: 9 April 1951 – 18 January 1970
Died: 18 January 1970

* * * * * * * * *

Relationship with the Constitution and U.S. Government

President David O. McKay was brought up with a respect for the U.S. Constitution, a respect which was deepened by his personal commitment to free agency. His tenure as President of the Church took place during the Cold War, the Korean War, and the Vietnam Conflict. These international events forcefully reminded President McKay of the serious threat of Communism. He expressed his hostility to this form of government, speaking out fearlessly in favor of free government, especially the American government. President McKay enjoyed amicable relations with government officials at every level.

Themes Discussed in the Quotations

Main theme: The Constitution guarantees free agency and other freedoms.
Minor themes:
1. The family as an institution will preserve the Constitution.

2. The Founding Fathers were inspired to write the Constitution through their faith in God.

Quotations

As an Apostle

9.1. I desire to call attention to the fact that the united, well-ordered American home is one of the greatest contributing factors to the preservation of the Constitution of the United States. It has been aptly said that "Out of the homes of America will come the future citizens of America, and only as those homes are what they should be will this nation be what it should be." (*CR* [Apr 1935] 110)

9.2. Our twelfth Article of Faith says:

> We believe in being subject to kings, presidents, rulers, and magistrates, in obeying, honoring, and sustaining the law....

... The three significant words used in the 12th Article of Faith express the proper attitude of the membership of the Church toward law. These words are—obey, honor and sustain....

We obey law from a sense of right.

We honor law because of its necessity and strength to society.

We sustain law by keeping it in good repute. (*CR* [Apr 1937] 27-28)

9.3. What really prompted me to emphasize this principle is the presence in our own United States of influences the avowed object of which is to sow discord and contention among men with the view of undermining, weakening, if not entirely destroying our constitutional form of government. If I speak plainly, and in condemnation lay bare reprehensible practices and aims of certain organizations, please do not think that I harbor ill-will or enmity in my heart towards other United States citizens whose views on political policies do not coincide with mine. But when acts and schemes are manifestly contrary to the revealed word of the Lord, we feel justified in warning people against them. We may be charitable and forbearing to the sinner, but must condemn the sin. . . .

. . . There is another danger even more menacing than the threat of invasion of a foreign foe. It is the unpatriotic activities and underhanded scheming of disloyal groups and organizations within our own borders. . . .

Latter-day Saints should have nothing to do with secret combinations and groups antagonistic to the Constitutional law of the land, which the Lord "suffered to be established," and which "should be maintained for the rights and protection of all flesh, according to just and holy principles;

> That every man may act in doctrine and principle pertaining to futurity, according to the moral agency which I have given unto him, that every man may be accountable for his own sins in the day of judgment.
>
> Therefore, it is not right that any man should be in bondage one to another.
>
> And for this purpose have I established the Constitution of this land, by the hands of wise men whom I raised up unto this very purpose, and redeemed the land by the shedding of blood. (D&C [101:]77-80)

Of course there are errors in government which some would correct, certainly there are manifest injustices and inequalities, and there will always be such in any government in the management of which enter the frailties of human nature. If you want changes go to the polls on election day, express yourself as an American citizen, and thank the Lord for the privilege that is yours to have a say as to who shall serve you in public office. (*CR* [Oct 1939] 102-05; also in *Statements on Communism and the Constitution of the United States* 3, 5-6)

9.4. If we would make the world better, let us foster a keener appreciation of the freedom and liberty guaranteed by the government of the United States as framed by the founders of this nation. Here again self-proclaimed progressives cry that such old-time adherence is out of date. But there are some fundamental principles of this Republic which, like eternal truths, never get out of date, and which are applicable at all times to liberty-loving peoples. Such are the underlying principles of the Constitution, a document framed by patriotic, freedom-loving men, who Latter-day Saints declare were inspired by the Lord.

This date, October 6, has been set apart by churches as "Loyalty Day." It is highly fitting, therefore, as a means of making the world better, not only to urge loyalty to the Constitution and to threatened fundamentals of the United States government, but to warn the people that there is evidence in the United States of disloyalty to tried and true fundamentals in government. There are unsound economic theories; there are European "isms," which, termite-like, secretly and, recently, quite openly and defiantly, are threatening to undermine our democratic institutions.

Today, as never before, the issue is clearly defined—liberty and freedom of choice, or oppression and subjugation for the individual and for nations.

As we contemplate the deplorable fact that within the brief space of one year, ten European nations have lost their independence, that over two hundred and fifty million people have surrendered all guarantees of personal liberty, deeper should be our gratitude, more intense our appreciation of the Constitution, and more strengthened our determination to resist at all costs any and all attempts to curtail our liberties, or to change the underlying system of our government. ("Essentials of a Better World" 698)

9.5. Throughout the ages advanced souls have yearned for a society in which liberty and justice prevail. Men have sought for it, fought for it, have died for it. Ancient freemen prized it; slaves longed for it; the Magna Charta demanded it; the Constitution of the United States declared it. ("The Church and the Present War" 341; also in *Gospel Ideals* 288)

9.6. We . . . warn our people in America of the constantly increasing threat against our inspired Constitution. . . . The proponents thereof are seeking to undermine our own form of government and to set up instead one of the forms of dictatorships [which] is now flourishing in other lands. These revolutionists are using a technique that is as old as the human race,—a fervid but false solicitude for the unfortunate over whom they thus gain mastery, and then enslave them. (Grant and McKay 273, 343)

9.7. Therefore, as against the tyranny and despotism of Totalitarianism and Dictatorships, let us willingly and heroically, defend the Constitution of this land that guarantees to every citizen of the republic, life, liberty, and the pursuit of happiness and favors the divine pronouncement that the souls of men are precious in the sight of God. ("Address to Marines Enlisted in Newest 'Mormon Battalion'" 4)

9.8. The Constitution of this government was written by men who accepted Jesus Christ as the Saviour of mankind. Let men and women in these United States then continue to keep their eyes centered upon Him who ever shines as a Light to all the world. ("The Light That Shines in Darkness" 750)

9.9. Men and women who live in America, "the land of Zion," have a responsibility greater than that yet borne by any other people. Theirs the duty, the obligation to preserve not only the Constitution of the land but the Christian principles from which sprang that immortal document. ("The Light That Shines in Darkness" 750)

9.10. Governments are the *servants*, not the *masters* of the people. All who love the Constitution of the United States can vow with Thomas Jefferson, who, when he was president, said,

> I have sworn upon the altar of God eternal hostility against every form of tyranny over the mind of man.

He later said:

> To preserve our independence, we must not let our rulers load us with perpetual debt. We must take our choice between economy and liberty, or profusion and servitude. If we run into such debts, we must be taxed in our meat and drink, in our necessities and in our comforts, in our labors and in our amusements.
> If we can prevent the government from wasting the labors of the people under pretense of caring for them, they will be happy. The same

prudence which in private life would forbid our paying our money for unexplained projects, forbids it in the disposition of public money. We are endeavoring to reduce the government to the practice of rigid economy to avoid burdening the people and arming the magistrate with a patronage of money which might be used to corrupt the principles of our government. . . .

In conclusion, I repeat that no greater immediate responsibility rests upon members of the Church, upon all citizens of this Republic and of neighboring Republics than to protect the freedom vouchsafed by the Constitution of the United States.

Let us, by exercising our privileges under the Constitution—

(1) Preserve our right to worship God according to the dictates of our conscience,

(2) Preserve the right to work when and where we choose. . . .

(3) Feel free to plan and to reap without the handicap of bureaucratic interference.

(4) Devote our time, means, and life if necessary, to hold inviolate those laws which will secure to each individual the free exercise of conscience, the right and control of property, and the protection of life. ("Free Agency . . . A Divine Gift" 367, 378)

As the President of the Church

9.11. A few hundred years afterward, came the Declaration of Independence, and then the Constitution of the United States, fundamental in which is the right of the individual to worship God, to speak as he feels, own his property, to take care of his family—his home, his castle. ("Principle of Choice Most Vital to World" 3; also in *Stepping Stones to an Abundant Life* 52)

9.12. The two most important documents affecting the destiny of America are the Declaration of Independence and the Constitution of the United States. Both these immortal papers relate primarily to the freedom of the individual. ("Favorable and Unfavorable Phases of Present-day Conditions" 407; also in *Gospel Ideals* 309)

9.13. No Latter-day Saint can be true to his country, true to his Church, true to his God, who will violate the laws which relate to the moral welfare and the spiritual advancement of mankind. The Latter-day Saints should uphold the law everywhere. And it is time that all of us—the leaders of this country, the politicians, the statesmen, the leaders in civic affairs in the state and in the cities, as well as parents and private citizens should so speak of and so uphold the constitutional law of the land that there will everywhere be a renewal of respect for it and a revival of the virtues of honor, honesty, and integrity. ("Honor, Honesty, Integrity" 566)

9.14. I am but repeating what we all know and feel when I say that our country's greatest asset is its manhood. Upon that depends not only the survival of the individual freedom vouchsafed by the Constitution and Bill of Rights, and all other ideals for which the founders of the Republic fought and died, but the survival of the best that we cherish in present-day civilization throughout the world. . . .
. . . Our educational system will radiate such principles just to the extent that we employ in our public schools, high schools, colleges, and universities men and women who are not only eminent in their particular professions, but loyal to the Constitution of our land, influential as leaders, noble in character. ("True Education: The Paramount Purpose of a Free People" 258)

9.15. Teachings and ideologies subversive to the fundamental principles of this great Republic, which are contrary to the Constitution of the United States, or which are detrimental to the progress of the Church of Jesus Christ of Latter-day Saints, will be condemned, whether advocated by Republicans or Democrats. ("Closing Address" 952)

9.16. We advocate the necessity of all members of the Church showing appreciation of your franchise, your citizenship, by voting, exercising your right to say who shall be your leaders. They become our servants. That is the spirit of the Constitution. ("Closing Address" 953)

9.17. I appreciate the Constitution of the United States and the Bill of Rights that grant unto each man individual liberty. . . . I have nothing but contempt in my heart for men who would disgrace that flag or would mar the standards of freedom and individual liberty. (Thompson 124; from an address given at Laguna Beard Ward, Laguna Beach, CA, 4 Jan 1953)

9.18. We pray, O Lord, that thou wilt inspire men to desire to make equal advancement in preserving and making applicable to society the principles of individual liberty and freedom of worship brought by the pioneers and vouchsafed by the Constitution of the United States. (Morrell 128; from the dedicatory prayer of the Mormon Pioneer Memorial Bridge, Omaha, NE, Jun 1953)

9.19. Next to the divine authority of the Priesthood I believe that no principle of the Gospel is more endangered today than is that principle which gives us individual freedom. . . .
    It was that very principle that induced our Founding Fathers to declare their independence from the countries in Europe and to establish the Constitution, giving to each individual the right to worship, the right to build, the right to work, the right to think, to speak, to preach, so long as each gave to other individuals that same privilege. (*Statements on Communism and the Constitution of the United States* 19; from the dedication of the Douglas Ward Chapel, Salt Lake City, UT, 18 Oct 1953)

9.20. By law, the public schools of this nation must be nondenominational. They can have no part in securing acceptance of any one of the numerous systems of belief regarding a supernatural power and the relation of mankind thereto. That restriction applies to the atheist as well as to the believer in God. The scientist who tells young people that religious faith is to be condemned because it is "unscientific" is violating the Constitution of the state and of the nation as much as he who would take advantage of his position to advocate the superiority of any religion. ("'Education for Citizenship'" 2; revised in *Pathways to Happiness* 66-67)

9.21. In education for citizenship, therefore, why should we not see to it that every child in America is taught the superiority of our Constitution and the sacredness of the freedom of the individual? Such definite instruction is not in violation of either the Federal or the State Constitution. . . .

Education for citizenship demands more emphasis upon moral and spiritual values. Our government was founded on faith in a Supreme Being as evidenced by the Mayflower Compact, the Declaration of Independence, by George Washington, and Benjamin Franklin in the Constitutional Convention, and by a hundred other incidents prior to, during, and following the birth of this Republic. Said the Father of our Country: "We have raised a standard to which the good and wise can repair; the event is in the hands of God." . . .

I love the Stars and Stripes, and the American Way of Life. I have faith in the Constitution of the United States. I believe that only through a truly educated citizenry can the ideals that inspired the Founding Fathers of our Nation be preserved and perpetuated. ("'Education for Citizenship'" 3; revised in *Statements on Communism and the Constitution of the United States* 20-21; *Pathways to Happiness* 70-71; from the inauguration ceremonies of the Utah State Agricultural College, Logan, UT, 8 Mar 1954)

9.22. I think we owe at least the consideration to be loyal to this country and to spurn with all the soul that is within us the scheming disloyal citizens who would undermine our Constitution, or who would deprive the individual of his liberty vouchsafed by that great document, and some of our men who have come up through the public schools are doing just that. Let every loyal member of the Church look down with scorn upon any man or woman who would undermine that Constitution. ("Safeguard in Loyalty" 3)

9.23. We are grateful for the Constitution of the United States of America which permitted the Church of Jesus Christ to be established through heavenly messengers, and which grants to every man the right to worship God according to the dictates of his own conscience. ("Dedicatory Address Delivered at Swiss Temple Dedication" 798; also in Morrell 167-68)

9.24. Next to being one in worshiping God, there is nothing in this world upon which this Church should be more united than in upholding and defending the Constitution of the United States!

May the appeal of our Lord in His intercessory prayer for unity be realized in our homes, our wards, and stakes, and in our support of the basic principles of our Republic. ("The Enemy Within" 34)

9.25. We are grateful for this land of America, "choice above all other lands" [2 Nephi 1:5]. The freedom vouchsafed by the Constitution of the United States, which guarantees to every man the right to worship Thee in accordance with the dictates of his own conscience, made possible the establishment of the Church of Jesus Christ of Latter-day Saints. O Father, may the American people not forget thee! Help us to see the greatness of this country and to minimize its weaknesses. . . . Government exists for the protection of the individual—not the individual for the government. Bless, we beseech Thee, the President of the United States, his Cabinet, the Houses of Congress and the Judiciary. Give the President health and wisdom needful for the world leadership now placed upon him. ("Dedicatory Prayer—Los Angeles Temple" 226; also in Thompson 125)

9.26. So the perpetuity of this land and nation depends upon faith. Any power or any influence that will destroy directly or indirectly this principle of faith in God is an enemy to the Constitution of the United States. ("Faith and Freedom: Two Guiding Principles of the Pilgrims" 322; also in *Treasures of Life* 143)

9.27. I should like to express gratitude this Thanksgiving season for this great country, for the Constitution of the United States which grants to each individual liberty, freedom to think and to speak and to act as he pleases, just so long as each gives to the other man that same privilege. I am thankful for this country which has given more persons opportunity to raise themselves under an individualistic, capitalistic, free enterprise system from menial to commanding positions than any other nation in the world, past or present. ("Faith and Freedom: Two Guiding Principles of the Pilgrims" 322; also in *Treasures of Life* 144-45)

9.28. The Church does not interfere, and has no intention of trying to interfere, with the fullest and freest exercise of the political franchise of its members, under and within our Constitution.

But Communism is not a political party nor a political plan under the Constitution; it is a system of government that is the opposite of our Constitutional government, and it would be necessary to destroy our government before Communism could be set up in the United States. . . .

. . . [Communism] even reaches its hand into the sanctity of the family circle itself, disrupting the normal relationship of parent and child, all in a manner unknown and unsanctioned under the Constitutional guarantees under which we in America live. (*Pathways to Happiness* 46)

9.29. Our founding fathers, despite some natural fears, clearly regarded the promulgation of the Constitution of the United States as their greatest triumph. ("The Gospel and the Individual" 901; revised in *Treasures of Life* 168)

9.30. Above all else, strive to support good and conscientious candidates of either party who are aware of the great dangers inherent in communism, and who are truly dedicated to the Constitution in the tradition of our founding fathers. ("The Gospel and the Individual" 903)

9.31. [One] principle that actuated the lives of the fathers who founded our Constitution was *faith in God*. (*Treasures of Life* 88)

9.32. Another fundamental for which we should be grateful is the free agency which God has given us—freedom and liberty vouchsafed by the Constitution of the United States.

I wonder if we appreciate this great gift. That free agency, the right to exercise that free agency, and the right of trial by your equals is vouchsafed by the Constitution of the United States. Let us have a spirit of gratitude in our hearts for the free exercise of our agency and the rights of liberty. (*Treasures of Life* 138)

9.33. By inheritance we enjoy liberty vouchsafed by the Constitution to speak, to work, to study, to pray as we wish, so long as we do not deprive others of the same privileges. (*Treasures of Life* 381)

9.34. As we celebrate the birthday of the Declaration of Independence on July 4, one hundred and eighty-eight years ago, let us catch the spirit of that morning and awaken appreciation for the blessings and privileges that are ours if we but remain loyal and true to the Constitution of the United States as established by our Founding Fathers. . . .

After the Revolutionary War was over and nine years after the Declaration of Independence was signed, the Founding Fathers met in that same Old State Hall to frame the Constitution of the United States.

The French historian, Francois Pierre Guillaume Guizot, while visiting in the United States, asked James Russell Lowell, *"How long will the American Republic endure?"* Lowell's answer was: *"As long as the ideas of the men who founded it continue dominant."*

And what were those ideas? Two fundamental principles were: *Freedom from Dictatorship* and *Freedom of the Individual!* This goes right back to our free agency, which is as precious as life itself. . . .

. . . Do we realize what it means to have a knock come at our door at night, and to have fear because it is the police, then to hear a voice commanding: "Open the Door!"? One woman who was alone got just such a command, and, scantily dressed, was taken, not down in the elevator, but rushed down four flights of stairs, put in a black wagon with guards on each side and carried off to prison. She was innocent, but the door closed behind her and that was the beginning of a nine-year prison sentence. This is a frequent happening in dictator countries in this the twentieth century!

That is the kind of treatment the spirit of man rebels against; that is why we had the Declaration of Independence; that is why we had the Constitution of the United States drawn up by men who were inspired; and that is why we have the Bill of Rights, granting protection to each individual. The government was established to protect the individual; the individual is not a part of the State, nor should he be used as part of the State. The government is set up to protect him in his rights.

What other fundamental prompted these men when they framed the Constitution—"the greatest instrument," said one man, "ever written by the hands of man"? I name it as *Faith in God*, next to free agency, or correlative with free agency. As an illustration, during the critical time when the representatives of the colonies were trying to frame the Constitution in that Old State Hall, Benjamin Franklin, the oldest man present, arose and stated his faith in an overruling Providence and in the power of prayer, and then said:

> I have lived, sir, a long time, and the longer I live, the more convincing proofs I see of this truth: That God governs in the affairs of men. And if a sparrow cannot fall to the ground without His notice, is it probable that an empire can rise without His aid?
>
> We have been assured, sir, in the sacred writings, that 'Except the Lord build the house, they labour in vain that build it.' I firmly believe this; and I also believe that without His concurring aid we shall succeed in this political building no better than the builders of Babel. . . .
>
> I therefore beg leave to move that henceforth prayers imploring the assistance of Heaven, and its blessings on our deliberations, be held in this Assembly every morning before we proceed to business, and that one or more of the clergy of this city be requested to officiate in that service.

. . . However, the point I wish to make is that Benjamin Franklin emphasized that faith in God is a fundamental principle of the Constitution of the United States. I should also like to refer to a remark made by George Washington, who, following the establishment of the Constitution, and the acceptance of it by the thirteen Colonies, wrote this:

> Of all the dispositions of habits which lead to political prosperity, religion and morality are indispensable supports. . . .

Actuated by these two fundamental and eternal principles—the free agency of the individual and faith in an overruling Providence—those 56 men who signed the Declaration of Independence, those who drew up the Constitution of the United States nine years later, gave to the world a concept of government which, if applied, will strike from the arms of downtrodden humanity the shackles of tyranny, and give hope, ambition, and freedom to the teeming millions throughout the world. ("The Founding of an American Republic" 249-51; also in *Statements on Communism and the Constitution of the United States* 31-37)

9.35. The First Presidency has previously issued a statement urging you as citizens to participate in the great democratic processes of our national election in accordance with your honest political convictions.

We have urged you, above all, to try to support good and conscientious candidates of either party who are aware of the great dangers inherent in communism and who are truly dedicated to the constitution in the tradition of our fathers. We have suggested also that you should support candidates who pledge their sincere fidelity to our liberty—a liberty which aims at the preservation of both personal and property rights. ("Vote Your Convictions" A1)

9.36. The Constitution of the United States, as given to us by our fathers, is the real government under which individuals may exercise free agency and individual initiative. ("Cherish Noble Aspirations" 1161)

9.37. In order that there may be no misunderstandings by bishops, stake presidents, and others regarding members of the Church participating in nonchurch meetings to study and become informed on the Constitution of the United States, Communism, etc., I wish to make the following statements that I have been sending out from my office for some time and that have come under question by some stake authorities, bishoprics, and others.

Church members are at perfect liberty to act according to their own consciences in the matter of safeguarding our way of life. They are, of course, encouraged to honor the highest standards of the gospel and to work to preserve their own freedoms. They are free to participate in nonchurch meetings that are held to warn people of the threat of Communism or any other theory or principle that will deprive us of our free agency or individual liberties vouchsafed by the Constitution of the United States.

The Church, out of respect for the rights of all its members to have their political views and loyalties, *must maintain the strictest possible neutrality.* We have no intention of trying to interfere with the fullest and freest exercise of the political franchise of our members under and within our Constitution, which the Lord declared he established "by the hands of wise men whom [he] raised up unto this very purpose" (D&C 101:80) and which, as to the principles thereof, the Prophet Joseph Smith, dedicating the Kirtland Temple, prayed should be "established forever." (D&C 109:54.) The Church does not yield any of its devotion to or convictions about safeguarding the American principles and the establishments of government under federal and state constitutions and the civil rights of men safeguarded by these.

. . . We therefore commend and encourage every person and every group who is sincerely seeking to study Constitutional principles and awaken a sleeping and apathetic people to the alarming conditions that are rapidly advancing about us. ("Statement Concerning the Position of the Church on Communism" 477)

9.38. We must not pick out that which will tear down a brother's character, nor the character of our Founding Fathers, nor the works of those great men who founded the Constitution of the United States. Let us be true to our nation! There is every reason to be true to it. (*Man May Know for Himself* 67)

9.39. We should be grateful for our Founding Fathers, for Washington and Lincoln, and for our boys and other great men who have fought and died for our freedom. (*Man May Know for Himself* 387-88)

9.40. We should feel grateful that we are not hampered nor hindered in any way by a government that would presume to tell us how to worship, what to worship, or how to build. I wonder how many of us kneel down and thank the Lord for that freedom vouch-safed to us by the Constitution of the United States, a step towards the liberty, the freedom mentioned by the Savior when he said, "If ye continue in my word . . . ye shall know the truth, and the truth shall make you free" [John 8:32].

Very seldom do we think of our God-given privileges to exercise the freedom which dates back to the Constitution, even to the Declaration of Independence.

William E. Gladstone, having read the Constitution one hundred years after it had been in force, said:

> The American Constitution is, so far as I can see, the most wonderful work ever struck off at a given time by the brain and purpose of men. It has had a century of trial, under the pressure of exigencies caused by an expansion unexampled in point of rapidity and range; and its exemption from formal change, though not entire, has certainly proved the sagacity of the constructors and the stubborn strength of the fabric. . . .

Do we feel to thank God for the freedom we have here in this country? (*Man May Know for Himself* 388-89)

9.41. There are some fundamental principles of this Republic which, like eternal truths, never get out of date, and which are applicable at all times to liberty-loving peoples. Such are the underlying principles of the Constitution, a document framed by patriotic, freedom-loving men. . . .

True Americans should have nothing to do with secret combinations and groups antagonistic to the Constitutional law of the land. (*Secrets of a Happy Life* 72-73)

9.42. In the United States of America, the Constitution vouchsafes individual freedom, and let us pray also that the Lord will frustrate the plans of the Communists who would deprive us of freedom. ("Let Virtue Garnish Thy Thoughts" 30)

9.43. The Magna Carta . . . was an expression of freedom-loving men against an usurping king. It was a guarantee of civil and personal liberty. These guarantees later found fuller and complete expression in the Constitution of the United States. (*Stepping Stones to an Abundant Life* 88)

9.44. Be true to the Constitution of the United States, to the Bill of Rights. Do not let any theories of immigrants or misguided politicians induce you to do anything that will deprive us of our liberties as vouchsafed by that immortal document. (*Stepping Stones to an Abundant Life* 112)

9.45. We should love the stars and stripes, and accept the constitution of these United States as divine. Don't hesitate to stand on the right side. (*Stepping Stones to an Abundant Life* 414)

9.46. It is a part of our "Mormon" theology that the Constitution of the United States was divinely inspired; that our Republic came into existence through wise men raised up for that very purpose. We believe it is the duty of the members of the Church to see that this Republic is not subverted either by any sudden or constant erosion of those principles which gave this Nation its birth.

In these days when there is a special trend among certain groups, including members of faculties of universities, to challenge the principles upon which our country has been founded and the philosophy of our Founding Fathers, I hope that Brigham Young University will stand as a bulwark in support of the principles of government as vouchsafed to us by our Constitutional Fathers. (Letter to Ernest L. Wilkinson 2)

Joseph Fielding Smith 10

Biographical Information

Born: 19 July 1876
Ordained an Apostle: 7 April 1910
Acting President of the Twelve: 30 September 1950
President of the Twelve: 9 April 1951
Additional Counselor in the First Presidency: 29 October 1965
President of the Church: 23 January 1970 – 2 July 1972
Died: 2 July 1972

* * * * * * * *

Relationship with the Constitution and U.S. Government

Joseph Fielding Smith strongly valued the U.S. Constitution. He was especially aware of the relationship between the restoration of the Church and the establishment of a free system of government under the American Constitution.

Joseph Fielding Smith was not very involved in politics, possibly because his extensive Church service left him little time for such activity. During his short term as President, relations between the LDS Church and Washington, D.C. were very favorable.

Themes Discussed in the Quotations

Main theme: We should uphold constitutional law.
Minor themes:
1. The Constitution is the greatest governmental document ever adopted by society.
2. We should be familiar with every part of the Constitution.

Quotations

As an Apostle

10.1. I believe that the fundamental things in our government, in the Constitution of the United States, are here to endure. Moreover, I believe that it is the business and responsibility of Latter-day Saints to uphold and sustain these sacred principles which bear the stamp of approval of God himself, and we should be loyal unto them. (*CR* [Apr 1935] 97)

10.2. All loyal citizens of the United States are very proud and jealous of their form of government. Especially is this true of Latter-day Saints. They have been taught that the Lord "established the Constitution of this land, by the hand of wise men" whom he raised up for this very purpose [D&C 101:80]. (*The Progress of Man* 240-41)

10.3. Under the "Articles of Confederation and Perpetual Union between the States," the union had no President, no supreme court, and consisted of one house of congress made up of delegates elected by the legislatures of the states, whose jurisdiction was greatly limited. There were so many defects and restrictions in the Federation that the wise men in the nation readily perceived that something more nearly perfect, more powerful and binding upon the colonies, was necessary if the union was to be preserved. . . .

The Constitution is the greatest document, so far as we know, ever adopted by organized society for their government, outside of the kingdom of God. It furnishes the nation a system of checks and balances for their protection so that any one department of the government, cannot, without losing its sacred foundations, be overcome or subordinated by another. (*The Progress of Man* 293, 295-96)

10.4. The people should with jealous care guard against the time ever coming when any one of these three branches may surrender its rights to any other, or be swallowed up and overcome by some other branch of the government. Today there are many who advocate the destruction of these safeguards given us by the framers of the Constitution who were men inspired to make this document as near to the fundamental doctrines of the kingdom of God as it was possible under the circumstances for it to be. (*The Progress of Man* 297)

10.5. The wisdom of these provisions in the Constitution which protect the liberties and inherent rights of the citizens, should be apparent to all. They should be guarded and protected with a jealous care. The Constitution is our assurance against anarchy and despotism. Every Latter-day Saint should be familiar with every part of this great document. Such knowledge is essential to an understanding of the significance of the word of the Lord in the Doctrine and Covenants. . . .

With this provision of the Constitution, that there should be no religious test, and that every person should have the right to worship according to the dictates of conscience, the fulness of religious liberty was born. This principle, we may see from a study of the past, has been of gradual growth and development since the days of the emancipation of the people from religious tyranny at the time of the Protestant revolution. It took several centuries for the seed to develop and bring forth the fully developed fruit which it did when the government of the United States was formed. In this way the Lord prepared the way for the restoration of the Gospel with all its keys and powers in a humble way in the Dispensation of the Fulness of Times. It would be wrong to say that it was impossible for the Lord to establish his work had not religious freedom come and been guaranteed as we find it in our Constitution. But it is a fact, nevertheless, that he, in his infinite wisdom, prepared the way, commencing several hundred years ago and working through brave and humble men, many of whom became martyrs to the cause of truth, when darkness ruled supreme over the face of the earth. (*The Progress of Man* 298-99)

10.6. From the very beginning of this latter-day work we have been taught that the Constitution of the United States was and still is an inspired document. Such it was when it came forth from the hands of the framers. Above all peoples on the face of the earth the Latter-day Saints should uphold, defend and cherish this sacred document. It has been predicted that the time will come when it will be threatened with destruction, and when that time comes the true Latter-day Saints will rally to its support.

Our attitude should be based on the word of the Lord given us for our guidance until the time shall come when the authority of the Redeemer shall be fully established in the earth. (*The Progress of Man* 299-300)

10.7. Since the Constitution was based upon correct principles founded, as the Prophet Joseph Smith has said, "on the wisdom of God" [*TPJS* 147], as he saw fit to give it to our fathers, we above all peoples on the earth should rally to its support in time of need and rejoice in its great protecting influence. (*The Progress of Man* 301-02)

10.8. The attitude of the members of the Church towards the Constitution of the United States and the fundamental principles of our Government has always been one of loyalty. Even in the days of our greatest tribulation, the Latter-day Saints have defended and sustained these sacred principles. Never have they lifted their hands or their voices against the fundamental principles upon which our nation with its liberty and freedom is based. It is well understood by all that the Constitution was given by inspiration of the Almighty to honorable and wise men raised up for this purpose. The character of our government has always been defended and sustained. The Prophet Joseph Smith, while suffering unjustly at the hands of officials who had sworn to uphold and defend the sacred principles of the Constitution, and who had violated their oath in the vilest manner, and who heaped upon him and his companions in tribulation cruelties which only fiends could inflict, wrote to the Saints to defend and sustain the constitutional law of the land and to be loyal to the fundamental principles of our government. (*The Progress of Man* 335)

10.9. Many great and glorious principles are contained within the constitution of our country. We do not say that it is perfect, but it is perfect so far as it pertains to the rights and privileges of the children of men. But there is a nucleus of a government, formed since that of the United States, which is perfect in its nature, having emanated from a Being who is perfect. (Orson Pratt quoted in *The Progress of Man* 417)

10.10. Some may enquire, is it right—is it lawful for another government to be organized within the United States, of a theocratical nature? Yes, perfectly so! Does not the constitution of our country guarantee to all religious societies the right of forming any ecclesiastical government they like? Certainly it does, and every intelligent man knows this to be the fact.

The nucleus of such a government is formed, and its laws have emanated from the throne of God, and it is perfect, having come from a pure fountain, but does this make us independent of the laws of the United States?

No, this new government does not come in contact with the government of the United States. In keeping our covenants and observing our religious laws and ceremonies, or the laws that God has given to the children of men, we are not required to violate the principles of right that are contained in the constitution and laws of the United States. (Orson Pratt quoted in *The Progress of Man* 417-18)

10.11. It was for this purpose, then, that a republic was organized upon this continent to prepare the way for a kingdom which shall have dominion over all the earth to the ends thereof. (Orson Pratt quoted in *The Progress of Man* 420)

10.12. No nation has been more greatly blessed than has the United States. We live in a land which has been called choice above all other lands by divine pronouncement. The Lord has watched over it with a jealous care and has commanded its people to serve him lest his wrath be kindled against them and his blessings be withdrawn. Our government came into existence through divine guidance. The inspiration of the Lord rested upon the patriots who established it, and inspired them through the dark days of their struggle for independence and through the critical period which followed that struggle when they framed our glorious Constitution which guarantees to all the self-evident truth proclaimed in the Declaration of Independence, "that all men are created equal: that they are endowed by their Creator with certain inalienable rights: that among these are life, liberty, and the pursuit of happiness." That is to say, it is the right of every soul to have equal and unrestricted justice before the law, equal rights to worship according to the dictates of conscience and to labor according to the individual inclinations, independently of coercion or compulsion. That this might be, the Lord has said, "I established the Constitution of this land, by the hands of wise men whom I raised up unto this very purpose and redeemed the land by the shedding of blood" (D&C 101:80).

The founders of this nation were men of humble faith. Many of them saw in vision a glorious destiny for our government, provided we would faithfully continue in the path of justice and right with contrite spirits and humble hearts, accepting the divine truths which are found in the Holy Scriptures. The appeal of these men has echoed down the passing years with prophetic warning to the succeeding generations, pleading with them to be true to all these standards which lay at the foundation of our government. This country was founded as a Christian nation, with the acceptance of Jesus Christ as the Redeemer of the world. ("Blessed Is the Nation Whose God Is the Lord" 274)

10.13. The art of printing along with the other inventions and discoveries which preceded the coming of Moroni and the restoration of the Gospel, had to be revealed before the Church could be established in the earth. The framing of the American Constitution, we well know, was by divine inspiration. And thus, revealing line upon line and precept upon precept, the Lord prepared the way for the restoration of His work in fulness in the earth. (*The Signs of the Times* 157)

10.14. I thought it would not be amiss or out of order to say something about the Constitution, to give a little history of it perhaps briefly; for I am convinced that the people generally of the United States have not studied it. Many of them have never read it, and some know nothing concerning what it is all about. ("Founded in the Wisdom of God" 370)

10.15. Now in this statement from *The Deseret News* we read: "We stand for the Constitution of the United States with its three departments of government as therein set forth, each one fully independent in its own field." I hope that every member of the Church subscribes to that declaration—also to *The Deseret News*. The preamble to the Constitution does not begin, *"I, the king"*; nor does it begin, *"I, the President of the United States."* It reads:

> We the people of the United States, in order to form a more perfect union, establish justice, insure domestic tranquility, provide for the common defense, promote the general welfare, and secure the blessings of liberty to ourselves and our posterity, do ordain and establish this Constitution for the United States of America.

It is *"We the people."*

It was understood that the people would govern; of course, it would have to be by representation, but the control of government would be in the hands of the people. As we read in the Book of Mormon, when the righteous rule, everything is well. King Mosiah gave up his throne with the idea that the people would have a republic, and he called attention to the dangers of a kingdom and a centralized government and the dangers that would arise should the wicked rule. The Lord has taught us to choose wise men and just men, and that was the understanding on the part of these men who formed the Constitution of the United States....

... I wish to read another statement. The English statesman, James Bryce, in his excellent work, *The American Commonwealth*, has said:

> The Constitution of 1789 deserves the veneration with which the Americans have been accustomed to regard it. It is true that many criticisms have been passed upon its arrangement, upon its omissions, upon its artificial character of some of the institutions it creates, ... Yet after all deductions it ranks above every other constitution for the intrinsic excellence of its scheme, its adaptation to

the circumstances of the people, the simplicity, brevity, and precision of its language, its judicious mixture of definiteness in principle with elasticity in detail. (*The American Commonwealth*, vol. 1, p 25.) ("Founded in the Wisdom of God" 412-14)

10.16. The statement has been made that the Prophet [Joseph Smith] said the time would come when this Constitution would hang as by a thread, and this is true. There has been some confusion, however, as to just what he said following this. I think that Elder Orson Hyde has given us a correct interpretation wherein he says that the Prophet said the Constitution would be in danger. Said Orson Hyde:

> I believe he said something like this—that the time would come when the Constitution and the country would be in danger of an overthrow; and said he: 'If the Constitution be saved at all, it will be by the Elders of this Church.' I believe this is about the language, as nearly as I can recollect it (*JD* 6:152).

Now I tell you it is time the people of the United States were waking up with the understanding that if they don't save the Constitution from the dangers that threaten it, we will have a change of government. ("Founded in the Wisdom of God" 416)

10.17. They were also advised that they were to uphold the constitutional law of the land, for it has been established by the will of God, therefore we are justified "in befriending that law which is the constitutional law of the land; and as pertaining to law of man, whatsoever is more or less than this cometh of evil" [D&C 98:6-7].

When we abide in the law which the Lord has approved, then we are free. It was his mighty hand which directed the founders of the government of the United States and gave this nation the constitution in the beginning. . . . The constitutional law was given by inspiration for the purpose of protecting the rights of the citizens of the country. The Lord delights in freedom. (*Church History and Modern Revelation* 1:433)

10.18. All of this had to be *before* the establishment of the Church of Jesus Christ of Latter-day Saints upon the earth. These things took place in Europe before the discovery of America.

After America was discovered liberty upon this land received an impetus which the old world could not give to it; and through the shedding of blood, the land was redeemed (the Lord has said it [D&C 101:80]) and freedom proclaimed in the constitution of the country, so that all peoples of the earth could find a place of refuge in America, the Land of Promise. When that was accomplished, the time had come for the bringing forth and establishing of the gospel of Jesus Christ upon the earth. *(Doctrines of Salvation* 1:179)

10.19. What of our own country? The Lord raised up honorable men to make it a land of freedom, and he declared: "It is not right that any man should be in bondage one to another. And for this purpose have I established the Constitution of this land, by the hands of wise men whom I raised up unto this very purpose, and redeemed the land by the shedding of blood" [D&C 101:79-80]. *(Doctrines of Salvation* 3:273)

10.20. Our duty is to keep the commandments of the Lord, to walk uprightly, to defend every principle of truth, to sustain and uphold the Constitution of this great country, to remember the Declaration of Independence, for, as we heard this morning from our President, upon these principles our country was based. *(Take Heed to Yourselves!* 164)

As the President of the Church

10.21. The Lord has said, "I established the Constitution of this land, by the hands of wise men whom I raised up unto this very purpose, and redeemed the land by the shedding of blood" [D&C 101:80]. *(Seek Ye Earnestly* 158)

Harold B. Lee   11

Biographical Information

Born: 28 March 1899
Ordained an Apostle: 10 April 1941
President of the Twelve: 23 January 1970
First Counselor to Joseph Fielding Smith: 23 January 1970
President of the Church: 7 July 1972 – 26 December 1973
Died: 26 December 1973

* * * * * * * * *

Relationship with the Constitution and U.S. Government

President Harold B. Lee was a champion of the Constitution and its attendant freedoms. He was one of only a few LDS Church Presidents to actually hold political office, serving on the City Commission in Salt Lake City as Commissioner of Streets and Public Improvements from 1932 to 1935, when he was called by the First Presidency to begin the Church Welfare Program. During his term as county commissioner he ran an efficient operation and saved the taxpayers a substantial amount of money. His relationship with the federal government while President of the Church was cordial and followed the pattern set by his immediate predecessors.

Themes Discussed in the Quotations

Main theme: The Constitution was established by the hands of wise men.

Minor Themes:
1. America will be saved by people who possess faith in her.
2. All nations should adopt a government similar to the U.S. government.
3. We should reflect more intently on the meaning of the Constitution.

Quotations

As an Apostle

11.1. Our anxiety has been increased when we have listened to the attempts of men in high stations to stir up class hatreds that contradict the age-old constitutional guarantee of free enterprise. (*True Patriotism* 1; revised in *Ye Are the Light of the World* 174)

11.2. Indeed, it has been said by a prophet in our generation that the time would come when the destiny of this nation would hang as by a single thread, but that it would be saved by the people who possessed faith in America and in her destiny. (*True Patriotism* 1-2; revised in *Ye Are the Light of the World* 174)

11.3. To the membership of The Church of Jesus Christ of Latter-day Saints, the Constitution of the United States is as a tree of liberty under whose cooling branches one might find a haven from the scorching sun of turmoil and oppression and have his rights protected according to just and holy principles. To them, the Constitution was established by the hands of wise men whom God raised up for this very purpose, and they devoutly believe that if it should be in danger of being overthrown, their lives, if need be, are to be offered in defense of its principles. (See D&C 101:77-80.) (*True Patriotism* 2; revised in *Ye Are the Light of the World* 176)

11.4. May I voice a plea for all Americans to love this country with a fervor that will inspire each to so live as to merit the favor of the Almighty during this time of grave uncertainties, as well as in times to come. I would that all men could believe in the destiny of America as did the early pioneers: that it is the land of Zion; that the founders of this nation were men of inspired vision; that the Constitution as written by the inspiration of heaven must be preserved at all costs. (*True Patriotism* 5; revised in *Ye are the Light of the World* 181-82)

11.5. Some time ago there appeared in a local newspaper an account of an interview with an elderly statesman who wielded great influence in American politics. This elderly statesman, in explaining the reason for his determination and zeal, told of a statement his own father—now long since dead—had made to his four sons just before he died. This is what the father said: "America, with its government and constitution, is the greatest institution invented by the mind of man. If you let them touch a stick or stone of it, I will come back and haunt you."

As I thought of that statement, my mind went back to our ancestors who pioneered in this dispensation an even greater constitution than that of the American nation, even the constitution of the kingdom of God, which might be said to be another definition of the gospel of Jesus Christ. As I thought of our pioneers, I was reminded of their virtues and their accomplishments and of the underlying principles that made them willing to leave all that they possessed and even willing to sacrifice their lives, if need be, to uphold and to maintain their beliefs. As I remembered that and thought of the statement of this aged American patriot, I wondered if we might not say: "The Lord help us to keep in memory our ancestors that we might be willing to uphold and sustain, by our lives and all that we possess, that for which they gave so much." ("The Spirit of Gathering" 281; also in *Ye Are the Light of the World* 163-64)

11.6. Patriotism and loyalty in defense of the Constitution of the United States is constantly enjoined upon us. President McKay again this morning has made reference to the cause of liberty in his remarks. To be effective in such teaching, we must begin by inspiring in each heart the faith that the Constitution of the United States was written by inspired men whom God raised up for that very purpose.

It was Joseph Smith who has been quoted as having said that the time would come when the Constitution would hang as by a thread, and at that time when it was thus in jeopardy, the elders of this Church would step forth and save it from destruction.

Why the elders of this Church? Would it be sacrilegious to paraphrase the words of the Apostle Peter, and say that the Constitution of the United States could be saved by the elders of this Church because this Church and this Church alone has the words of eternal life? We alone know by revelation as to how the Constitution came into being, and we, alone, know by revelation the destiny of this nation. The preservation of "life, liberty and the pursuit of happiness" can be guaranteed upon no other basis than upon a sincere faith and testimony of the divinity of these teachings. ("Faith—An Effective Weapon Against Wickedness in Men and Nations" 912-13)

11.7. The question is now whether or not we can make a Republican form of government work, not merely for America but for the world, as all other nations under Heaven may be persuaded of the blessings of freedom enjoyed by the people of this land and to adopt similar governmental systems, thus fulfilling the ancient prophecy of Isaiah "that out of Zion might go forth the law and the word of the Lord from Jerusalem" [Isa 2:3]. ("'I Dare You to Believe'" 4)

11.8. In such a system, the individual is told in effect, "You are free to make your life what you will, and we will try to see that you are rewarded for worthwhile service." These lofty concepts did not spring from governments, but from the Creator Himself, penned into tenets for a stabilized government by men whom God raised up for this very purpose. The basic principles underlying these concepts of human government are contained in that great state paper, the Constitution of the United States of America.

Written into the Constitution as we have it today are three prime safeguards:

1. There are unique restraints on power that governmental authority may exercise upon citizens, embodied in what is known as the Bill of Rights.

2. There is outlined a division of power between the federal and state governments.

3. There is defined a distinct separation of power among three branches of government—the executive, the legislative, and the judicial—in such a way as to provide checks and balances to control the exercise of governmental power.

In the wisdom of the Almighty, this ensign of liberty was raised to the nations to fulfill an ancient prophecy that "out of Zion [should] go forth the law, and the word of the Lord from Jerusalem" (Isa 2:3). How could this be? The answer is clear: through the Constitution, kings and rulers and the peoples of all nations under heaven may be informed of the blessings enjoyed by the people of this land of Zion by reason of their freedom under Divine guidance, and be constrained to adopt similar governmental systems and thus fulfill the ancient law to which I have already referred.

My visits to underprivileged countries and among subjugated peoples who have placed their trust in governments of dominating men, rather than in governments of constitutional law, have shown me the importance and the great blessed privilege that is ours to live in this country where the basic law of the Constitution safeguards us in our God-given rights. (*Ye Are the Light of the World* 232-33; from a memorial service for President John F. Kennedy, Salt Lake City, UT, 25 Nov 1963)

11.9. The kingdom of God must be a continuing revolution against the norms of the society that fall below the standards that are set for us in the gospel of Jesus Christ. In the field of public life, it must be a continuing revolution against proposals that contradict the fundamental principles as laid down in the Constitution of the United States, which was written by men whom God raised up for this very purpose. If we remember that, we will be in the forefront of every battle against the things that are tearing down our society. ("Keep Your Lamp Lighted" 104)

11.10. Brethren of the priesthood, if we will be united and let our light shine, and not hide our light under a bushel but exercise it righteously, and let our priesthood callings be an eternal revolution against the norms of society or against any proposals that fall below the standards as set forth in the gospel of Jesus Christ or as laid down by the Constitution of the United States written by inspired men, then we will be a force in the world that will be "the marvelous work and wonder" which the Lord said the kingdom of God was to be. ("Keep Your Lamp Lighted" 105)

11.11. We would hope that we might be instrumental in developing statesmen—men not only with unsurpassed excellence of training in the law, but also with an unwavering faith that the Constitution of the United States was divinely inspired and written by men whom God raised up for this very purpose [D&C 101:80].

Teachers, hold up before your students the prophetic statement of the Prophet Joseph Smith—that if and when our inspired Constitution should hang as by a thread, there would be prepared, well-qualified defenders of the faith of our fathers, the elders of this church, who would step forth and save the Constitution from destruction. (*Ye Are the Light of the World* 118; from the inauguration of President Dallin H. Oaks, Brigham Young University, Provo, UT, 12 Nov 1971)

11.12. May we keep always a deep sense of gratitude for our pioneer heritage, a love for this country, and a deep-seated reverence for the Constitution of the United States, to the end that we will never forget our civic and political obligations. (*Ye Are the Light of the World* 120; from the inauguration of President Dallin H. Oaks, Brigham Young University, Provo, UT, 12 Nov 1971)

11.13. The Constitution of the United States has been mentioned several times by speakers in this conference as the basis of wise decisions in fundamental principles as applied to all matters pertaining to law and order, because it was framed by men whom God raised up for this very purpose. But in addition to that inspired document, we must always keep in mind that the greatest weapons that can be forged against any false philosophy are the positive teachings of the gospel of Jesus Christ. ("A Time of Decision" 32)

As the President of the Church

11.14. I concluded by calling attention to the prophecy of Joseph Smith that "the constitution would hang as by a thread." I then pointed out that the basic principles of the three separate and independent branches of government were being threatened in the demands of the present Senate investigation. I then read a statement of President J. Reuben Clark, Jr., pointing this out that if either the executive, the legislative, or the judicial were to presume to make the law, enforce it, and then pass judgement, we would approach tyranny. At least the audience heard and listened to this last statement. I finally said that if the basic principles laid down in the Constitution were to be threatened, as is now a possibility, that we might come to [such] a time as when Abraham bargained with the Lord to save Sodom and Gomorrah from destruction, if he could find some righteous souls. Similarly, if such a downfall of the Constitution were imminent, the righteousness of this people might again importune the Almighty to save it because of their pleadings. (Goates 531-32)

11.15. We are living in a time of great crisis. The country is torn with scandal and with criticism, with faultfinding and condemnation. There are those who have downgraded the image of this nation as probably never before in the history of the country. It is so easy to clamber onto the bandwagon and to join the extremists in condemnation, little realizing that when they commit their actions, they are not just tearing down a man; they are tearing down a nation, and they are striking at the underpinnings of one of the greatest of all the nations of all the world—a nation that was founded upon an inspired declaration we call the Constitution of the United States. The Lord said it was written by men whom He raised up for that very purpose, and that Constitution stands today as a model to all nations to pattern their lives [D&C 101:77, 80]. (*Ye Are the Light of the World* 340)

11.16. Some time ago the First Presidency and the Council of the Twelve were engaged in a meeting of serious import, and I said something at that time unpremeditated, but I couldn't have said it better had I taken a month to prepare it. I said: . . .

> . . . We should not be concerned about finding out what is wrong with America, but we should be finding what is right about America and should be speaking optimistically and enthusiastically about America. (*Ye Are the Light of the World* 341-42)

11.17. Men may fail in this country, earthquakes may come, seas may heave beyond their bounds, there may be great drought, disaster, and hardship, but this nation, founded on principles laid down by men whom God raised up, will never fail. This is the cradle of humanity, where life on this earth began in the Garden of Eden. This is the place of the new Jerusalem. This is the place that the Lord said is favored above all other nations in all the world. This is the place where the Savior will come to His temple. This is the favored land in all the world. Yes, I repeat, men may fail, but this nation won't fail. I have faith in America; you and I must have faith in America, if we understand the teachings of the gospel of Jesus Christ. We are living in a day when we *must* pay heed to these challenges.

I plead with you not to preach pessimism. Preach that this is the greatest country in all the world. This is the favored land. This is the land of our forefathers. It is the nation that will stand despite whatever trials or crises it may yet have to pass through. (*Ye Are the Light of the World* 350-51)

11.18. We urge members of the Church and all Americans to begin now to reflect more intently on the meaning and importance of the Constitution, and of adherence to its principles. ("News of the Church" 90)

11.19. I have faith in the future of this promised land of America and in its institutions of representative government, but more than that, I have faith in you, the youth of America, to build even more securely on the foundations laid by the faith and devotion of your pioneer fathers. That you as the youth of the Church would have an important part to play in preserving the ideals of this great country as quoted by one who was very close to him. I quote the words of Eliza R. Snow: "I heard the Prophet Joseph Smith say 'that the time would come when this nation would so far depart from its original purity, its glory, and its love of freedom and the protection of civil and religious rights, that the Constitution of our country would hang, as it were, by a thread.' He also said that this people, the sons of Zion, would rise up and save the Constitution and bear it off triumphantly." (Eliza R. Snow, 1870, *Women of Mormondom* by Tullidge.)

So today is no time for youth to whimper the refrain of the defeated and retire to the fancied security of the regimented state. Today is the day for youth to gird themselves with the armor of peace, having as their weapons "the shield of faith . . . and the sword of the Spirit, which is the word of God." (Eph 6:16-17.) (*Decisions for Successful Living* 209)

11.20. Youth must never forget that this the government of the United States was established "According to the laws and constitution of the people, which (God) has suffered to be established. . . . That every man may act in doctrine and principle . . . according to the moral agency which (God) has given unto him, that every man may be accountable for his own sins in the day of judgment. Therefore, it is not right that any man should be in bondage one to another." It was to accomplish this lofty purpose basic to all liberty that God "established the Constitution of this land by the hands of wise men whom (he) raised up unto this very purpose." (D&C 101:77-80.) Contained within the principles of that great heaven-inspired document is the message of this Church to the world in this fateful hour. Except the spirit of the Gospel of Jesus Christ and principles contained within the Constitution of the United States are inherent in world plans now being formulated, they are but building on sand and the Lord is not in that building. (*Decisions for Successful Living* 217)

Spencer W. Kimball   12

Biographical Information

Born: 28 March 1895
Ordained an Apostle: 7 October 1943
Acting President of the Twelve: 23 January 1970
President of the Twelve: 7 July 1972
President of the Church: 30 December 1973 – 5 November 1985
Died: 5 November 1985

*   *   *   *   *   *   *   *

Relationship with the Constitution and U.S. Government

President Spencer W. Kimball grew up in a home where patriotism and love of country were taught. He carried those early lessons into his administration as Church President.

President Kimball was a highly visible Church President, making numerous pronouncements on public policy. One example was his opposition to the MX Missile system which had been proposed for the Utah desert. President Kimball spoke out vigorously on this issue and buttressed his arguments both with scriptural and constitutional evidence. The Church also strongly opposed the passage of the ERA (Equal Rights Amendment) as the wrong way to gain a desirable end. Involvement in these issues presented a high political profile for the Church.

Themes Discussed in the Quotations

Main theme: The Constitution was established to prepare the way for the restoration of the gospel.

Minor themes:
1. Every Latter-day Saint should sustain, honor, and obey the law of the land.
2. The only way to keep our freedom is to work at it.
3. The Mormon people are loyal to the Constitution.

Quotations

As an Apostle

12.1. Early in this dispensation the Lord made clear the position his restored church should take with respect to civil government. In the revelation he gave to the Prophet Joseph Smith, he said: "And now, verily I say unto you concerning the . . . law of the land which is constitutional, supporting that principle of freedom in maintaining rights and privileges, [that it] belongs to all mankind, and is justifiable before me.

"Therefore, I, the Lord, justify you . . . in befriending that law which is the constitutional law of the land." (D&C 98:4-6.)

Every Latter-day Saint should sustain, honor, and obey the constitutional law of the land in which he lives. ("Guidelines to Carry Forth the Work of God in Holiness" 4-5)

As the President of the Church

12.2. We are grateful that thou didst cause this land to be rediscovered and settled by people who founded a great nation with an inspired constitution guaranteeing freedom in which there could come the glorious restoration of the gospel and the Church of thy Beloved Son. ("President Kimball Dedicates Temple" 81)

12.3. The Church of Jesus Christ of Latter-day Saints was restored in 1830 after numerous revelations from the divine source; and this is the kingdom, set up by the God of heaven, that would never be destroyed nor superseded, and the stone cut out of the mountain without hands that would become a great mountain and would fill the whole earth.

History unfolded and the world powers came and went after ruling the world for a little season, but in the early nineteenth century the day had come. The new world of America had been discovered and colonized and was being settled. Independence had been gained and a constitution approved and freedom given to men, and people were now enlightened to permit truth to be established and to reign.

No king or set of rulers could divine this history; but a young, pure, and worthy prophet could receive a revelation from God.

There was purpose for this unveiling of the history of the world so that the honest in heart might be looking forward to its establishment, and numerous good men and women, knowing of the revelations of God and the prospects for the future, have looked forward to this day. ("The Stone Cut Without Hands" 9)

12.4. The only way we can keep our freedom is to work at it. Not some of us. All of us. Not some of the time, but all of the time.

So if you value your citizenship and you want to keep it for yourself and your children and their children, give it your faith, your belief, and give it your active support in civic affairs. (*TSWK* 405; from an address given at the Rotary Club, Salt Lake City, UT, 8 Jun 1976)

12.5. This restoration was preceded by a long period of preparation. The Pilgrims and other Europeans were inspired to find this American haven of refuge and thus people this land with honest and God-fearing citizens. Washington and his fellows were inspired to revolt from England and bring political liberty to this land, along with the more valuable treasure of religious liberty so that the soil might be prepared for the seed of the truth when it should again be sown. ("Absolute Truth" 7)

12.6. Few men have enjoyed more of the guidance of the Holy Spirit than did President Woodruff. He was an apostle of the Lord

Jesus Christ, was valiant and true all his days, and, in the provinces of the Lord, he was the fourth president of The Church of Jesus Christ of Latter-day Saints. He is the one who dedicated the Salt Lake Temple in 1893, and it was to him that the founders of the American nation appeared in the St. George Temple, seeking to have the temple ordinances performed for them. That was very unusual, brethren, and those kinds of miracles and visions and revelations were rather unusual, as you would know. These men of the American Constitution had lived in a day when the gospel was not upon the earth, but they were upright, good men who were entitled to all of the blessings which come to us. ("Preparing for Service in the Church" 47)

12.7. The Mormon people who are citizens of [the United States of] America today are intensely loyal to its Constitution and desire in every way to promote the God-given freedoms it was designed to protect. They have had experience with the tragedy that results when those freedoms are not protected, but this only feeds their determination to do all within their power to protect these freedoms, both for themselves and others, everywhere. (*TSWK* 405; from an address given at the rededication of the Mormon Pioneer Memorial Bridge, Omaha, NE, 21 Apr 1979)

12.8. We encourage all members, as citizens of the nation, to be actively involved in the political process, and to support those measures which will strengthen the community, state, and nation—morally, economically, and culturally. (Quoted in Benson, "A Witness and a Warning" 33; from a letter from the First Presidency, 29 Jun 1979)

12.9. President Ronald Reagan has proclaimed the week beginning Sept. 17 (the 195th anniversary of the signing of the Constitution of Sept. 17, 1787) as Constitution Week and has urged all Americans to observe that week by stressing the importance of the Constitution to our individual freedoms and form of government.
    In view of this proclamation and because of the high esteem in which the Constitution has been held by members of The

Church of Jesus Christ of Latter-day Saints since the days of the Prophet Joseph Smith, we encourage leaders and members of the Church in the United States to heed President Reagan's proclamation and during this week to remember with appreciation before the Lord the great blessings of liberty and opportunity which are guaranteed to the citizens of the United States. The First Presidency. ("First Presidency Urges Support of Constitution Week" 4)

Ezra Taft Benson 13

Biographical Information

Born: 4 August 1899
Ordained an Apostle: 7 October 1943
President of the Twelve: 30 December 1973
President of the Church: 10 November 1985

* * * * * * * *

Relationship with the Constitution and U.S. Government

As a young man, President Ezra Taft Benson was imbued with a fervent love for the Constitution. This love has been a hallmark of his public career both in government and in the Church.

President Benson has spent more time in public office than any of his predecessors; most notable were his eight years as Secretary of Agriculture in the Eisenhower administration. He has written more and said more about the U.S. Constitution than any other of his fellow Church Presidents. He has been known as a staunch foe of Communism and as an advocate of the Constitution as envisioned by the Founding Fathers. During the U.S. Constitution Bicentennial celebration he gave several major addresses and published a book on the American Constitution entitled The Constitution: A Heavenly Banner.

Themes Discussed in the Quotations

Main theme: We should sustain and support the Constitution.

Minor Themes:
  1. The Founding Fathers were inspired.
  2. We should study and teach the Constitution.
  3. The Constitution is threatened today.
  4. Our duty is to defend and restore constitutional principles.

Quotations

As an Apostle

13.1. In framing that great document which Gladstone declared "the most wonderful work ever struck off at a given time by the brain and purpose of man," our early leaders called upon a kind Providence. Later the product of the constitutional convention was referred to as our God-inspired Constitution. They had incorporated within its sacred paragraphs eternal principles supported by the holy scriptures with which they were familiar. It was established "for the rights and protection of all flesh according to just and holy principles" [D&C 101:77]. Later the Lord himself declared, "I established the Constitution of this land, by the hands of wise men whom I raised up unto this very purpose" [D&C 101:80]. ("America: A Choice Land" 674; compare *RC* 284)

13.2. Twenty-five years later, another prophet [Jacob], son of the first one quoted [Lehi], was privileged to see into the future regarding this land and to proclaim that God would fortify the land against other nations; that he that fought against Zion would perish; that no king would ever be raised on these shores; that the Lord would be their king and be a light unto the people forever who accepted and listened to his words.

    And so this great nation, has come into being under the inspiration of the Almighty to accomplish his purposes. Through modern revelation we have had made very plain to us something of the mission of America and the establishment of our national Constitution in this dispensation. ("America: Land of the Blessed" 283; revised in *RC* 109)

13.3. And so, every true Latter-day Saint has a deep love and respect for the Constitution of this land. ("America: Land of the Blessed" 342)

13.4. This same modern prophet [Joseph Smith] said—even though he knew he would suffer martyrdom in this land—"The Constitution of the United States is a glorious standard; it is founded in the wisdom of God. It is a heavenly banner" [*TPJS* 147].

According to this prophet's contemporaries, he foresaw the time when the destiny of the nation would be in danger and would hang as by a thread. Thank God he did not see the thread break. He also indicated the important part his people should yet play in standing for the principles embodied in these sacred documents— the Declaration of Independence and the Constitution. ("America: Land of the Blessed" 342; compare *RC* 110)

13.5. We stand firmly in support of the principles enunciated in the Constitution and the Declaration of Independence, and every Latter-day Saint would defend to the last those eternal principles. ("America: Land of the Blessed" 343)

13.6. Our Constitution and Bill of Rights guarantee to all our people the greatest freedom ever enjoyed by the public of any great nation. This system guarantees freedom of individual enterprise, freedom to own property, freedom to start one's own business and to operate it according to one's own judgment so long as the enterprise is honorable. The individual has power to produce beyond his needs, to provide savings for the future protection of himself and family. He can live where he wishes and pick any job he wants and select any educational opportunity. (*So Shall Ye Reap* 151; also in *TETB* 605; from a baccalaureate address given at the University of Wyoming, Laramie, WY, 4 Jun 1950)

13.7. In concluding, I said: "I love this nation. It is my firm belief that the God of Heaven raised up the founding fathers and inspired them to establish the Constitution of this land. This is part of my religious faith." To me this is not just another nation. It is a great and glorious nation with a divine mission to perform for liberty-loving people everywhere. (*CF* 79; from an address given at the 16th Annual National Farm Institute, Des Moines, IA, 21 Feb 1953)

13.8. My one fear, and my one anxiety is that I may inadvertently sometime do something or say something that will cast an unfavorable light or bring discredit upon the Church and kingdom of God and the people whom I love so dearly, and upon this great nation which we all love. I pray that this may never happen.

I love this nation of which we are a part. To me it is not just another nation, not just a member of a family of nations. It is a great and glorious nation with a divine mission and it has been brought into being under the inspiration of heaven. It is truly a land choice above all others. I thank God for the knowledge which we have regarding the prophetic history and the prophetic future of this great land of America. . . .

I am grateful for the Founding Fathers of this land and for the freedom they have vouchsafed to us. I am grateful that they recognized, as great leaders of this nation have always recognized, that the freedom which we enjoy did not originate with the Founding Fathers; that this glorious principle, this great boon of freedom and respect for the dignity of man, came as a gift from the Creator. The Founding Fathers, it is true, with superb genius welded together the safeguards of these freedoms. It was necessary, however, for them to turn to the scriptures, to religion, in order to have this great experiment make sense to them. And so our freedom is God-given. It antedates the Founding Fathers. ("Our Duty as Citizens" 918, 920)

13.9. I am grateful for the Constitution of this land. I am grateful that the Founding Fathers made it clear that our allegiance runs to that Constitution and the glorious eternal principles embodied therein. Our allegiance does not run to any man, to a king, or a dictator, or a president, although we revere and honor those whom we elect to high office. Our allegiance runs to the Constitution and to the principles embodied therein. The Founding Fathers made that clear and provided well for checks and balances and safeguards in an attempt to guarantee this freedom to those of us who live in this land.

I am grateful that the God of heaven saw fit to put his stamp of approval upon the Constitution and to indicate that it had come into being through wise men whom he raised up unto this very purpose. He asked the Saints, even in the dark days of their persecution and hardship to continue to seek for redress from their enemies "According," he said, "to the laws and constitution . . . which I have suffered to be established and should be maintained for the rights and protection of all flesh." (D&C 101:77.) And then he made this most impressive declaration:

> And for this purpose have I established the Constitution of this land, by the hands of wise men whom I raised up unto this very purpose, and redeemed the land by the shedding of blood. (D&C 101:80.)

It is gratifying that the Constitutions in many of the other lands of our neighbors in the Americas are patterned very much after this divinely-appointed Constitution, which the God of heaven directed in the founding of this nation. It isn't any wonder, therefore, that Joseph Smith, the Prophet—a truly great American—referring to the Constitution, said,

> "[It] is a glorious standard; it is founded in the wisdom of God. It is a heavenly banner." (*Teachings of the Prophet Joseph Smith*, p. 147.) ("Our Duty as Citizens" 920)

13.10. Wherefore, honest men and wise men should be sought for diligently, and good men and wise men ye should observe to uphold; otherwise whatsoever is less than these cometh of evil. (D&C 98:10.)

Now that is a commandment to his Church and to his Saints. To me it means that we have a responsibility as Latter-day Saints to use our influence so honest men and wise men and good men will be elected to public office in the community, in the county, in the state, and in the nation. To me this commandment of God is just as binding upon the Latter-day Saints as is the law of tithing, or the Word of Wisdom, or any other commandment which the God of heaven has given us.

As I read that for the first time some years ago I thought, "What an indictment of corrupt would-be political leaders in many parts of the world—demagogues who deal in half-truths, innuendos, and falsehoods! Here the God of heaven has pointed out the type of men he wants elected to public office among his people." It is not enough, my brethren and sisters, just to stand on the sidelines and criticize what is taking place, and to point the finger of scorn at some political leader. It is our job, our duty, and our responsibility to take an active interest in these matters, and carry out the admonition and the commandment which God has given us to see to it that men of character—good men, as measured by the standards of the gospel—are elected to public office.

So, today, I would like to throw out a challenge to the elders of Israel, my brethren of the priesthood, that we put forth an effort to prepare ourselves for statesmanlike work. The Prophet Joseph, as you will recall, had something to say regarding the important part which the elders of Israel would play in the safeguarding, if not the saving, of the Constitution of this land.

It is my conviction that only in this land, under this God-inspired Constitution, under an environment of freedom, could it have been possible to have established the Church and kingdom of God and restored the gospel in its fulness. It is our responsibility, my brethren and sisters, to see that this freedom is maintained, so that the Church can flourish in the future. ("Our Duty as Citizens" 920, 922)

13.11. Today I would like to propose four questions which every Latter-day Saint might well ask as he attempts to appraise any program, policy, or idea promoted by any would-be political leader. I mention these because I think they will provide a safeguard in electing to office men who will meet the requirements which the Lord has set forth in the revelations.

Firstly, is the proposal, the policy, or the idea being promoted right as measured by the gospel of Jesus Christ? I assure you it is much easier for one to measure a proposed policy by the gospel of Jesus Christ if he has accepted the gospel and is living it.

Secondly, is it right as measured by the Constitution of this land and the glorious principles embodied in that Constitution? Now that suggests that we must read and study the Constitution, the Declaration of Independence, and the Bill of Rights, that we might know what principles are embodied therein.

Thirdly, we might well ask the question: Is it right as measured by the counsel of the living oracles of God? It is my conviction, my brethren and sisters, that these living oracles are not only authorized, but are obligated to give counsel to this people on any subject which is vital to the welfare of this people and the upbuilding of the kingdom of God. So, that measure should be applied. Is it right as measured by the counsel of the living oracles of God?

Fourthly, what will be the effect on the morale and the character of the people if this or that policy is adopted? After all, as a Church we are interested in building men and women, building character, because character is the one thing we make in this world and take with us into the next. It must never be sacrificed for expediency. ("Our Duty as Citizens" 922)

13.12. The Founding Fathers did not invent this priceless boon of individual freedom and respect for the dignity of man. That great gift to mankind sprang from the Creator and not from government. But the Founding Fathers with superb genius, I believe, welded together certain safeguards which we must always protect to the very limit if we would preserve and strengthen the blessings of freedom.

. . . They were guided by allegiance to basic principles. These principles must be kept in mind always by those who are here today and reaping the benefits and the blessings which they so wisely provided. We must be careful that we do not trade freedom for security. Whenever that is attempted, usually we lose both. There is always a tendency when nations become mature for the people to become more interested in preserving their luxuries and their comforts than in safeguarding the ideals and principles which made these comforts and luxuries possible. ("Responsibilities of Citizenship" 8; also in *TETB* 599-600)

13.13. Second to their duty to God, youth should realize their duty to our country. They should love and honor the Constitution of the United States, the basic concepts and principles upon which this nation has been established. Yes, they need to develop a love for our free institutions. (*GFC* 219; from an address delivered at the second annual meeting of the President's Council on Youth Fitness, Camp Ritchie, Cascade, MD, 8 Sep 1958)

13.14. Free agency is an eternal principle vouchsafed to us in the perfect law of liberty—the gospel of Jesus Christ. Freedom of choice is more to be treasured than any earthly possession. It is guaranteed in our heaven-inspired Constitution. Yes, freedom is an inherited, inalienable, divine gift to men. . . .

The inspired founding fathers formulated a system of government with checks and balances protecting the freedom of the people. But even this was not enough. The first order of the new congress was to draw up a Bill of Rights—ten amendments guaranteeing for all time the fundamental freedoms that the American people insist are theirs by the will of God, not by the will of government.

Yes, the founders of this nation bequeathed to us a heritage of freedom and unity that is our most priceless political possession. . . .

. . . Under the constitutional concept, powers not granted to the federal government are reserved to the states or to the people [U.S. Const. Amend. X]. . . .

The founding fathers, inspired though they were, did not invent the priceless blessing of individual freedom and respect for the dignity of man. No, that priceless gift to mankind sprang from the God of heaven and not from government. Yes, the founding fathers welded together the safeguards as best they could, but freedom must be continually won to be enjoyed. Let us never forget these facts.

This is America—the land of opportunity! A land choice above all other lands. Let us keep it so! . . .

. . . It is my firm conviction that the Constitution of this land was established by men whom the God of heaven raised up unto this very purpose.

The days ahead are sobering and challenging and will demand the faith, prayers, and loyalty of every American. Our challenge is to keep America strong and free—strong socially, strong economically, and above all, strong spiritually, if our way of life is to endure. There is no other way. Only in this course is there safety for our nation. ("The Heritage of Freedom" 954-55, 957)

13.15. Some day we may be called upon as a people to exert great influence in helping to preserve the liberties and freedoms and blessings vouchsafed to us as a people in the Constitution of this land. Some of our inspired leaders have had words to say on that subject. I hope and pray that we will be ready when the time comes—in fact, I am inclined to feel sometimes it is going to be a gradual process. Maybe it is underway now. We will not be able to discharge our obligations unless we adhere strictly to the standards and ideals of the church and kingdom of God. (*GFC* 87; from an address delivered at the Mutual Improvement Association [hereafter MIA] Conference, Salt Lake City, UT, 14 Jun 1959)

13.16. To every Latter-day Saint, we have a tremendous obligation to be good citizens, to uphold the Constitution of this land, to adhere to its basic concepts, to do all in our power to protect the freedoms and the liberties and the basic rights which are associated with citizenship. The Lord has said even in our day, through the Prophet Joseph Smith, that we have an obligation. He has not only spoken about the Constitution being inspired, he has said that if we are to be good Latter-day Saints, we also have to take an interest in this country in which we live and we are to see to it that good men are upheld and sustained in public office. (*TETB* 615-16; from an address given at Short Hills, NJ, 15 Jan 1961)

13.17. I would to God that every citizen of this land might read the Book of Mormon prayerfully and learn something of the prophecies made regarding this land—the promises made and the conditions upon which they are made—that we might as an American people so live that these great promises could be fully realized; that we might come to know that the Constitution of this land has been established by men whom the God of heaven raised up unto that very purpose. ("A World Message" 432; also in *TL* 213)

13.18. We have heard that the Prophet Joseph said something about the time when the Constitution would be in danger. We do not know just what turn that will take. He also said something about the Elders of Israel rising to the challenge and helping to save the Constitution of this land. It is entirely possible that that may come about in a rather natural way. Our young people—as they mature and develop and take their positions in industry, in the professions, and in agriculture clear across this land—might represent the balance of power in a time of crisis, when they will stand up and defend those eternal principles upon which this Constitution has been established. ("A Four-Fold Hope" 7)

13.19. Under our system there has been released great creative capacity, because we have been free, unrestricted. What have we achieved? A standard of living unequalled anywhere in the world. Not because we are smarter, not because we are more brilliant, not because we have greater capacity than people of other nations, but because we have had a system which is superior—a system which was wisely provided by the Founding Fathers. We must protect and safeguard that system. Sometimes we find people who almost apologize for it—the free enterprise system. Of course it is not perfect; it is operated by human beings, but it is the best system in operation in this world today. If we are wise, we will preserve it, we will strengthen it and we will safeguard it for our children and our children's children. ("A Four-Fold Hope" 8)

13.20. No true Latter-day Saint can be a Communist or a Socialist because Communist principles run counter to the revealed word of God and to the Constitution of this land which was established by men whom the God of Heaven raised up unto that very purpose [D&C 101:80]. ("A Four-Fold Hope" 11)

13.21. One of the first considerations given after my appointment to serve as Secretary of Agriculture was to formulate with my close associates and other interested parties a basic statement on agricultural policy. Among the fundamental concepts stated were the following:

"Freedom is a God-given, eternal principle vouchsafed to us under the Constitution. It must be guarded continually as something more precious than life itself." ...

... How do we stand with reference to our belief in those freedoms safeguarded for us under the Constitution of the United States? What is our attitude toward our government—toward the free enterprise system and our American Way of Life?

... I trust you are leaving this institution [Brigham Young University] with faith in the Constitution of the United States. ("Paramount Issue Today" 13)

13.22. Every member of the priesthood should understand the divine plan designed by the Lord to raise up the first free people in modern times. Here is how scripture says it was achieved: ...

Sixth: Having declared America to be a land of liberty, God undertook to raise up a band of inspired and intelligent leaders who could write a constitution of liberty and establish the first free people in modern times. The hand of God in this undertaking is clearly indicated by the Lord himself, in a revelation to the Prophet Joseph Smith in these words:

> I established the Constitution of this land, by the hands of wise men whom I raised up unto this very purpose.... (D&C 101:80.)

Seventh: God declared that the United States Constitution was divinely inspired for the specific purpose of eliminating bondage and the violation of the rights and protection which belong to "all flesh." (D&C 101:77-80.)

Eighth: God placed a mandate upon his people to befriend and defend the constitutional laws of the land and see that the rights and privileges of all mankind are protected. He verified the declaration of the founding fathers, that God created all men free. He also warned against those who would enact laws encroaching upon the sacred rights and privileges of free men. He urged the election of honest and wise leaders and said that evil men and laws were of Satan. (D&C 98:5-10.) . . .

Eleventh: In connection with the attack on the United States, the Lord told the Prophet Joseph Smith there would be an attempt to overthrow the country by destroying the Constitution. Joseph Smith predicted that the time would come when the Constitution would hang as it were by a thread, and at that time, "this people will step forth and save it from the threatened destruction." (*Journal History*, Jul 4, 1854.)

It is my conviction that the elders of Israel, widely spread over the nation, will, at the crucial time, successfully rally the righteous of our country and provide the necessary balance of strength to save the institutions of constitutional government. ("The American Heritage of Freedom" 952; also in *The American Heritage of Freedom* 1, 3-4; *TL* 179-81)

13.23. If the Gentiles on this land reject the word of God and conspire to overthrow the liberty and the Constitution, then their doom is fixed, and they "shall be cut off from among my people who are of the covenant." (3 Nephi 21:11, 14, 21; 1 Nephi 14:6; D&C 84:114, 115, 117.) ("The American Heritage of Freedom" 952-53; also in *The American Heritage of Freedom* 5; *TL* 181)

13.24. What are these fundamental principles which have allowed the United States to progress so rapidly and yet remain free?

First, a written Constitution clearly defining the limits of government so that government will not become more powerful than the people. (*TL* 168; from an address given at Los Angeles, CA, 11 Dec 1961)

13.25. We should pay no attention to the recommendations of men who call the Constitution an eighteenth-century agrarian document—who apologize for capitalism and free enterprise. We should refuse to follow their siren song of concentrating, increasingly, the powers of government in the Chief Executive, of delegating American sovereign authority to non-American institutions in the United Nations, and pretending that it will bring peace to the world by turning our armed forces over to a U.N. world-wide police force. (*TL* 176; from an address given at Los Angeles, CA, 11 Dec 1961)

13.26. I thank God for freedom—the right of choice. I am grateful for this great nation. Every true Latter-day Saint throughout the world loves the USA. The Constitution of this land is part of every Latter-day Saint's religious faith.

This is not just another nation, not just a member of a family of nations. This is a great and glorious nation with a divine mission and a prophetic history and future. It has been brought into being under the inspiration of heaven.

It is our firm belief, as Latter-day Saints, that the Constitution of this land was established by men whom the God of heaven raised up unto that very purpose. It is our conviction also that the God of heaven guided the founding fathers in establishing it for his particular purpose.

The founders of this republic were deeply spiritual men. They believed men are capable of self-government and that it is the job of government to protect freedom and foster private initiative.

Our earliest American fathers came here with a common objective—freedom of worship and liberty of conscience.

They were familiar with the sacred scriptures, and they believed that liberty is a gift of heaven. To them, man as a child of God emphasized the sacredness of the individual and the interest of a kind Providence in the affairs of men and nations.

These leaders recognized the need for divine guidance and the importance of vital religion and morality in the affairs of men and nations. ("The Lord's Base of Operations" 454-55; also in *TL* 86)

13.27. To achieve his purposes the Lord had to have a base of operations. Later he revealed to a modern prophet that the Constitution of this land was established by "wise men" whom the Lord "raised up unto this very purpose." (See D&C 101:80.) The Lord also directed that the constitutional laws of the land, supporting the principle of freedom, should be upheld and that honest and wise men should be sought for and upheld in public office [D&C 98:10]. ("The Lord's Base of Operations" 456; also in *TL* 87)

13.28. God, through his power has established a free people in this land as a means of helping to carry forward his purposes. . . .

It was here under a free government and a strong nation that protection was provided for his restored Church.

Now God will not permit America, his base of operations, to be destroyed. He has promised protection to this land if we will but serve the God of the land. He has also promised protection to the righteous even, if necessary, to send down fire from heaven to destroy their enemies. (1 Nephi 22.)

No, God's base of operations will not be destroyed. But it may be weakened and made less effective. ("The Lord's Base of Operations" 456; also in *TL* 88-89)

13.29. We must return to a love and respect for the basic spiritual concepts upon which this nation has been established. We must study the Constitution and the writings of the founding fathers. ("The Lord's Base of Operations" 457; also in *TL* 91)

13.30. Our Constitution and Bill of Rights vouchsafe to all our people the greatest freedom ever enjoyed by the people of any great nation. This system safeguards freedom of individual enterprise, freedom to own property, freedom to start one's own business and to operate it according to one's own judgment so long as the enterprise is honorable. (*RC* 89-90)

13.31. In the providence of God, governments were intended to be the servants, not the masters of the people. This eternal truth needs to be emphasized and re-emphasized. (*RC* 91)

13.32. The men who wrote the Declaration of Independence, the Constitution and the Bill of Rights were under no illusion that their work was done. They had carried freedom up to a new high, but had no idea that a pinnacle had been reached, that having reached the summit there was no more to be done. They were confident that we of succeeding generations would carry on.

Along with the political freedom so dearly won came a climate which challenged man's intellect and ingenuity. People began to move freedom forward along lines possibly not envisaged by the men who drafted the Declaration of Independence, the Constitution and the Bill of Rights. Freedom from backbreaking toil came with the invention and development of labor-saving devices in factories and on farms. (*RC* 94)

13.33. The Founding Fathers, it is true, with superb genius welded together the safeguards of our freedom. It was necessary, however, for them to turn to the scriptures, to religion, to prayer, in order to have this great experiment make sense to them. And so our freedom is God-given. It ante-dates the Founding Fathers.

It is my belief that ours is not just another nation, not just a member of a family of nations. It is a great and glorious nation with a divine mission and it has been brought into being under the inspiration of heaven. I thank God for the knowledge which I have regarding the prophetic history and the prophetic future of this land of America.

It is my firm belief that the Constitution of the land was established by men whom the God of Heaven raised up unto that very purpose. It is my firm belief, also, that the God of Heaven guided the Founding Fathers in establishing it for His particular purposes. But God's purpose is to build people of character, not physical monuments to their material accumulations.

The founders of this republic had deeply spiritual beliefs. Their concept of man had a solidly religious foundation. They believed "it is not right that any man should be in bondage one to another" [D&C 101:79]. They believed that men were capable of self-government and that it was the job of government to protect freedom and foster private initiative. (*RC* 101-02)

13.34. The Founding Fathers, I repeat, in order that their new experiment—establishment of a new nation of freemen—make sense, had to turn to religion and to the scriptures. They turned to the prophecies, the Decalogue, the Sermon on the Mount.

Then when time came for the establishment of the Constitution, and when the time came for them to issue their Declaration of Independence, a sacred document issued in white heat on the anvil of defiance, they appealed to the Almighty. Both at the opening of that document and at its closing they spoke of eternal truths. They spoke of the fact that men are endowed by their Creator with certain inalienable rights. At the close they said:

". . . with a firm reliance on Divine Providence we mutually pledge to each other our lives, our fortunes, and our sacred honor." (*RC* 106)

13.35. And so this great nation has come into being under the inspiration of the Almighty to accomplish his purposes. Through modern revelation we have had made very plain to us something of the mission of America and the establishment of our national Constitution. (*RC* 109)

13.36. Surely the preservation and enjoyment of the freedoms vouchsafed to us by the Constitution of the United States will require eternal vigilance even to the guarding of it with our lives.

. . . We must ever be on our guard against the unsound theories that would strike at our Constitutional freedoms.

We must ever keep faith with our founding fathers by keeping faith with our Constitution.

I trust that we all have faith in the Constitution of the United States, and that that faith is born of an assurance that this great document came into being through the inspiration of God to wise men, embodying as it does, eternal principles. This nation has a spiritual foundation which must be preserved at any cost of sweat and blood. May we recognize our debt and responsibility and be ever vigilant.

The need for this eternal and constant vigilance is seen in some prophetic words of Daniel Webster, given in 1802:

"Next to correct morals and watchful guardianship over the Constitution is the proper means for its support. No human advantage is indefensible. The fairest productions of man have in themselves or receive from accident a tendency to decay. Unless the Constitution be constantly fostered on the principles which created it, its excellency will fade; and it will feel, even in its infancy, the weakness and decrepitude of age.

"Our form of government is superior to all others, inasmuch as it provides, in a fair and honorable manner for its own amendment. But it requires no gift or prophecy to foresee that this privilege may be seized on by demagogues, to introduce wild and destructive innovations. Under the gentle name of amendments, changes may be proposed which, if unresisted, will undermine the national compact, mar its fairest features, and reduce it finally to a dead letter. It abates nothing of the danger to say that alterations may be trifling and inconsiderable. If the Constitution be picked away by piecemeal, it is gone—and gone as effectually as if some military despot had grasped it at once, trampled it beneath his feet, and scattered its loose leaves in the wild winds."

If we are to keep faith with our Constitution, we must know it. Since it is the basis of our American way of life and our liberties every American should be familiar with it. We should read it periodically.

How can people who are ignorant of the principles and guarantees of American government stand up in defense of it and our rights under the Constitution? The fundamentals and processes of free government should be known to every school boy— and his parents. No free people can ever survive if they are ignorant of and fail to understand the principles of free government! *(RC* 201-02)

13.37. We pay lip service to the principles embodied in the Declaration of Independence and the Constitution without realizing what they are and the danger of ignoring them. *(RC* 263)

13.38. [Political and economic rights] are the things we are inclined to take for granted as American citizens.

The rights as listed included the right to worship God in one's own way, rights to free speech and a free press, the right to assemble and freely to speak our own minds without any fear whatever. There are many countries of this world where you cannot do that today.

The right to petition for grievances, the right to privacy in our homes, the right to trial by jury, and to know that we are innocent until we are proven guilty. The right to move freely at home and abroad, the right to own private property, the right to free elections and personal secret ballot. The right to work in callings and localities of our choice. The right to bargain with our employees and employers. The right to go into business, to compete, to make a profit. The right to bargain for goods and services in a free market. The right to contract about our affairs.

These are an impressive list of rights which lay at the very foundation of the American way of life and preserve the dignity of the individual. Our constitutional government desires to serve the people, and basic in our beliefs is our fundamental belief in God and in the eternal principle of free agency, the right of choice. (*RC* 266; also in *TETB* 606)

13.39. "Our real enemies," said President [J. Reuben] Clark, "are *communism* and its running mate, *socialism. . . .*"

" . . . Its purpose is to destroy the Constitution and our Constitutional government." ("Righteousness Exalteth a Nation" 516-17; also in *TL* 109-10)

13.40. Every Latter-day Saint has spiritual obligations in four basic areas: his home, his church, his job, and his citizenship responsibility. Each of these areas should receive consistent attention although not necessarily equal time. Are we doing our duty in these important fields? What about our citizenship responsibility—our obligation to safeguard our freedom and preserve the Constitution?

The Prophet Joseph Smith said the time would come when the Constitution would hang, as it were, by a thread. Modern-day prophets for the past several decades have been warning us that we have been rapidly moving in that direction. Fortunately, the

Prophet Joseph Smith saw the part the elders of Israel would play in this crisis. Will there be some of us who won't care about saving the Constitution, others who will be blinded by the craftiness of men, and some who will knowingly be working to destroy it? He who has ears to hear and eyes to see can discern by the Spirit and through the words of God's mouthpiece that our liberties are being taken. ("Righteousness Exalteth a Nation" 517; also in *TL* 112-13; *GFC* 398-99; revised in *TETB* 623)

13.41. Teach them to love their country, and here in America to love the Constitution and the founding fathers, and to know that this is the Lord's base of operations in these last days, and that that operation will be world-wide. (*TL* 207; from an address given at the MIA Conference, Salt Lake City, UT, 14 Jun 1963)

13.42. Freedom of choice is more to be treasured than any earthly possession. As a United States citizen I believe it is guaranteed in our heaven-inspired Constitution. ("Let Us Live to Keep Men Free" 2; also in *TL* 3)

13.43. I do not believe an American citizen can be patriotic and loyal to his own country and its God-inspired Constitution of freedom without being anti-communist—anti-socialist. ("Let Us Live to Keep Men Free" 10; also in *TL* 15)

13.44. It is my firm conviction that the Constitution of this land was established by men whom the God of heaven raised up unto this very purpose. This is part of my religious faith. ("Let Us Live to Keep Men Free" 13; also in *TL* 20-21)

13.45. President McKay has said a lot about our tragic trends towards socialism and communism and the responsibilities liberty-loving people have in defending and preserving our Constitution. (see *Conference Report*, Apr 1963, pp. 112-13.) Have we read these words from God's mouthpiece and pondered on them? ("Be Not Deceived" 1064; compare *GFC* 340)

13.46. Let us not be deceived in the sifting days ahead. Let us rally together on principle behind the prophet as guided by the promptings of the Spirit. We should continue to speak out for freedom and against socialism and communism. We should continue to come to the aid of patriots, programs, and organizations that are trying to save our Constitution through every legal and moral means possible. ("Be Not Deceived" 1065; compare *GFC* 342)

13.47. That great and wise American, Thomas Jefferson, warned us of the danger of conferring unwarranted power upon our government administrators in these sobering words:

". . . Our Constitution has accordingly fixed the limits to which, and no further, our confidence may go. . . . In questions of power, then, let not more be heard of confidence in man, but bind him down from mischief by the chains of the Constitution." ("A Race Against Time" 5; also in *TL* 65)

13.48. They [our forefathers] believed that we must have some government, but it must be bound down by the chains of our Constitution so that it will not slip farther and farther over into the realm of *governmentism.* ("A Race Against Time" 11; also in *TL* 72-73)

13.49. I urge all to read the solid volume, *Stand Fast by Our Constitution* [by J. Reuben Clark, Jr.]. ("A Race Against Time" 16; also in *TL* 79)

13.50. Today it is becoming an increasing handicap, it seems, to one's career in government for a man or woman to take seriously his pledge of allegiance to our Constitution. ("A Race Against Time" 16; also in *TL* 79)

13.51. The scriptures also tell about our inspired Constitution. If you accept these scriptures, you will automatically reject the counsel of men who depreciate our Constitution. If you use the scriptures as a guide, you know what the Book of Mormon has to say regarding murderous conspiracies in the last day and how we are to awake to our awful situation today (see Ether 8:18-25). I find certain elements in the Church do not like to read the Book of Mormon and Doctrine and Covenants so much—they have too much to say about freedom. ("A Race Against Time" 17; also in *TL* 80-81; *TETB* 81)

13.52. On this basis may I give to you my own personal recommendation of some reading which will help you in the fight to save our Constitution.

First, for a number of years President J. Reuben Clark, Jr., served on the board of trustees of the Foundation for Economic Education while he was a member of the First Presidency. President Clark, as you probably know, was an Under Secretary of State and Ambassador to Mexico. He wrote the famous memorandum on the Monroe Doctrine. In 1923 in the Salt Lake Tabernacle he warned us of the communist-socialist menace and what it was going to do—and he was right. No one in the Church has shown greater insight regarding our Constitution and the socialist-communist threat to it. The Foundation for Economic Education with which he served puts out some of the most enlightening freedom literature available. They also put out a free monthly magazine, entitled *The Freeman*, which is excellent. They will be happy to send you a free catalog of their literature. May I mention some of the books which they distribute: *The Federalist*, written by Alexander Hamilton, John Jay and James Madison, three of our inspired founding fathers, explaining why the need of a constitution; *The Constitution of the United Sates*, by Mussatti; *The Clichés of Socialism*; *The Mainspring of Human Progress*, by Weaver; *Economics in One Lesson*, by Hazlitt; and *The Admiral's Log*, by Admiral Ben Moreell, which book is also on the MIA reading list. ("A Race Against Time" 18; also in *TL* 82)

13.53. It is not, however, enough to be acquainted with the grave dangers facing these United States. We must also instruct ourselves, and others, in the great spiritual values underlying our divinely inspired Constitution and our American free-enterprise system. ("A Race Against Time" 19; also in *TL* 84)

13.54. Not cheap politicians but statesmen are needed today. Not opportunists but men and women of principle must be demanded by the people. In this time of great stress and danger we must place [in office] only those dedicated to the preservation of our Constitution, our American Republic, and responsible freedom under God. "Oh, God, give us men with a mandate higher than the ballot box." ("A Race Against Time" 20; also in *TL* 85; *TETB* 685)

13.55. I quote the great American, J. Edgar Hoover: "I confess to a real apprehension so long as communists are able to secure ministers of the gospel to promote their evil work and espouse a cause that is alien to the religion of Christ and Judaism. I do fear so long as school boards and parents tolerate conditions whereby communists and fellow travelers under the guise of academic freedom can teach our youth a way of life that eventually will destroy the sanctity of the home, that undermines faith in God, that causes them to scorn respect for constituted authority and sabotage our revered Constitution." (*Menace of Communism*, p. 11.) (*TL* 44; from an address given at Logan, UT, 13 Dec 1963)

13.56. I believe one of the most serious mistakes a President could make would be to weaken the Constitution.

From the time I was a small boy I was taught that the American Constitution is an inspired document. I was also taught that the day will come when the Constitution will be endangered and hang as it were by a single thread. I was taught that we should study the Constitution. . . . I expect to continue my efforts to help protect and safeguard our inspired Constitution. (*TL* 28; compare *Enemy* 37; *TETB* 614-15; from an address given at Boise, ID, 19 Dec 1963)

13.57. At this particular moment in history the United States Constitution is definitely threatened, and every citizen should know about it. The warning of this hour should resound through the corridors of every American institution—schools, churches, the halls of Congress, press, radio, and TV, and so far as I am concerned it will resound—with God's help.

Wherever possible I have tried to speak out. It is for this very reason that certain people in Washington have bitterly criticized me. They don't want people to hear the message. It embarrasses them. The things which are destroying the Constitution are the things they have been voting for. (*TL* 30; compare *Enemy* 39-40; from an address given at Boise, ID, 19 Dec 1963)

13.58. I think it is time for every patriotic American to join with neighbors to study the Constitution and the conspiracy. Subscribe to several good patriotic magazines. (*TL* 40; compare *Enemy* 44; from an address given at Boise, ID, 19 Dec 1963)

13.59. With all my heart I love our great nation. I have lived and traveled abroad just enough to make me appreciate rather fully what we have in America. To me the U. S. is not just another nation. It is not just one of a family of nations. The U. S. is a nation with a great mission to perform for the benefit and blessing of liberty-loving people everywhere. (*Enemy* 28; from an address given at a luncheon of the American Chamber of Commerce in Frankfurt, Germany, 12 May 1964)

13.60. Students, study the writings of the prophets. Fortunately, the constistent position taken over the years by the prophets of the Church on vital issues facing this nation have recently been compiled in an excellent book entitled *Prophets, Principles and National Survival* [by Jerreld L. Newquist]. ("Three Threatening Dangers" 1068).

13.61. The Founding Fathers recognized the importance of vital religion and morality in the affairs of individuals and governments, and they turned to religion in order to give their new experiment a sense of direction. They were well aware that the principles of moral, intellectual, and spiritual integrity taught and exemplified by the Savior are the perfect guide for the conduct of countries and of individuals. It is no accident that the principles of Christian religion are the foundation of the Constitution of the United States. (*TETB* 600; from an address given at Frankfurt am Main, Germany, 1964)

13.62. Now, the Lord knew that before the gospel could flourish there must first be an atmosphere of freedom. This is why he first established the Constitution of this land through gentiles whom he raised up before he restored the gospel. ("Not Commanded in All Things" 538; also in *GFC* 385)

13.63. The devil knows that if the elders of Israel should ever wake up, they could step forth and help preserve freedom and extend the gospel. Therefore the devil has concentrated, and to a large extent successfully, in neutralizing much of the priesthood. He has reduced them to sleeping giants. His arguments are clever.

Here are a few samples:

First: "We really haven't received much instruction about freedom," the devil says. . . .

Second: "You're too involved in other church work," says the devil. . . .

Third: "You want to be loved by everyone," says the devil, "and this freedom battle is so controversial you might be accused of engaging in politics." . . .

Fourth: "Wait until it becomes popular to do," says the devil, "or, at least until everybody in the Church agrees on what should be done." . . .

Fifth: "It might hurt your business or your family," says the devil, "and besides why not let the gentiles save the country? They aren't as busy as you are." . . .

Sixth: "Don't worry," says the devil, "the Lord will protect you, and besides the world is so corrupt and heading toward destruction at such a pace that you can't stop it, so why try." . . .

And now as to the last neutralizer that the devil uses most effectively—it is simply this: "Don't do anything in the fight for freedom until the Church sets up its own specific program to save the Constitution." This brings us right back to the scripture I opened with today—to those slothful servants who will not do anything until they are "compelled in all things" [D&C 58:26]. Maybe the Lord will never set up a specific church program for the purpose of saving the Constitution. Perhaps if he set one up at this time it might split the Church asunder, and perhaps he does not want that to happen yet for not all the wheat and tares are fully ripe.

The Prophet Joseph Smith declared it will be the elders of Israel who will step forward to help save the Constitution, not the Church. And have we elders been warned? Yes, we have. And have we elders been given the guidelines? Yes indeed, we have. And besides, if the Church should ever inaugurate a program, who do you think would be in the forefront to get it moving? It would not be those who were sitting on the sidelines prior to that time or those who were appeasing the enemy. It would be those choice spirits who, not waiting to be "commanded in all things" [D&C 58:26], used their own free will, the counsel of the prophets, and the Spirit of the Lord as guidelines and who entered the battle "in a good cause" [D&C 58:27] and brought to pass much righteousness in freedom's cause. . . .

Brethren, if we had done our homework and were faithful, we could step forward at this time and help save this country. The fact that most of us are unprepared to do it is an indictment we will have to bear. The longer we wait, the heavier the chains, the deeper the blood, the more the persecution, and the less we can carry out our God-given mandate and worldwide mission. The war in heaven is raging on the earth today. Are you being neutralized in the battle? ("Not Commanded in All Things" 538-39; also in *GFC* 385-89)

13.64. We had better take our small pain now than our greater loss later. There were souls who wished afterwards that they had stood and fought with Washington and the founding fathers, but they waited too long—they passed up eternal glory. There has never been a greater time than now to stand up against entrenched evil. And while the gentiles established the Constitution, we have a divine mandate to preserve it. But unfortunately today in this freedom struggle, many gentiles are showing greater wisdom in their generation than the children of light. ("Not Commanded in All Things" 538; also in *GFC* 387)

13.65. The Lord raised up the Founding Fathers. He it was who established the Constitution of this land—the greatest document of freedom ever written. This God-inspired Constitution is not outmoded. It is not an outdated "agrarian document" as some of our would-be statesmen, socialists, and fellow travelers of the godless conspiracy would have us believe. It was the Lord God who established the foundation of this nation; and woe be unto those—members of the Supreme Court and others—who would weaken this foundation. ("America—A Man and an Event" 1150)

13.66. *The sad and shocking story of what has happened in America in recent years must be told. Our people must have the facts. There is safety in an informed public.* There is real danger in a complacent, uninformed citizenry. This is our real danger today. Yes, the truth must be told even at the risk of destroying, in large measure, the influence of men who are widely respected and loved by the American people. The stakes are high. *Freedom and survival is the issue.* (*Enemy* 91; from an address given at a meeting sponsored by the American Wake Up Committee, St. Louis, MO, 28 Feb 1966)

13.67. *Leaders of youth, teach our young people to love freedom, to know that it is God-given.* . . . Teach them to love their country, to know that it has a spiritual foundation, that it has a prophetic history, that it is the Lord's base of operation.

Teach them that the Constitution of the United States was established by men whom God raised up for that very purpose, that it is not outmoded, that it is not an old-fashioned agrarian document, as some men in high places are calling it today. (*Enemy* 303-04; from an address delivered at the MIA Conference, Salt Lake City, UT, Jun 1966)

13.68. About two hundred years ago some inspired men walked this land. Not perfect men, but men raised up by the Perfect Man to perform a great work. Foreordained were they to lay the foundation of this republic. Blessed by the Almighty in their struggle for liberty and independence, the power of heaven rested on these founders as they drafted that great document for governing men—the Constitution of the United States. Like the Ten

Commandments, the truths on which the Constitution was based were timeless; and also as with the Decalogue—the hand of the Lord was in it. They filled their mission well. From them we were endowed with a legacy of liberty—a constitutional republic. ("Prepare, Then Fear Not" 57; revised in *Enemy* 53; *GFC* 326; *TETB* 595; from an address given at the New England Rally for God, Family, and Country; Boston, MA, 4 Jul 1966)

13.69. The question as to whether we may save our constitutional republic is simply based on two factors: the number of patriots and the extent of their obedience.

That the Lord desires to save this nation which he raised up there is no doubt. But that he leaves it up to us, with his help, is the awful reality. ("Prepare, Then Fear Not" 58; revised in *Enemy* 55; *GFC* 327; from an address given at the New England Rally for God, Family, and Country; Boston, MA, 4 Jul 1966)

13.70. Jefferson warned that we should not talk about confidence in men but that we should inhibit their power through the Constitution. [Thomas Jefferson, Draft of Kentucky Resolutions of 1798; *Works* 9:470-71.] ("Our Immediate Responsibility" 9; also in *Enemy* 313)

13.71. For years we have heard of the role the elders could play in saving the Constitution from total destruction. But how can the elders be expected to save it if they have not studied it and are not sure if it is being destroyed or what is destroying it?

An informed patriotic gentile was dumbfounded when he heard of Joseph Smith's reported prophecy regarding the mission our elders could perform in saving the Constitution. He lived in a Mormon community with nice people who were busily engaged in other activities but who had little concern in preserving their freedom. He wondered if maybe a letter should not be sent to President McKay, urging him to release some of the elders from their present Church activities so there would be a few who could help step forward to save the Constitution.

Now it is not so much a case of a man giving up all his other duties to fight for freedom, as it is a case of a man getting his life

*in balance so he can discharge all of his God-given respon-
sibilities.* And of all these responsibilities President McKay has
said that we have "no greater immediate responsibility" than "to
protect the freedom vouchsafed by the Constitution of the United
States."

There is no excuse that can compensate for the loss of liberty.

Satan is anxious to neutralize the inspired counsel of the
Prophet and hence keep the priesthood off balance, ineffective
and inert in the fight for freedom. He does this through diverse
means, including the use of perverse reasoning. . . .

The cause of freedom is a most basic part of our religion.
Our position on freedom helped get us to this earth and it can
make the difference as to whether we get back home or not. . . .

Now part of the reason why we do not have sufficient
Priesthood bearers to save the Constitution, let alone to shake the
powers of hell, is, I fear, because unlike Moroni, our souls do not
joy in keeping our country free and we are not firm in the faith
of Christ, nor have we sworn with an oath to defend our rights.
("Our Immediate Responsibility" 10-11; also in *Enemy* 313-15)

13.72. Here in America, the Lord's base of operations—so
designated by the Lord Himself through His holy prophets—we
of the priesthood, members of His restored Church, might well
provide the balance of power to save our freedom. Indeed we
might, if we go forward as Moroni of old, and raise the standard
of liberty throughout the land [Alma 62:4]. My brethren, we can
do the job that must be done. We can, as a priesthood, provide
the balance of power to preserve our freedom and save this nation
from bondage.

The Prophet Joseph Smith is reported to have prophesied the
role the priesthood might play to save our inspired Constitution.
Now is the time to move forward courageously—to become
alerted, informed, and active. . . .

We know, as do no other people, that the Constitution of the
United States is inspired—established by men whom the Lord
raised up for that very purpose [D&C 101:80]. We cannot—we
must not—shirk our sacred responsibility to rise up in defense of

our God-given freedom. ("Our Immediate Responsibility" 17; compare *Enemy* 321; *TETB* 620)

13.73. Another standard I use in determining what law is good and what is bad is the Constitution of the United States. I regard this inspired document as a solemn agreement between the citizens of this nation which every officer of government is under a sacred duty to obey. (*Enemy* 133; also in *GFC* 288-89; compare *TETB* 615; from an address delivered at the Utah Forum for the American Idea, Salt Lake City, UT, 29 Feb 1968)

13.74. I believe that God has endowed men with certain inalienable rights as set forth in the Declaration of Independence and that no legislature and no majority, however great, may morally limit or destroy these; that the sole function of government is to protect life, liberty, and property, and anything more than this is usurpation and oppression.

I believe that the Constitution of the United States was prepared and adopted by men acting under inspiration from Almighty God; that it is a solemn compact between the peoples of the states of this nation that all officers of government are under duty to obey; that the eternal moral laws expressed therein must be adhered to or individual liberty will perish. . . .

I am hereby resolved that under no circumstances shall the freedoms guaranteed by the Bill of Rights be infringed. In particular I am opposed to any attempt on the part of the federal government to deny the people their right to bear arms, to worship, and to pray when and where they choose, or to own and control private property. (*Enemy* 143-44; also in *GFC* 299-300; revised in *TETB* 617; from an address given at the Utah Forum for the American Idea, Salt Lake City, UT, 29 Feb 1968)

13.75. Do we dare ask ourselves if the United States, though cast in the role of a leader to preserve and strengthen world civilization, isn't itself tottering internally because too many of its citizens have abandoned the virtues that comprised the basic format of its own civilization? For instance, if spiritual faith, courage, and the willingness of our forbears to work hard were the sustaining virtues, and if, solely because of them, they were able to create our own civilization, can we now in the United States substitute for these virtues the human weaknesses of selfishness, complacency, apathy, and fear—and still hope to survive as a civilized nation? (*Enemy* 118; from an address given at the Annual Boy Scouts Banquet, Commerce, TX, 13 May 1968)

13.76. It is my conviction that the Constitution of the United States was established by the hands of wise men whom the Lord raised up unto this very purpose.

The Lord expects us to safeguard this sacred and inspired document for the blessing of all of us and our posterity. If we fail so to do we will not only lose our priceless freedom but jeopardize the cause of truth throughout the entire world. (*Enemy* 268)

13.77. With independence won, another body of men assembled; and under the inspiration of heaven, they too drafted a document, probably the greatest instrument ever struck off at a given time by the mind of man: the Constitution of the United States. (*GFC* 371; from an address given at the New England Rally for God, Family, and Country; Boston, MA, 4 Jul 1970)

13.78. I support the doctrine of separation of church and state as traditionally interpreted to prohibit the establishment of an official national religion. But this does not mean that we should divorce government from any formal recognition of God. To do so strikes a potentially fatal blow at the concept of the divine origin of our rights, and unlocks the door for an easy entry of future tyranny. If Americans should ever come to believe that their rights and freedoms are instituted among men by politicians and bureaucrats, they will no longer carry the proud inheritance of their forefathers, but will grovel before their masters seeking favors and dispensations—a throwback to the feudal system of the Dark Ages. (*TETB* 609; from an address given at the LDS Business and Professional Men's Association, Glendale, CA, 10 Nov 1970)

13.79. We honor these partners [friends outside the Church] because their devotion to correct principles overshadowed their devotion to popularity, party, or personalities.

We honor our founding fathers of this republic for the same reason. God raised up these patriotic partners to perform their mission, and he called them "wise men." (see D&C 101:80.) The First Presidency acknowledged that wisdom when they gave us the guideline a few years ago of supporting political candidates "who are truly dedicated to the Constitution in the tradition of our Founding Fathers." (*Deseret News*, November 2, 1964.) . . .

Our wise founders seemed to understand, better than most of us, our own scripture, which states that "it is the nature and disposition of almost all men, as soon as they get a little authority . . . they will immediately begin to exercise unrighteous dominion." (D&C 121:39.)

To help prevent this, the founders knew that our elected leaders should be bound by certain fixed principles. Said Thomas Jefferson: "In questions of power, then, let no more be heard of confidence in man, but bind him down from mischief by the chains of the Constitution."

These wise founders, our patriotic partners, seemed to appreciate more than most of us the blessings of the boundaries that the Lord set within the Constitution, for he said, "And as pertaining to law of man, whatsoever is more or less than this, cometh of evil." (D&C 98:7.)

In God the founders trusted, and in his Constitution—not in the arm of flesh. "O Lord," said Nephi, "I have trusted in thee, and I will trust in thee forever. I will not put my trust in the arm of flesh; . . . cursed is he that putteth his trust in man or maketh flesh his arm." (2 Nephi 4:34.) ("Civic Standards for the Faithful Saints" 59-60)

13.80. It is a part of my religious belief that America is a land choice above all others, that we are not just another of the family of nations, but that we have been singled out to perform a divine mission for liberty-loving people everywhere. Those who founded this republic were wise men raised up by our Father in heaven to perform that very task, and the Constitution of this land was inspired by God. We have a divine duty—even a destiny—to preserve that Constitution from destruction and hold it aloft to the world. (*GFC* 405; from an address given at the New England Rally for God, Family, and Country honor banquet; Boston, MA, 4 Jul 1972)

13.81. May we pledge anew that the divine principles embodied in the divinely inspired documents that govern our country be written on the tablets of our own hearts. I pray that our eyes might be single to the will of God, that we might thereby bless our families and our country and that we shall, with increased devotion, work for less government, more individual responsibility, and, with God's help, a better world. (*GFC* 407; also in *TETB* 594-95; from an address given at the New England Rally for God, Family, and Country honor banquet; Boston, MA, 4 Jul 1972)

13.82. It is good at all times to remember a few of the many gifts we have received from our Lord, Jesus Christ, and to think of what we in turn might give to him. . . .

. . . In addition to the gifts of the life of Christ, his prophet, his church, and the Book of Mormon is the gift of the Constitution. The Lord said, "I established the Constitution of this land, by the hands of wise men whom I raised up" (D&C 101:80). . . .

The elders of this church have a prophetic mission yet to perform so far as the Constitution is concerned. In a discourse by Joseph Smith on July 19, 1840, he said:

"Even this nation will be on the very verge of crumbling to pieces and tumbling to the ground, and when the Constitution is upon the brink of ruin, this people will be the staff upon which the nation shall lean, and they shall bear the Constitution away from the very verge of destruction." (Joseph Smith Collection, LDS Church Historical Department)

Now, how are the elders going to prepare for that mission? How are they going to know what the Constitution is so they will know when it is on the brink of ruin? . . .

To the Lord, his prophets, and the founding fathers we must go to learn of this divine document so our efforts will be to preserve and not destroy the Constitution. ("Jesus Christ—Gifts and Expectations" 16, 19)

13.83. Thank God for the constitution. And may God bless the elders of Israel that when, as President John Taylor said, "The people shall have torn to shreds the Constitution of the United States, the Elders of Israel will be found holding it up to the nations of earth and proclaiming liberty" (*Journal of Discourses,* 21:8). ("Jesus Christ—Gifts and Expectations" 19; also in *TETB* 614)

13.84. Before we go to our ailments and disorders, it is well to review the elements of our health and strength that we have acquired under our divinely inspired Constitution, the liberties it guarantees, and the free institution it sets up. . . .

No country has been more concerned with "due process" in its judicial system than ours. The protection of human rights, as granted by our Constitution and Bill of Rights, is not just theory. History will record that we bent over backwards to protect the rights of the individual, sometimes even to a fault. (*A Plea for America* 2)

13.85. It must be remembered that the founding fathers of this great nation were men imbued with these principles [the Ten Commandments]. There are those in the land whose faith it is that these were "wise men whom [God] raised up" for the purpose of establishing the Constitution of the United States. They recognized that there are two possible sources to the origin of our freedoms that we have come to know as human rights. Rights are either God-given as part of a *divine* plan or they are granted as part of the political plan. Reason, necessity, and religious conviction and belief in the sovereignty of God led these men to accept the *divine* origin of these rights. To God's glory and the credit of these men, our nation was uniquely born. (*A Plea for America* 9)

13.86. We urge people to support the Constitution of the United States and our free institutions set up under it.

It is a part of our faith that the Constitution of the United States was inspired by God. We reverence it akin to the revelations that have come from God. . . . We have no intention of trying to interfere with the fullest and freest exercise of the political franchise of our members under and within our Constitution, which the Lord declared He established "by the hands of wise men whom [He] raised up unto this very purpose" (D&C 109:54). (*A Plea for America* 26)

13.87. As a means of emphasizing this during this Bicentennial year, we have prepared four Bicentennial family home evening lessons, which will be distributed to all Church members in the United States of America. We are asking fathers and mothers to teach the story of America to their children, to tell of its spiritual foundation, and to emphasize how that freedom can be preserved. (*A Plea for America* 30)

13.88. Tonight I will speak to you about our beloved republic and the inspired agents whom God raised up to establish the foundation upon which our liberty rests. . . . I speak to you as members of the "household of faith," the Lord's true church, and remind you of your solemn charge to uphold, sustain, and defend the kingdom of God.

The destiny of America was divinely decreed. The events that established our great nation were foreknown to God and revealed to prophets of old. As in an enacted drama, the players who came on the scene were rehearsed and selected for their parts. Their talent, abilities, capacities, and weaknesses were known before they were born. ("God's Hand in Our Nation's History" 297-98; revised in *This Nation Shall Endure* 11)

13.89. The Lord has also decreed that this land should be "the place of the new Jerusalem, which should come down out of heaven, and the holy sanctuary of the Lord." (Ether 13:3.) Here is our nation's destiny! To serve God's eternal purposes and to prepare this land and the people for America's eventual destiny, He "established the Constitution of this land, by the hands of wise men whom [He] raised up unto this very purpose, and redeemed the land by the shedding of blood." (D&C 101:80.) ("God's Hand in Our Nation's History" 301; *This Nation Shall Endure* 13)

13.90. The charge [has been made] that the founders designed the Constitution primarily to benefit themselves and their class (property owners) financially, and that the economic motif was their dominant incentive. Such was the thesis of the American historian, Dr. Charles Beard. Yet Madison said: "There was never an assembly of men . . . who were more pure in their motives." We must remember that these were men who had sacrificed in many cases their fortunes and their sacred honor.

Shortly after the turn of this century, Charles Beard published his work *An Economic Interpretation of the Constitution of the United States.* This book marked the beginning of a trend to defame the motives and integrity of the founders of the Constitution. It also grossly distorted the real intent of the founders by suggesting their motivation was determined by economics—a thesis that had originated with Karl Marx. Beard himself was not a Marxist, but he was a socialist in his thinking, and he admitted there was much we could learn from Marx's ideas. Before his death Beard recanted his own thesis, but the damage had been done. This began a new trend in educational and intellectual circles in the United States. ("God's Hand in Our Nation's History" 304-05; revised in *This Nation Shall Endure* 16)

13.91. The temple work for the 56 signers of the Declaration of Independence and other Founding Fathers has been done. All these appeared to Wilford Woodruff when he was president of the St. George Temple. President George Washington was ordained a high priest at that time. You will also be interested to know that, according to Wilford Woodruff's journal, John Wesley, Benjamin Franklin, and Christopher Columbus were also ordained high priests at that time. When one casts doubt about the character of these noble sons of God, I believe he or she will have to answer to the God of heaven for it. Yes, with Lincoln, I say: "To add brightness to the sun or glory to the name of Washington is . . . impossible. Let none attempt it. In solemn awe pronounce the name and in its naked deathless splendor, leave it shining on."

If ever this country needed the timeless wisdom of the father of our country, it is today. How much our country could benefit by following the wisdom of our country's first president. Here are a few among many maxims:

> "Let the reins of government then be braced and held with a steady hand, and every violation of the constitution be reprehended. If defective, let it be amended, but not suffered to be trampled upon whilst it has an existence." (To Henry Lee, October 31, 1786, *Writings* 29:34.)

> "To be prepared for war is one of the most effectual means of preserving peace." (First Annual Address, January 8, 1790, *Writings* 12:8.)

> " ... the love of my country will be the ruling influence of my conduct." (Answer to the New Hampshire Executive, November 3, 1789, *Writings* 12:175.)

> " ... a good moral character is the first essential in a man. ... It is therefore highly important, that you should endeavor not only to be learned but virtuous." (To George Steptoe Washington, December 5, 1790, *Writings* 10:123-24.)

> "Let us unite, therefore, in imploring the Supreme Ruler of nations, to spread his holy protection over these United States; to turn the machinations of the wicked to confirming of our constitution; to enable us at all times to root out internal sedition, and put invasion to flight; to perpetuate to our country that prosperity, which his goodness has already conferred; and to verify the anticipation of this government being a safeguard to human rights." (To the Senate and the House of Representatives, November 19, 1794, *Writings* 12:54.)

It would profit all of us as citizens to read again Washington's Farewell Address to his countrymen. The address is prophetic. I believe it ranks alongside the Declaration of Independence and the Constitution.

My feelings about this tendency to discredit our Founding Fathers are well summarized by the late President J. Reuben Clark in these words: "These were the horse and buggy days as they have been called in derision; these were the men who traveled in the horsedrawn buggies and on horseback; but these were the men who carried under their hats, as they rode in the buggies and on their horses, a political wisdom garnered from the ages. As giants to pygmies are they when placed alongside our political emigres and their fellow travelers of today, who now traduce them with slighting word and contemptuous phrase." (*Stand Fast by Our Constitution*, pp. 136-37.) ("God's Hand in Our Nation's History" 307-09; revised in *This Nation Shall Endure* 18-19)

13.92. May we be wise—prayerfully wise—in the electing of those who would lead us. May we select only those who understand and will adhere to constitutional principles. To do so, we need to understand these principles ourselves. . . .

. . . We should understand the Constitution as the founders meant that it should be understood. We can do this by reading their words about it, such as those contained in the Federalist Papers. Such understanding is essential if we are to preserve what God has given us. . . .

. . . I testify that the God of heaven selected and sent some of his choicest spirits to lay the foundation of this government as prologue to the restoration of the gospel and the second coming of our Savior. ("The Constitution—A Glorious Standard" 93)

13.93. Our forefathers left us a free government which is a miracle of faith—strong, durable, marvelously workable. Yet it can remain so only as long as we understand it, believe in it, devote ourselves to it, and, when necessary, fight for it. (Hillam v)

13.94. Learn about the Constitution, the Declaration of Independence, and other basic documents of our great country so that you can sustain them and the free institutions set up under them. The greatest watchdog of our freedom is an informed electorate. ("America at the Crossroads" 39; compare *TETB* 616)

13.95. When I became President of the Twelve and Spencer W. Kimball became President of the Church, we met, just the two of us, every week after our Thursday meetings in the temple, just to be sure that things were properly coordinated between the Twelve and the First Presidency. After one of those first meetings, we talked about the many sacred documents in some of the older temples. St. George was mentioned in particular because St. George is our oldest temple in Utah. I had a stake conference down there about that time, and it was agreed that I would go into the archives—the walk-in vault—of that great temple and review the sacred documents that were there. We were planning for the remodeling and renovating of the St. George Temple and thought that the records might possibly be moved to Salt Lake for safekeeping. And there in the St. George Temple I saw what I had always hoped and prayed that someday I would see. Ever since I returned as a humble missionary and first learned that the Founding Fathers had appeared in that temple, I wanted to see the record. And I saw the record. They did appear to Wilford Woodruff twice and asked why the work hadn't been done for them. They had founded this country and the Constitution of this land, and they had been true to those principles. Later the work was done for them.

In the archives of the temple, I saw in a book, in bold handwriting, the names of the Founding Fathers and others, including Columbus and other great Americans, for whom the work had been done in the house of the Lord. This is all one great program on both sides of the veil. We are fortunate to be engaged in it on this side of the veil. I think the Lord expects us to take an active part in preserving the Constitution and our freedom. (*TETB* 603; from an address given at Sandy, UT, 30 Dec 1978)

13.96. The Constitution of this land, with which we should all be familiar, is the only constitution in the world bearing the stamp of approval of the Lord Jesus Christ (D&C 101:76-80). (*TETB* 596; from an address given at a Young Adult Fireside, Logan, UT, 11 Feb 1979)

13.97. You must keep your honor. You cannot yet speak officially for the country, but you can become informed. You can speak your mind. You may think you can do little about the national economy or the actions of our government and the moral weakness all about us, but we must all remember that the Lord has placed great responsibilities upon the elders of Israel in the preservation of our Constitution. (*TETB* 622; from an address given at a Young Adult Fireside, Logan, UT, 11 Feb 1979)

13.98. To serve God's eternal purposes and to prepare this land for Zion, God "established the Constitution of this land, by the hands of wise men whom [He] raised up . . . and redeemed the land by the shedding of blood" (D&C 101:80).

The Constitution of the United States was ratified in 1789. The priesthood of God was restored in 1829. Between those two dates is an interval of forty years. It is my conviction that God, who knows the end from the beginning, provided that period of time so the new nation could grow in strength to protect the land of Zion. ("A Witness and a Warning" 31; compare *TETB* 596)

13.99. Men who are wise, good, and honest, who will uphold the Constitution of the United States in the tradition of the Founding Fathers, must be sought for diligently. This is our hope to restore government to its rightful role.

I fully believe that we can turn things around in America if we have the determination, the morality, the patriotism, and the spirituality to do so. . . .

. . . I further witness that this land—the Americas—must be protected, its Constitution upheld, for this is a land foreordained to be the Zion of our God. He expects us as members of the Church and bearers of His priesthood to do all we can to preserve our liberty. ("A Witness and a Warning" 33)

13.100. Before the gospel could again shine forth its resplendent light, religious and political freedom first had to be restored. This land had been preserved as a continent apart from the religious oppression, tyranny, and intolerance of Europe. In time, emigrants came to the new land and established colonies. By and large, they were a God-fearing people. A war was fought for their independence, and by God's intervention, victory was achieved (see 1 Nephi 13:16-19). By that same omnipotent power the Constitution was born (see D&C 101:80), which guaranteed religious and political liberty (see D&C 98:5-8). Only then was the time propitious for the kingdom of God—that "stone cut out without hands"—to be restored (see Dan 2:34). (*This Nation Shall Endure* 116; compare *TETB* 109)

13.101. Our Creator endowed each one of us with certain rights at birth, among which are the rights to life, liberty, speech, and conscience, to name a few. These are not just human rights; they are divine rights. When these rights are not permitted expression by a nation, that nation becomes inhibited in its progress and development, and its leaders are responsible before God for suffocating sacred rights.

This native endowment is what separates man from the animals. It causes men to want to be good and to seek higher aspirations. It creates in man a desire to better his life and his station in life. (*TETB* 593; from an address given at Brigham Young University-Hawaii, 11 Feb 1983)

As the President of the Church

13.102. We must study and learn for ourselves the principles laid down in the Constitution which have preserved our freedoms for the last two hundred years. If we do not understand the role of government and how our rights are protected by the Constitution, we may accept programs or organizations that help erode our freedoms. An informed citizenry is the first line of defense against anarchy and tyranny. (*TETB* 594; from an address given at the Provo Freedom Festival, Provo, UT, 29 Jun 1986)

13.103. The Founding Fathers had no problems seeing the hand of the Lord in the birth of the nation. George Washington gave direct credit to God for the victory over the British in the Revolutionary War. But that did not end the need for inspiration and divine help.

A constitution was drafted. And thirty-nine of fifty delegates signed it. I would ask: Why is it that the references to God's influence in the noble efforts of the founders of our republic are not mentioned by modern historians?

The fact that our Founding Fathers looked to God for help and inspiration should not surprise us, for they were men of great faith. These men had been raised up specifically by the Lord so they could participate in the great political drama unfolding in America. (*TETB* 599; from an address given at the Provo Freedom Festival, Provo, UT, 29 Jun 1986)

13.104. The Founding Fathers understood the principle that "righteousness exalteth a nation" (Prov 14:34), and helped to bring about one of the greatest systems ever used to govern men. But unless we continue to seek righteousness and preserve the liberties entrusted to us, we shall lose the blessings of heaven. Thomas Jefferson said, "The price of freedom is eternal vigilance." The price of freedom is also to live in accordance with the commandments of God. The early Founding Fathers thanked the Lord for His intervention in their behalf. They saw His hand in their victories in battle and believed strongly that He watched over them.

The battles are not over yet, and there will yet be times when this great nation will need the overshadowing help of Deity. Will we as a nation be worthy to call upon Him for help? (*TETB* 601; from an address given at the Provo Freedom Festival, Provo, UT, 29 Jun 1986)

13.105. Our Founding Fathers, with solemn and reverent expression, voiced their allegiance to the sovereignty of God, knowing that they were accountable to Him in the day of judgment. Are we less accountable today? I think not. I urge you to keep the commandments and to pray for our nation and its leaders. (*TETB* 602; from an address given at the Provo Freedom Festival, Provo, UT, 29 Jun 1986)

13.106. On the 17th day of September 1987 we commemorate the two hundredth birthday of the Constitutional Convention which gave birth to the document that Gladstone said is "the most wonderful work ever struck off at a given time by the brain and purpose of man."

I heartily endorse this assessment. . . .

We pay honor—honor to the document itself, honor to the men who framed it, and honor to the God who inspired it and made possible its coming forth. . . .

. . . God himself has borne witness to the fact that He is pleased with the final product of the work of these great patriots [our Founding Fathers]. (*CHB* 1, 15; revised in *TETB* 593)

13.107. The War that began in heaven is not yet over. The conflict continues on the battlefield of mortality. And one of Lucifer's primary strategies has been to restrict our agency through the power of earthly governments. . . .

. . . We must appreciate that we live in one of history's most exceptional moments—in a nation and a time of unprecedented freedom. Freedom as we know it has been experienced by perhaps less than one percent of the human family. (*CHB* 3-4)

13.108. History is not an accident. Events are foreknown to God. His superintending influence is behind the actions of his righteous children. Long before America was even discovered, the Lord was moving and shaping events that would lead to the coming forth of the remarkable form of government established by the Constitution. America had to be free and independent to fulfill this destiny. (*CHB* 10; compare *TETB* 587)

13.109. George Washington referred to this document [the Constitution] as a miracle. This miracle could only have been performed by exceptional men. (*CHB* 11; compare *TETB* 598)

13.110. The coming forth of the Constitution is of such transcendent importance in the Lord's plan that ancient prophets foresaw this event and prophesied of it. In the dedicatory prayer for the Idaho Falls Temple, President George Albert Smith indicated that the Constitution fulfilled the ancient prophecy of Isaiah that "out of Zion shall go forth the law" (Isa 2:3). (*CHB* 16; also in *TETB* 595)

13.111. In order to avoid a concentration of power in any one branch, the Founding Fathers created a system of government that provided checks and balances. Congress could pass laws, but the president could check these laws with a veto. Congress, however, could override the veto and, by its means of initiative in taxation, could further restrain the executive department. The Supreme Court could nullify laws passed by the Congress and signed by the president, but Congress could limit the court's appellate jurisdiction. The president could appoint judges for their lifetime with the consent of the Senate.

The use of checks and balances was deliberately designed, first, to make it difficult for a minority of the people to control the government, and, second, to place restraint on the government itself. (*CHB* 20; also in *TETB* 607)

13.112. The Founding Fathers well understood human nature and its tendency to exercise unrighteous dominion when given authority [D&C 121:39-40]. A Constitution was therefore designed to limit government to certain enumerated functions, beyond which was tyranny. (*CHB* 21; also in *TETB* 600)

13.113. In recognizing God as the source of their rights, the Founding Fathers declared Him to be the ultimate authority for their basis of law. This led them to the conviction that people do not make law but merely acknowledge preexisting law, giving it specific application. The Constitution was conceived to be such an expression of higher law. And when their work was done, James Madison wrote: "It is impossible for the man of pious reflection not to perceive in it a finger of that Almighty hand which has been so frequently and signally extended to our relief in the critical stages of the revolution" (*The Federalist*, no. 37). (*CHB* 23; compare *TETB* 597)

13.114. It is now two hundred years since the Constitution was written. Have we been wise beneficiaries of the gift entrusted to us? Have we valued and protected the principles laid down by this great document?

At this bicentennial celebration we must, with sadness, say that we have not been wise in keeping the trust of our Founding Fathers. For the past two centuries, those who do not prize freedom have chipped away at every major clause of our

Constitution until today we face a crisis of great dimensions. (*CHB* 24-25; compare *TETB* 612)

13.115. To all who have discerning eyes, it is apparent that the republican form of government established by our noble forefathers cannot long endure once fundamental principles are abandoned. Momentum is gathering for another conflict—a repetition of the crisis of two hundred years ago. This collision of ideas is worldwide. Another monumental moment is soon to be born. The issue is the same that precipitated the great premortal conflict—will men be free to determine their own course of action or must they be coerced?

We are fast approaching that moment prophesied by Joseph Smith when he said: "Even this nation will be on the very verge of crumbling to pieces and tumbling to the ground, and when the Constitution is upon the brink of ruin, this people will be the staff upon which the nation shall lean, and they shall bear the Constitution away from the very verge of destruction." (July 19, 1840, Joseph Smith Collection, LDS Church Historical Department.) (*CHB* 27-28; revised in *TETB* 623-24)

13.116. Will we be prepared? Will we be among those who will "bear the Constitution away from the very verge of destruction?" If we desire to be numbered among those who will, here are some things we must do:

1. *We must be righteous and moral.* We must live the gospel principles—all of them. We have no right to expect a higher degree of morality from those who represent us than what we ourselves are. In the final analysis, people generally get the kind of government they deserve. To live a higher law means we will not seek to receive what we have not earned by our own labor. It means we will remember that government owes us nothing. It means we will keep the laws of the land. It means we will look to God as our Lawgiver and the Source of our liberty.

2. *We must learn the principles of the Constitution and then abide by its precepts.* We have been instructed again and again to reflect more intently on the meaning and importance of the Constitution and to adhere to its principles. What have we done

about this instruction? Have we read the Constitution and pondered it? Are we aware of its principles? Could we defend it? Can we recognize when a law is constitutionally unsound? The Church will not tell us how to do this, but we are admonished to do it. I quote Abraham Lincoln: "Let [the Constitution] be taught in schools, in seminaries, and in colleges, let it be written in primers, in spelling books and in almanacs, let it be preached from the pulpit, proclaimed in legislative halls, and enforced in courts of justice. And, in short, let it become the political religion of the nation."

3. *We must become involved in civic affairs.* As citizens of this republic, we cannot do our duty and be idle spectators. It is vital that we follow this counsel from the Lord: "I, the Lord God, make you free, therefore ye are free indeed; and the law also maketh you free. Nevertheless, when the wicked rule the people mourn. Wherefore, honest men and wise men should be sought for diligently, and good men and wise men ye should observe to uphold; otherwise whatsoever is less than these cometh of evil. And I give unto you a commandment, that ye shall forsake all evil and cleave unto all good, that ye shall live by every word which proceedeth forth out of the mouth of God" (D&C 98:8-11).

Note the qualities that the Lord demands in those who are to represent us. They must be good, wise, and honest. Some leaders may be honest and good but unwise in legislation they choose to support. Others may possess wisdom but be dishonest and unvirtuous. We must be concerted in our desires and efforts to see men and women represent us who possess all three of these qualities.

4. *We must make our influence felt by our vote, our letters, and our advice.* We must be wisely informed and let others know how we feel. We must take part in local precinct meetings and select delegates who will truly represent our feelings.

I have faith that the Constitution will be saved as prophesied by Joseph Smith. But it will not be saved in Washington. It will be saved by the citizens of this nation who love and cherish freedom. It will be saved by enlightened members of this Church—men and women who will subscribe to and abide the principles of the Constitution. (*CHB* 28-31)

13.117. I reverence the Constitution of the United States as a sacred document. To me its words are akin to the revelations of God, for God has placed His stamp of approval on the Constitution of this land [D&C 101:76-80]. I testify that the God of Heaven sent some of His choicest spirits to lay the foundation of this government, and He has sent other choice spirits—even you who read my words—to preserve it. (*CHB* 31; compare *TETB* 614)

13.118. We encourage Latter-day Saints throughout the nation to familiarize themselves with the Constitution. They should focus attention on it by reading and studying it. They should ponder the blessings that come through it. They should recommit themselves to its principles and be prepared to defend it and the freedom it provides. (D&C 109:54.) . . .

Because some Americans have not kept faith with our Founding Fathers, the Constitution faces severe challenges. Those who do not prize individual freedom are trying to erode its great principles. We believe the Constitution will stand, but it will take the efforts of patriotic and dedicated Americans to uphold it. . . . We, as Latter-day Saints, must be vigilant in doing our part to preserve the Constitution and safeguard the way of life it makes possible.

This bicentennial year affords us renewed opportunities to learn more about this divinely inspired charter of our liberty, to speak in its defense, and to preserve and protect it against evil or destruction. ("First Presidency Urges Observance of Bicentennial of the Constitution" 11)

13.119. May we be worthy of the freedoms that have been provided us in our Constitution, and equal to the trials and tests that shall surely come. We truly have special and individual responsibilities to befriend and to defend that "glorious standard," our Constitution.

Our Heavenly Father raised up the men who founded this government (see D&C 101:80), thereby fulfilling the prophecy of His Beloved Son that the people "should be established in this land and be set up as a free people by the power of the Father"

(3 Nephi 21:4). (*TETB* 594; from an address given at the Bicentennial Ball, Salt Lake City, UT, 18 Sep 1987)

13.120. The restoration of the gospel and the establishment of the Lord's Church could not come to pass until the Founding Fathers were raised up and completed their foreordained missions. Those great souls who were responsible for the freedoms we enjoy acknowledged the guiding hand of Providence. For their efforts we are indebted, but we are even more indebted to our Father in Heaven and to His Son, Jesus Christ. How fortunate we are to live when the blessings of liberty and the gospel of Jesus Christ are both available to us. (*TETB* 604; from an address given at the Bicentennial Ball, Salt Lake City, UT, 18 Sep 1987)

13.121. The United States Constitution has been in existence longer than any written constitution in history. It has been a blessing, not only to our land, but to the world as well. Many nations have wisely adopted concepts and provisions of our Constitution, just as was prophesied (D&C 101:77). (*TETB* 624; from an address given at the Bicentennial Ball, Salt Lake City, UT, 18 Sep 1987)

13.122. How then can we best befriend the Constitution in this critical hour and secure the blessings of liberty and ensure the protection and guidance of our Father in Heaven?
First and foremost, we must be righteous. . . .
Two great American Christian civilizations—the Jaredites and the Nephites—were swept off this land because they did not "serve the God of the land, who is Jesus Christ" (Ether 2:12). What will become of our civilization?
Second, We must learn the principles of the Constitution in the tradition of the Founding Fathers.
Have we read the *Federalist* papers? Are we reading the Constitution and pondering it? Are we aware of its principles? Are we abiding by these principles and teaching them to others? Could we defend the Constitution? Can we recognize when a law is constitutionally unsound? Do we know what the prophets have said about the Constitution and the threats to it? . . .

We, the blessed beneficiaries of the Constitution, face difficult days in America, "a land which is choice above all other lands" (Ether 2:10).

May God give us the faith and the courage exhibited by those patriots who pledged their lives, their fortunes, and their sacred honor.

May we be equally as valiant and as free. ("Our Divine Constitution" 6-7)

13.123. On September 17, 1987, we commemorate the two-hundredth birthday of the signing of the United States Constitution. The group of inspired men assembled for that convention produced the document that the Prophet Joseph Smith referred to as "a glorious standard" and "a heavenly banner" [*TPJS* 147].

In commemoration of this important event, we are providing this booklet, which contains three family home evening lessons, activity ideas, and a copy of the Constitution. We encourage you to prepare and teach each lesson prayerfully so that family members may feel the divine significance of the Constitution in their minds and hearts. Faithfully, your brethren, The First Presidency. (*Family Home Evening Lessons for the Bicentennial of the Constitution* 2)

13.124. I testify that America is a choice land. (See 2 Nephi 1:5.) God raised up the founding fathers of the United States of America and established the inspired Constitution. (See D&C 101:77-80.) This was the required prologue for the restoration of the gospel. (See 3 Nephi 21:4.) America will be a blessed land unto the righteous forever, and is the base from which God will continue to direct the worldwide latter-day operations of His kingdom. (See 2 Nephi 1:7.) ("I Testify" 87)

Appendix

The Constitution of the United States of America

PREAMBLE

We the People of the United States, in Order to form a more perfect Union, establish Justice, insure domestic Tranquility, provide for the common defence, promote the general Welfare, and secure the Blessings of Liberty to ourselves and our Posterity, do ordain and establish this CONSTITUTION for the United States of America.

ARTICLE I

SECTION 1. All legislative Powers herein granted shall be vested in a Congress of the United States which shall consist of a Senate and House of Representatives.

SECTION 2. The House of Representatives shall be composed of Members chosen every second Year by the People of the several States, and the Electors in each State shall have the Qualifications requisite for Electors of the most numerous Branch of the State Legislature.

No Person shall be a Representative who shall not have attained to the Age of twenty-five Years, and been seven Years a Citizen of the United States, and who shall not, when elected, be an Inhabitant of that State in which he shall be chosen.

[Representatives and direct Taxes shall be apportioned among the several States which may be included within this Union, according to their respective Numbers, which shall be determined by adding to the whole Number of free Persons, including those bound to Service for a Term of Years, and excluding Indians not taxed, three fifths of all other Persons.] The actual Enumeration shall be made within three Years after the first Meeting of the Congress of the United States, and within every subsequent Term of ten Years, in such Manner as they shall by Law direct. The Number of Representatives shall not exceed one for every thirty Thousand, but each State shall have at least one Representative; and until such enumeration shall be made, the State of New Hampshire shall be entitled to chuse three, Massachusetts eight, Rhode-Island and Providence Plantations one, Connecticut five, New York six, New Jersey four, Pennsylvania eight, Delaware one, Maryland six, Virginia ten, North Carolina five, South Carolina five, and Georgia three.

When vacancies happen in the Representation from any State, the Executive Authority thereof shall issue Writs of Election to fill such Vacancies.

The House of Representatives shall chuse their Speaker and other Officers; and shall have the sole Power of Impeachment.

SECTION 3. The Senate of the United States shall be composed of two Senators from each State, chosen by the Legislature thereof, for six Years; and each Senator shall have one Vote.

Immediately after they shall be assembled in Consequence of the first Election, they shall be divided as equally as may be into three Classes. The Seats of the Senators of the first Class shall be vacated at the Expiration of the second Year, of the second Class at the Expiration of the fourth Year, and of the third Class at the Expiration of the sixth Year, so that one third may be chosen every second Year; and if Vacancies happen by Resignation, or otherwise, during the Recess of the Legislature of any State, the Executive thereof may make temporary Appointments until the next Meeting of the Legislature, which shall then fill such Vacancies.

No Person shall be a Senator who shall not have attained to the Age of thirty Years, and been nine Years a Citizen of the United States, and who shall not, when elected, be an Inhabitant of that State for which he shall be chosen.

The Vice President of the United States shall be President of the Senate, but shall have no Vote, unless they be equally divided.

The Senate shall chuse their other Officers, and also a President pro tempore, in the Absence of the Vice President, or when he shall exercise the Office of President of the United States.

The Senate shall have the sole Power to try all Impeachments. When sitting for that Purpose, they shall be on Oath or Affirmation. When the President of the United States is tried, the Chief Justice shall preside: And no Person shall be convicted without the Concurrence of two thirds of the Members present.

Judgment in Cases of Impeachment shall not extend further than to removal from Office, and disqualification to hold and enjoy any Office of honor, Trust or Profit under the United States: but the Party convicted shall nevertheless be liable and subject to Indictment, Trial, Judgment, and Punishment, according to Law.

SECTION 4. The Times, Places and Manner of holding Elections for Senators and Representatives, shall be prescribed in each State by the Legislature thereof; but the Congress may at any time by Law make or alter such Regulations, except as to the Place of chusing Senators.

The Congress shall assemble at least once in every Year, and such Meeting shall be on the first Monday in December, unless they shall by Law appoint a different Day.

SECTION 5. Each House shall be the Judge of the Elections, Returns and Qualifications of its own Members, and a Majority of each shall constitute a quorum to do Business; but a smaller Number may adjourn from day to day, and may be authorized to compel the Attendance of absent Members, in such Manner, and under such Penalties as each House may provide.

Each House may determine the Rules of its Proceedings, punish its members for disorderly Behavior, and, with the Concurrence of two thirds, expel a Member.

Each House shall keep a Journal of its Proceedings, and from time to time publish the same, excepting such Parts as may in their Judgment require Secrecy; and the Yeas and Nays of the Members of either House on any question shall, at the Desire of one fifth of those Present, be entered on the Journal.

Neither House, during the Session of Congress, shall, without the Consent of the other, adjourn for more than three days, nor to any other Place than that in which the two Houses shall be sitting.

SECTION 6. The Senators and Representatives shall receive a Compensation for their Services, to be ascertained by Law, and paid out of the Treasury of the United States. They shall in all Cases, except Treason, Felony and Breach of the Peace, be privileged from Arrest during their Attendance at the Session of their respective Houses, and in going to and returning from the same; and for any Speech or Debate in either House, they shall not be questioned in any other Place.

No Senator or Representative shall, during the Time for which he was elected, be appointed to any civil Office under the Authority of the United States, which shall have been created, or the Emoluments whereof shall have been encreased during such time; and no Person holding any Office under the United States, shall be a Member of either House during his Continuance in Office.

SECTION 7. All Bills for raising Revenue shall originate in the House of Representatives; but the Senate may propose or concur with Amendments as on other Bills.

Every Bill which shall have passed the House of Representatives and the Senate, shall, before it become a Law, be presented to the President of the United States; If he approve he shall sign it, but if not he shall return it, with his Objections to the House in which it shall have originated, who shall enter the Objections at large on their Journal, and proceed to reconsider it. If after such Reconsideration two thirds of that House shall agree to pass the Bill, it shall be sent, together with the Objections, to the other House, by which it shall likewise be reconsidered, and if approved by two thirds of that House, it shall become a Law. But in all such Cases the Votes of both Houses shall be determined by Yeas and Nays, and the Names of the Persons voting for and against the Bill shall be entered on the Journal of each House respectively. If any Bill shall not be returned by the President within ten Days (Sundays excepted) after it shall have been presented to him, the Same shall be a Law, in like Manner as if he had signed it, unless the Congress by their Adjournment prevent its Return, in which Case it shall not be a Law.

Every Order, Resolution, or Vote to Which the Concurrence of the Senate and House of Representatives may be necessary (except on a question of Adjournment) shall be presented to the President of the United States; and before the Same shall take Effect, shall be approved by him, or being disapproved by him, shall be repassed by two thirds of the Senate and House of Representatives, according to the Rules and Limitations prescribed in the Case of a Bill.

SECTION 8. The Congress shall have Power To lay and collect Taxes, Duties, Imposts and Excises, to pay the Debts and provide for the common Defence and general Welfare of the United States; but all Duties, Imposts and Excises shall be uniform throughout the United States;

To borrow money on the credit of the United States;

To regulate Commerce with foreign Nations, and among the several States, and with the Indian Tribes;

To establish an uniform Rule of Naturalization, and uniform Laws on the subject of Bankruptcies throughout the United States;

To coin Money, regulate the Value thereof, and of foreign Coin, and fix the Standard of Weights and Measures;

To provide for the Punishment of counterfeiting the Securities and current Coin of the United States;

To establish Post Offices and Post Roads;

To promote the Progress of Science and useful Arts, by securing for limited Times to Authors and Inventors the exclusive Right to their respective Writings and Discoveries;

To constitute Tribunals inferior to the Supreme Court;

To define and punish Piracies and Felonies committed on the high Seas, and Offenses against the Law of Nations;

To declare War, grant Letters of Marque and Reprisal, and make Rules concerning Captures on Land and Water;

To raise and support Armies, but no Appropriation of Money to that Use shall be for a longer Term than two Years;

To provide and maintain a Navy;

To make Rules for the Government and Regulation of the land and naval Forces;

To provide for calling forth the Militia to execute the Laws of the Union, suppress Insurrections and repel Invasions;

To provide for organizing, arming, and disciplining, the Militia, and for governing such Part of them as may be employed in the Service of the United States, reserving to the States respectively, the Appointment of the Officers, and the Authority of training the Militia according to the discipline prescribed by Congress;

To exercise exclusive Legislation in all Cases whatsoever, over such District (not exceeding ten Miles square) as may, by Cession of particular States, and the acceptance of Congress, become the Seat of the Government of the United States, and to exercise like Authority over all Places purchased by the Consent of the Legislature of the State in which the Same shall be, for the Erection of Forts, Magazines, Arsenals, dock-Yards, and other needful Buildings;—And

To make all Laws which shall be necessary and proper for carrying into Execution the foregoing Powers, and all other Powers vested by this Constitution in the Government of the United States, or in any Department or Officer thereof.

SECTION 9. The Migration or Importation of such Persons as any of the States now existing shall think proper to admit, shall not be prohibited by the Congress prior to the Year one thousand eight hundred and eight, but a Tax or duty may be imposed on such Importation, not exceeding ten dollars for each Person.

The privilege of the Writ of Habeas Corpus shall not be suspended, unless when in Cases of Rebellion or Invasion the public Safety may require it.

No Bill of Attainder or ex post facto Law shall be passed.

No capitation, or other direct, Tax shall be laid, unless in Proportion to the Census or Enumeration herein before directed to be taken.

No Tax or Duty shall be laid on Articles exported from any State.

No Preference shall be given by any Regulation of Commerce or Revenue to the Ports of one State over those of another: nor shall Vessels bound to, or from, one State, be obliged to enter, clear, or pay Duties in another.

No Money shall be drawn from the Treasury, but in Consequence of Appropriations made by Law; and a regular Statement and Account of the Receipts and Expenditures of all public Money shall be published from time to time.

No Title of Nobility shall be granted by the United States: And no Person holding any Office of Profit or Trust under them, shall, without the Consent of the Congress, accept of any present, Emolument, Office, or Title, of any kind whatever, from any King, Prince, or foreign State.

SECTION 10. No State shall enter into any Treaty, Alliance, or Confederation; grant Letters of Marque and Reprisal; coin Money; emit Bills of Credit; make any Thing but gold and silver Coin a Tender in Payment of Debts; pass any Bill of Attainder, ex post facto Law, or Law impairing the Obligation of Contracts, or grant any Title of Nobility.

No State shall, without the Consent of the Congress, lay any Imposts of Duties on Imports or Exports, except what may be absolutely necessary for executing its inspection Laws: and the net Produce of all Duties and Imposts, laid by any State on Imports and Exports, shall be for the Use of the Treasury of the United States; and all such Laws shall be subject to the Revision and Control of the Congress.

No State shall, without the Consent of Congress, lay any duty of Tonnage, keep Troops, or Ships of War in time of Peace, enter into any Agreement or Compact with another State, or with a foreign Power, or engage in War, unless actually invaded, or in such imminent Danger as will not admit of delay.

ARTICLE II

SECTION 1. The executive Power shall be vested in a President of the United States of America. He shall hold his Office during the Term of four Years, and, together with the Vice-President, chosen for the same Term, be elected, as follows

Each State shall appoint, in such Manner as the Legislature thereof may direct, a Number of Electors, equal to the whole Number of Senators and Representatives to which the State may be entitled in the Congress: but no Senator or Representative, or Person holding an Office of Trust or Profit under the United States, shall be appointed an Elector.

[The Electors shall meet in their respective States, and vote by Ballot for two persons, of whom one at least shall not be an Inhabitant of the same State with themselves. And they shall make a List of all the Persons voted for, and of the Number of Votes for each; which List they shall sign and certify, and transmit sealed to the Seat of the Government of the United States, directed to the President of the Senate. The President of the Senate shall, in the Presence of the Senate and House of Representatives, open all the Certificates, and the Votes shall then be counted. The Person having the greatest Number of Votes shall be the President, if such Number be a Majority of the whole Number of Electors appointed; and if there be more than one who have such Majority, and have an equal Number of Votes, then the House of Representatives shall immediately chuse by Ballot one of them for President; and if no Person have a Majority, then from the five highest on the List the said House shall in like Manner chuse the President. But in chusing the President, the Votes shall be taken by States, the Representation from each State having one Vote; A quorum for this Purpose shall consist of a Member or Members from two-thirds of the States, and a Majority of all the States shall be necessary to a Choice. In every Case, after the Choice of the President, the Person having the greater Number of Votes of the Electors shall be the Vice President. But if there should remain two or more who have equal Votes, the Senate shall chuse from them by Ballot the Vice-President.]

The Congress may determine the Time of chusing the Electors, and the Day on which they shall give their Votes; which Day shall be the same throughout the United States.

No person except a natural born Citizen, or a Citizen of the United States, at the time of the Adoption of this Constitution, shall be eligible to the Office of President; neither shall any Person be eligible to that Office who shall not have attained to the Age of thirty-five Years, and been fourteen Years a Resident within the United States.

In Case of the removal of the President from Office, or of his Death, Resignation, or Inability to discharge the Powers and Duties of the said Office, the same shall devolve on the Vice President, and the Congress may by Law provide for the Case of Removal, Death, Resignation or Inability, both of the President and Vice President, declaring what Officer shall then act as President, and such Officer shall act accordingly, until the Disability be removed, or a President shall be elected.

The President shall, at stated Times, receive for his Services, a Compensation, which shall neither be encreased nor diminished during the Period for which he shall have been elected, and he shall not receive within that Period any other Emolument from the United States, or any of them.

Before he enter on the Execution of his Office, he shall take the following Oath or Affirmation:—"I do solemnly swear (or affirm) that I will faithfully execute the Office of President of the United States, and will to the best of my Ability, preserve, protect and defend the Constitution of the United States."

SECTION 2. The President shall be Commander in Chief of the Army and Navy of the United States, and of the Militia of the several States, when called into the actual Service of the United States; he may require the Opinion in writing, of the principal Officer in each of the executive Departments, upon any subject relating to the Duties of their respective Offices, and he shall have Power to Grant Reprieves and Pardons for Offenses against the United States, except in Cases of Impeachment.

He shall have Power, by and with the Advice and Consent of the Senate, to make Treaties, provided two-thirds of the Senators present concur; and he shall nominate, and by and with the Advice and Consent of the Senate, shall appoint Ambassadors, other public Ministers and Consuls, Judges of the supreme Court, and all other Officers of the United States, whose Appointments are not herein otherwise provided for, and which shall be established by Law: but the Congress may by Law vest the Appointment of such inferior Officers, as they think proper, in the President alone, in the Courts of Law, or in the Heads of Departments.

The President shall have Power to fill up all Vacancies that may happen during the Recess of the Senate, by granting Commissions which shall expire at the End of their next Session.

SECTION 3. He shall from time to time give to the Congress Information of the State of the Union, and recommend to their Consideration such Measures as he shall judge necessary and expedient; he may, on extraordinary Occasions, convene both Houses, or either of them, and in Case of Disagreement between them, with Respect to the Time of Adjournment, he may adjourn them to such time as he shall think proper; he shall receive Ambassadors and other public Ministers; he shall take Care that the Laws be faithfully executed, and shall Commission all the Officers of the United States.

SECTION 4. The President, Vice President and all civil Officers of the United States, shall be removed from Office on Impeachment for, and Conviction of, Treason, Bribery, or other high Crimes and Misdemeanors.

ARTICLE III

SECTION 1. The judicial Power of the United States, shall be vested in one supreme Court, and in such inferior Courts as the Congress may from time to time ordain and establish. The Judges, both of the supreme and inferior Courts, shall hold their Offices during good Behavior, and shall, at stated Times, receive for their Services a Compensation which shall not be diminished during their Continuance in Office.

SECTION 2. The judicial Power shall extend to all Cases, in Law and Equity, arising under this Constitution, the Laws of the United States, and Treaties made, or which shall be made, under their Authority;—to all Cases affecting Ambassadors, other public Ministers and Consuls;—to all Cases of admiralty and maritime Jurisdiction;—to Controversies to which the United States shall be a Party;—to Controversies between two or more States;—between a State and Citizens of another State;—between Citizens of different States;—between Citizens of the Same State claiming Lands under the Grants of different States, and between a State, or the Citizens thereof, and foreign States, Citizens or Subjects.

In all Cases affecting Ambassadors, other public Ministers and Consuls, and those in which a State shall be a Party, the supreme Court shall have original Jurisdiction. In all the other Cases before mentioned, the supreme Court shall have appellate Jurisdiction, both as to Law and Fact, with such Exceptions, and under such Regulations as the Congress shall make.

The trial of all Crimes, except in Cases of Impeachment, shall be by Jury; and such Trial shall be held in the State where the said Crimes shall have been committed; but when not committed within any State, the Trial shall be at such Place or Places as the Congress may by Law have directed.

SECTION 3. Treason against the United States, shall consist only in levying War against them, or in adhering to their Enemies, giving them Aid and Comfort. No Person shall be convicted of Treason unless on the Testimony of two Witnesses to the same overt Act, or on Confession in open Court.

The Congress shall have power to declare the Punishment of Treason, but no Attainder of Treason shall work Corruption of Blood, or Forfeiture except during the Life of the Person attained.

ARTICLE IV

SECTION 1. Full Faith and Credit shall be given in each State to the Public Acts, Records, and judicial Proceedings of every other State. And the Congress may by general Laws prescribe the Manner in which such Acts, Records and Proceedings shall be proved and the Effect thereof.

SECTION 2. The Citizens of each State shall be entitled to all Privileges and Immunities of Citizens in the several States.

A Person charged in any State with Treason, Felony, or other Crime, who shall flee from Justice, and be found in another State, shall on demand of the executive Authority of the State from which he fled, be delivered up, to be removed to the State having Jurisdiction of the Crime.

No Person held to Service or Labour in one State, under the Laws thereof, escaping into another, shall, in Consequence of any Law or Regulation therein, be discharged from such Service or Labour, but shall be delivered up on Claim of the Party to whom such Service or Labour may be due.

SECTION 3. New States may be admitted by the Congress into this Union; but no new State shall be formed or erected within the Jurisdiction of any other State; nor any State be formed by the Junction of two or more States, or parts of States, without the Consent of the Legislatures of the States concerned as well as of the Congress.

The Congress shall have Power to dispose of and make all needful Rules and Regulations respecting the Territory or other Property belonging to the United States; and nothing in this Constitution shall be so construed as to Prejudice any Claims of the United States, or of any particular State.

SECTION 4. The United States shall guarantee to every State in this Union a Republican Form of Government, and shall protect each of them against Invasion; and on Application of the Legislature, or of the Executive (when the Legislature cannot be convened) against domestic Violence.

ARTICLE V

The Congress, whenever two-thirds of both Houses shall deem it necessary, shall propose Amendments to this Constitution, or, on the Application of the Legislatures of two-thirds of the several States, shall call a Convention for proposing Amendments, which, in either Case, shall be valid to all Intents and Purposes, as part of this Constitution, when ratified by the

Legislatures of three-fourths of the several States, or by Conventions in three-fourths thereof, as the one or the other Mode of Ratification may be proposed by the Congress; Provided that no Amendment which may be made prior to the Year One thousand eight hundred and eight shall in any Manner affect the first and fourth Clauses in the Ninth Section of the first Article; and that no State, without its Consent, shall be deprived of its equal Suffrage in the Senate.

ARTICLE VI

All Debts contracted and Engagements entered into, before the Adoption of this Constitution, shall be as valid against the United States under this Constitution, as under the Confederation.

This Constitution, and the Laws of the United States which shall be made in Pursuance thereof; and all Treaties made, or which shall be made, under the Authority of the United States, shall be the supreme Law of the Land; and the Judges in every State shall be bound thereby, any Thing in the Constitution or Laws of any State to the Contrary notwithstanding.

The Senators and Representatives before mentioned, and the Members of the several State Legislatures, and all executive and judicial Officers, both of the United States and of the several States, shall be bound by Oath or Affirmation, to support this Constitution; but no religious Test shall ever be required as a Qualification to any Office or public Trust under the United States.

ARTICLE VII

The Ratification of the Conventions of nine States shall be sufficient for the Establishment of this Constitution between the States so ratifying the Same.

DONE in Convention by the Unanimous Consent of the States present the Seventeenth Day of September in the Year of our Lord one thousand seven hundred and Eighty seven and of the Independence of the United States of America the Twelfth. In Witness whereof We have hereunto subscribed our Names.

Go Washington
Presidt and deputy from Virginia

New Hampshire
John Langdon
Nicholas Gilman

Massachusetts
Nathaniel Gorham
Rufus King

Connecticut
Wm Saml Johnson
Roger Sherman

New York
Alexander Hamilton

New Jersey
Wil: Livingston
David Brearley
Wm Patterson
Jona: Dayton

Pennsylvania
B. Franklin
Robt. Morris
Thos Fitzsimons
James Wilson
Thomas Mifflin
Geo. Clymer
Jared Ingersoll
Gouv Morris

Delaware
Geo: Read
John Dickinson
Jaco: Broom
Gunning Bedford jun
Richard Bassett

Maryland
James McHenry
Danl Carroll
Dan: of St Thos Jenifer

Virginia
John Blair—
James Madison Jr.

North Carolina
Wm Blount
Hu Williamson

South Carolina
J. Rutledge
Charles Pinckney
Charles Cotesworth Pinckney
Pierce Butler

Georgia
William Few
Abr Baldwin

Attest: William Jackson, *Secretary*

ARTICLES IN ADDITION TO, AND AMENDMENT OF, THE
CONSTITUTION OF THE UNITED STATES OF AMERICA,
PROPOSED BY CONGRESS, AND RATIFIED BY THE
LEGISLATURES OF THE SEVERAL STATES, PURSUANT TO THE
FIFTH ARTICLE OF THE ORIGINAL CONSTITUTION.

AMENDMENT I [1791]

Congress shall make no law respecting an establishment of religion, or prohibiting the free exercise thereof; or abridging the freedom of speech, or of the press; or the right of the people peaceably to assemble, and to petition the Government for a redress of grievances.

AMENDMENT II [1791]

A well regulated Militia, being necessary to the security of a free State, the right of the people to keep and bear Arms, shall not be infringed.

AMENDMENT III [1791]

No Soldier shall, in time of peace be quartered in any house, without the consent of the Owner, nor in time of war, but in a manner to be prescribed by law.

AMENDMENT IV [1791]

The right of the people to be secure in their persons, houses, papers, and effects, against unreasonable searches and seizures, shall not be violated, and no Warrants shall issue, but upon probable cause, supported by Oath or affirmation, and particularly describing the place to be searched, and the persons or things to be seized.

AMENDMENT V [1791]

No person shall be held to answer for a capital, or otherwise infamous crime, unless on a presentment or indictment of a Grand Jury, except in cases arising in the land or naval forces, or in the Militia, when in actual service in time of War or public danger; nor shall any person be subject for the same offence to be twice put in jeopardy of life or limb; nor shall be compelled in any criminal case to be a witness against himself, nor be deprived of life, liberty, or property, without due process of law; nor shall private property be taken for public use, without just compensation.

AMENDMENT VI [1791]

In all criminal prosecutions, the accused shall enjoy the right to a speedy and public trial, by an impartial jury of the State and district wherein the crime shall have been committed, which district shall have been previously ascertained by law, and to be informed of the nature and cause of the accusation; to be confronted with the witnesses against him; to have compulsory process for obtaining witnesses in his favor, and to have the Assistance of Counsel for his defence.

AMENDMENT VII [1791]

In suits at common law, where the value in controversy shall exceed twenty dollars, the right of trial by jury shall be preserved, and no fact tried by jury, shall be otherwise re-examined in any Court of the United States, than according to the rules of the common law.

AMENDMENT VIII [1791]

Excessive bail shall not be required, nor excessive fines imposed, nor cruel and unusual punishment inflicted.

AMENDMENT IX [1791]

The enumeration in the Constitution, of certain rights, shall not be construed to deny or disparage others retained by the people.

AMENDMENT X [1791]

The powers not delegated to the United States by the Constitution, nor prohibited by it to the States, are reserved to the States respectively, or to the people.

AMENDMENT XI [1798]

The Judicial power of the Untied States shall not be construed to extend to any suit in law or equity, commenced or prosecuted against one of the Untied States by Citizens of another State, or by Citizens or Subjects of any foreign State.

AMENDMENT XII [1804]

The Electors shall meet in their respective states and vote by ballot for President and Vice-President, one of whom, at least, shall not be an inhabitant of the same state with themselves; they shall name in their ballots the person voted for as President, and in distinct ballots the person voted for as Vice-President, and they shall make distinct lists of all persons voted for as President, and of all persons voted for as Vice-President, and of the number of votes for each, which lists they shall sign and certify, and transmit sealed to the President of the Senate;—The President of the Senate shall, in the presence of the Senate and House of Representatives, open all the certificates and the votes then be counted; —The person having the greatest number of votes for President, shall be the President, if such number be a majority of the whole number of Electors appointed; and if no person have such a majority, then from the persons having the highest numbers not exceeding three on the list of those voted for as President, the

House of Representatives shall choose immediately, by ballot, the President. But in choosing the President, the votes shall be taken by states, the representation from each state having one vote; a quorum for this purpose shall consist of a member or members from two-thirds of the states, and majority of all the states shall be necessary to a choice. And if the House of Representatives shall not choose a President whenever the right of choice shall devolve upon them, before the fourth day of March next following, then the Vice-President shall act as President, as in the case of the death or other constitutional disability of the President.—The person having the greatest number of votes as Vice-President, shall be the Vice-President, if such number be a majority of the whole number of Electors appointed, and if no person have a majority, then from the two highest numbers on the list, the Senate shall choose the Vice-President; a quorum for the purpose shall consist of two-thirds of the whole number of Senators, and a majority of the whole number shall be necessary to a choice. But no person constitutionally ineligible to the office of President shall be eligible to that of Vice-President of the United States.

AMENDMENT XIII [1865]

SECTION 1. Neither slavery nor involuntary servitude, except as a punishment for crime whereof the party shall have been duly convicted, shall exist within the United States, or any place subject to their jurisdiction.

SECTION 2. Congress shall have power to enforce this article by appropriate legislation.

AMENDMENT XIV [1868]

SECTION 1. All persons born or naturalized in the United States, and subject to the jurisdiction thereof, are citizens of the United States and of the State wherein they reside. No State shall make or enforce any law which shall abridge the privileges or immunities of citizens of the United States; nor shall any State deprive any person of life, liberty, or property, without due process of law; nor deny to any person within its jurisdiction the equal protection of the laws.

SECTION 2. Representatives shall be apportioned among the several States according to their respective numbers, counting the whole number of persons in each State excluding Indians not taxed. But when the right to vote at any election for the choice of electors for President and Vice-President of the United States, Representatives in Congress, the Executive and Judicial officers of a State, or the members of the Legislature thereof, is denied to any of the male inhabitants of such State, being twenty-one years of age, and citizens of the United States, or in any way abridged, except for participation in rebellion, or other crime, the basis of representation therein shall be reduced in the proportion which the number of such male citizens shall bear to the whole number of male citizens twenty-one years of age in such State.

SECTION 3. No person shall be a Senator or Representative in Congress, or elector of President and Vice-President, or hold any office, civil or military, under the United States, or under any State, who, having previously taken an oath, as a member of Congress, or as an officer of the United States, or as a member of any State legislature, or as an executive or judicial officer of any State, to support the Constitution of the United States, shall have engaged in insurrection or rebellion against the same, or given aid or comfort to the enemies thereof. But Congress may by a vote of two-thirds of each House, remove such disability.

SECTION 4. The validity of the public debt of the United States, authorized by law, including debts incurred for payment of pensions and bounties for services in suppressing insurrection or rebellion, shall not be questioned. But neither the United States nor any State shall assume or pay any debt or obligation incurred in aid of insurrection or rebellion against the United States, or any claim for the loss or emancipation of any slave; but all such debts, obligations and claims shall be held illegal and void.

SECTION 5. The Congress shall have power to enforce, by appropriate legislation, the provisions of this article.

AMENDMENT XV [1870]

SECTION 1. The right of citizens of the United States to vote shall not be denied or abridged by the United States or by any State on account of race, color, or previous condition of servitude—

SECTION 2. The Congress shall have power to enforce this article by appropriate legislation.

AMENDMENT XVI [1913]

The Congress shall have power to lay and collect taxes or incomes, from whatever source derived, without apportionment among the several States, and without regard to any census or enumeration.

AMENDMENT XVII [1913]

The Senate of the United States shall be composed of two Senators from each State, elected by the people thereof, for six years; and each Senator shall have one vote. The electors in each State shall have the qualifications requisite for electors of the most numerous branch of the State legislatures.

When vacancies happen in the representation of any State in the Senate, the executive authority of such State shall issue writs of election to fill such vacancies: *Provided*, That the legislature of any State may empower the executive thereof to make temporary appointments until the people fill the vacancies by election as the legislature may direct.

This amendment shall not be so construed as to affect the election or term of any Senator chosen before it becomes valid as part of the Constitution.

AMENDMENT XVIII [1919]

SECTION 1. After one year from the ratification of this article the manufacture, sale, or transportation of intoxicating liquors therein, the importation thereof into, or the exportation thereof from the United States and all territory subject to the jurisdiction thereof for beverage purposes is hereby prohibited.

SECTION 2. The Congress and the several States shall have concurrent power to enforce this article by appropriate legislation.

SECTION 3. This article shall be inoperative unless it shall have been ratified as an amendment to the Constitution by the legislatures of the several States, as provided in the Constitution, within seven years from the date of the submission hereof to the States by the Congress.

AMENDMENT XIX [1920]

The right of citizens of the United States to vote shall not be denied or abridged by the United States or by any State on account of sex.

Congress shall have power to enforce this article by appropriate legislation.

AMENDMENT XX [1933]

SECTION 1. The terms of the President and Vice President shall end at noon on the 20th day of January, and the terms of Senators and Representatives at noon on the 3d day of January, of the years in which such terms would have ended if this article had not been ratified; and the terms of their successors shall then begin.

SECTION 2. The Congress shall assemble at least once in every year, and such meeting shall begin at noon on the 3d day of January, unless they shall by law appoint a different day.

SECTION 3. If, at the time fixed for the beginning of the term of the President, the President elect shall have died, the Vice President elect shall become President. If a President shall not have been chosen before the time fixed for the beginning of his term, or if the President elect shall have failed to qualify, then the Vice President elect shall act as President until a President shall have qualified; and the Congress may by law provide for the case wherein neither a President elect nor a Vice President elect shall have qualified, declaring who shall then act as President, or the manner in which one who is to act shall be selected, and such person shall act accordingly until a President or Vice President shall have qualified.

SECTION 4. The Congress may by law provide for the case of the death of any of the persons from whom the House of Representatives may choose a President whenever the right of choice shall have devolved upon them, and for the case of the death of any of the persons from whom the Senate may choose a Vice President whenever the right of choice shall have devolved upon them.

SECTION 5. Sections 1 and 2 shall take effect on the 15th day of October following the ratification of this article.

SECTION 6. This article shall be inoperative unless it shall have been ratified as an amendment to the Constitution by the legislatures of three-fourths of the several States within seven years from the date of its submission.

AMENDMENT XXI [1933]

SECTION 1. The eighteenth article of amendment to the Constitution of the United States is hereby repealed.

SECTION 2. The transportation or importation into any State, Territory, or possession of the United States for delivery or use therein of intoxicating liquors, in violation of the laws thereof, is hereby prohibited.

SECTION 3. The article shall be inoperative unless it shall have been ratified as an amendment to the Constitution by conventions in the several States, as provided in the Constitution, within seven years from the date of the submission hereof to the States by the Congress.

AMENDMENT XXII [1951]

SECTION 1. No person shall be elected to the office of President more than twice, and no person who has held the office of President, or acted as President, for more than two years of a term to which some other person was elected President shall be elected to the office of President more than once. But this Article shall not apply to any person holding the office of President when this Article was proposed by the Congress, and shall not prevent any person who may be holding the office of President, or acting as President, during the term within which this Article becomes operative from holding the office of President or acting as President during the remainder of such term.

SECTION 2. This article shall be inoperative unless it shall have been ratified as an amendment to the Constitution by the legislatures of three-fourths of the several States within seven years from the date of its submission to the States by the Congress.

AMENDMENT XXIII [1961]

SECTION 1. The District constituting the seat of Government of the United States shall appoint in such manner as the Congress may direct:

A number of electors of President and Vice President equal to the whole number of Senators and Representatives in Congress to which the District would be entitled if it were a State, but in no event more than the least populous State; they shall be in addition to those appointed by the States, but they shall be considered, for the purposes of the election of President and Vice President, to be electors appointed by a State; and they shall meet in the District and perform such duties as provided by the twelfth article of amendment.

SECTION 2. The Congress shall have power to enforce this article by appropriate legislation.

AMENDMENT XXIV [1964]

SECTION 1. The right of citizens of the United States to vote in any primary or other election for President or Vice-President, or for Senator or Representative in Congress, shall not be denied or abridged by the United States or any State by reason of failure to pay any poll tax or other tax.

SECTION 2. The Congress shall have power to enforce this article by appropriate legislation.

AMENDMENT XXV [1967]

SECTION 1. In case of removal of the President from office or of his death or resignation, the Vice-President shall become President.

SECTION 2. Whenever there is a vacancy in the office of the Vice-President, the President shall nominate a Vice-President who shall take office upon confirmation by a majority of both Houses of Congress.

SECTION 3. Whenever the President transmits to the President pro tempore of the Senate and the Speaker of the House of Representatives his written declaration that he is unable to discharge the powers and duties of his office, and until he transmits to them a written declaration to the contrary, such powers and duties shall be discharged by the Vice-President as Acting President.

SECTION 4. Whenever the Vice-President and a majority of either the principal officers of the executive departments or of such other body as Congress may by law provide, transmit to the President pro tempore of the Senate and the Speaker of the House of Representatives their written declaration that the President is unable to discharge the powers and duties of his office, the Vice-President shall immediately assume the powers and duties of the office as Acting President.

Thereafter, when the President transmits to the President pro tempore of the Senate and the Speaker of the House of Representatives his written declaration that no inability exists, he shall resume the powers and duties of his office unless the

Vice-President and a majority of either the principal officers of the executive department or of such other body as Congress may by law provide, transmit within four days to the President pro tempore of the Senate and the Speaker of the House of Representatives their written declaration that the President is unable to discharge the powers and duties of his office. Thereupon Congress shall decide the issue, assembling within forty-eight hours for that purpose if not in session. If the Congress, within twenty-one days after receipt of the latter written declaration, or, if Congress is not in session, within twenty-one days after Congress is required to assemble, determines by two-thirds vote of both Houses that the President is unable to discharge the power and duties of his office, the Vice-President shall continue to discharge the same as Acting President; otherwise, the President shall resume the powers and duties of his office.

AMENDMENT XXVI [1971]

SECTION 1. The right of citizens of the United States, who are eighteen years of age or older, to vote shall not be denied or abridged by the United States or by any State on account of age.

SECTION 2. The Congress shall have power to enforce this article by appropriate legislation.

Bibliography

Benson, Ezra Taft. "America: A Choice Land." *Improvement Era* (Nov 1944) 47:674-75, 726; also in *Conference Report* (Oct 1944) 128-35.

———. "America—A Man and an Event." *Improvement Era* (Dec 1965) 68:1150-52; also in *Conference Report* (Oct 1965) 121-25.

———. "America at the Crossroads: The Ten Commandments." *New Era* (Jul 1978) 8:36-39.

———. "America: Land of the Blessed." *Improvement Era* (May 1948) 51:283, 342-43; also in *Conference Report* (Apr 1948) 82-87.

———. "The American Heritage of Freedom — A Plan of God." *Improvement Era (Dec 1961) 64:952-57; also in Conference Report* (Oct 1961) 69-75.

———. *The American Heritage of Freedom— A Plan of God.* Salt Lake City: Deseret Book, 1961.

———. "Be Not Deceived." *Improvement Era* (Dec 1963) 66:1063-65; also in *Conference Report* (Oct 1963) 15-19.

———. "Civic Standards for the Faithful Saints." *Ensign* (Jul 1972) 2:59-60; also in *Conference Report* (Apr 1972) 48-53.

———. *The Constitution—A Glorious Standard. Ensign* (May 1976) 6:91-93; also in *Conference Report* (Apr 1976) 134-38.

———. *The Constitution: A Heavenly Banner.* Salt Lake City: Deseret Book, 1986. [Also printed in BYU *Speeches of the Year 1986-87.*]

———. *Cross Fire: The Eight Years with Eisenhower.* Garden City, NY: Doubleday, 1962.

———. *An Enemy Hath Done This.* Comp. Jerreld L. Newquist. Salt Lake City: Parliament, 1969.

————. *Family Home Evening Lessons for the Bicentennial of the Constitution.* Salt Lake City: The Church of Jesus Christ of Latter-day Saints, 1987.

————. "First Presidency Urges Observance of Bicentennial of Constitution." *Church News* (31 Jan 1987) 11.

————. "A Four-Fold Hope." *Brigham Young University Speeches of the Year.* Provo, UT, 24 May 1961.

————. *God, Family, Country: Our Three Great Loyalties.* Salt Lake City: Deseret Book, 1974.

————. "God's Hand in Our Nation's History." In *Speeches of the Year, 1976.* Provo, UT: Brigham Young Univ, 1977.

————. "The Heritage of Freedom." *Improvement Era* (Dec 1958) 61:954-57; also in *Conference Report* (Oct 1958) 98-102.

————. "I Testify." *Ensign* (Nov 1988) 18:86-87; also in *Conference Report* (Oct 1988) 101-04.

————. "Jesus Christ—Gifts and Expectations." *New Era* (May 1975) 5:16-21.

————. "Let Us Live to Keep Men Free." Testimonial Banquet for Robert Welch. Los Angeles, 23 Sep 1963. Ts. Special Collections. Harold B. Lee Library, Brigham Young Univ, Provo, UT.

————. "The Lord's Base of Operations." *Improvement Era* (Jun 1962) 65:454-57; also in *Conference Report* (Apr 1962) 103-06.

————. "Not Commanded in All Things." *Improvement Era* (Jun 1965) 68:537-39; also in *Conference Report* (Apr 1965) 121-25.

————. "Our Divine Constitution." *Ensign* (Nov 1987) 17:4-7; also in *Conference Report* (Oct 1987) 3-7.

————. "Our Duty as Citizens." *Improvement Era* (Dec 1954) 57:918+; also in *Conference Report* (Oct 1954) 118-23.

————. "Our Immediate Responsibility." *Brigham Young University Speeches of the Year.* Provo, UT, 25 Oct 1966.

―――. "Paramount Issue Today—Liberty Against Creeping Socialism." *Church News* (2 Sep 1961) 13-14.

―――. *A Plea for America*. Salt Lake City: Deseret Book, 1975.

―――. "Prepare, Then Fear Not." *Improvement Era* (Jun 1967) 70:57-60; also in *Conference Report* (Apr 1967) 58-62.

―――. "A Race Against Time." *Brigham Young University Speeches of the Year*. Provo, UT, 10 Dec 1963.

―――. *The Red Carpet*. Salt Lake City: Bookcraft, 1962.

―――. "Responsibilities of Citizenship." *Brigham Young University Speeches of the Year*. Provo, UT, 22 Oct 1954.

―――. "Righteousness Exalteth a Nation." *Improvement Era* (Jun 1963) 66:514-17; also in *Conference Report* (Apr 1963) 109-14.

―――. . . . *So Shall Ye Reap*. Comp. Reed A. Benson. Salt Lake City: Deseret Book, 1960.

―――. *This Nation Shall Endure*. Salt Lake City: Deseret Book, 1977.

―――. "Three Threatening Dangers." *Improvement Era* (Dec 1964) 65:1067-69; also in *Conference Report* (Oct 1964) 56-60.

―――. *Title of Liberty*. Comp. Mark A. Benson. Salt Lake City: Deseret Book, 1964.

―――. "A Witness and a Warning." *Ensign* (Nov 1979) 9:31-33; also in *Conference Report* (Oct 1979) 43-47.

―――. "A World Message." *Improvement Era* (Jun 1961) 64:430-33; also in *Conference Report* (Apr 1961) 110-14.

Brown, Hugh B. *Eternal Quest*. Comp. and ed. Charles Manley Brown. Salt Lake City: Bookcraft, 1956.

Clark, James R., comp. *Messages of the First Presidency of The Church of Jesus Christ of Latter-day Saints*. 6 vols. Salt Lake City: Bookcraft, 1965-75.

"The Constitution Is an Inspired Document." *Liahona: The Elders' Journal* (30 Mar 1915) 12:644.

"Constitution Topic of Tabernacle Sermons." *Deseret News* (20 Sep 1920) sec 2:8.

Discourses Delivered by Presidents Joseph Smith and Brigham Young, on the Relation of the "Mormons" to the Government of the United States. Salt Lake City: Deseret News Office, 1855.

"Ecclesiastical Control in Utah." *North American Review* (Jan 1884) 138:1-23.

Goates, L. Brent. *Harold B. Lee: Prophet and Seer*. Salt Lake City: Bookcraft, 1985.

"Gov. West Is Baffled." *Salt Lake Tribune* (14 May 1886) 4.

Grant, Heber J., and David O. McKay. "The Message of the First Presidency to the Church." *Improvement Era* (May 1942) 45:272+; also in "Message of the First Presidency." *Conference Report* (Apr 1942) 88-97.

Grant, Heber J. "Admonition and Blessing." *Improvement Era* (Nov 1944) 47:654, 694-95; also in *Conference Report* (Oct 1944) 6-13.

———. *Conference Report* (Oct 1919) 15-35.

———. *Conference Report* (Oct 1927) 2-6.

———. *Conference Report* (Oct 1928) 2-12.

———. *Conference Report* (Oct 1935) 118-22.

———. *Conference Report* (Oct 1936) 2-16.

———. "Lincoln and Law." *Improvement Era* (Feb 1940) 43:73, 127.

———. "President Heber J. Grant's Conference Message." *Improvement Era* (May 1926) 29:677-85; also in *Conference Report* (Apr 1926) 4-5.

———. "Speech of Hon. H. J. Grant . . . What Has the Republican Party Done for Utah?" Democratic Territorial Convention. Salt Lake City, 15 Sep 1894.

————. "The Upholding of Constituted Law and Order." *Improvement Era* (Apr 1928) 31:508-15.

————. "Warning to Church Members." *Improvement Era* (Aug 1936) 39:488.

Hansen, Klaus J. *Quest for Empire.* East Lansing, MI: Michigan State Univ, 1967.

Henry, D. "The Prophets on the Christ." *Liahona: The Elders' Journal* (26 Dec 1908) 6:674-79.

Hillam, Ray C., ed. *By the Hands of Wise Men.* Provo, UT: Brigham Young Univ, 1979.

History of the Church. 7 vols. Salt Lake City: Deseret Book, 1980.

Hollister, O. J. *The Supreme Court Decision in the Reynold's Case.* Salt Lake City: n.p., 1879.

Johnson, Patriarch Benjamin F. "An Interesting Letter from Patriarch Benjamin F. Johnson to Elder George S. Gibbs." 1903. Ts. Americana Collection. Harold B. Lee Library. Brigham Young University, Provo, UT.

Joseph Smith Collection. LDS Church Archives. The Church of Jesus Christ of Latter-day Saints. Salt Lake City.

Journal History of the Church. Salt Lake City: Historical Department, The Church of Jesus Christ of Latter-day Saints, 1906- .

Journal of Discourses. 26 vols. 1854-86.

Kimball, Spencer W. "Absolute Truth." *Ensign* (Sep 1978) 9:3-8.

————. "First Presidency Urges Support of Constitution Week." *Church News* (18 Sep 1982) 4.

————. "Guidelines to Carry Forth the Work of God in Holiness: A Plea to Forsake the Ways of the World." *Ensign* (May 1974) 4:4-8; also in *Conference Report* (Apr 1974) 4-10.

————. "Preparing for Service in the Church." *Ensign* (May 1979) 9:47-49; also in *Conference Report* (Apr 1979) 66-70.

————. "President Kimball Dedicates Temple." *Ensign* (Feb 1975) 5:79-83.

————. "The Stone Cut Without Hands." *Ensign* (May 1976) 6:4-9; also in *Conference Report* (Apr 1976) 4-12.

Lee, Harold B. *Decisions for Successful Living.* Salt Lake City: Deseret Book, 1973.

————. "Faith—An Effective Weapon Against Wickedness in Men and Nations." *Improvement Era* (Dec 1952) 55:912-13; also in *Conference Report* (Oct 1952) 16-19.

————. "'I Dare You to Believe.'" *Church News* (6 Jun 1953) 4+.

————. "Keep Your Lamp Lighted." *Improvement Era* (Dec 1970) 73:103-05; also in *Conference Report* (Oct 1970) 109-12.

————. "News of the Church: Constitutional Responsibility Encouraged by First Presidency as Elder L. Tom Perry Appointed Chairman of Bicentennial Committee." *Ensign* (Nov 1973) 3:90.

————. "The Spirit of Gathering." *Improvement Era* (May 1948) 51:281, 320-322; also in *Conference Report* (Apr 1948) 52-58.

————. "A Time of Decision." *Ensign* (Jul 1972) 2:29-33; also in *Conference Report* (Apr 1972) 120-25.

————. *True Patriotism—An Expression of Faith.* N.p.: Columbia Broadcast System, 1941.

————. *Ye Are the Light of the World.* Salt Lake City: Deseret Book, 1974.

McKay, David O. "Address to Marines Enlisted in Newest 'Mormon Battalion.'" *Church News* (18 Jul 1942) 4.

————. "Cherish Noble Aspirations." *Improvement Era* (Dec 1965) 68:1160-61; also in *Conference Report* (Oct 1965) 144-46.

————. "The Church and the Present War." *Improvement Era* (May 1942) 45:276, 340-42; also in *Conference Report* (Apr 1942) 70-74.

————. "Closing Address." *Improvement Era* (Dec 1952) 55:952-54; also in *Conference Report* (Oct 1952) 128-31.

————. *Conference Report* (Apr 1935) 110-16.

————. *Conference Report* (Apr 1937) 27-31.

————. *Conference Report* (Oct 1939) 101-05.

————. "Dedicatory Address Delivered at Swiss Temple Dedication." *Improvement Era* (Nov 1955) 58:795+.

————. "Dedicatory Prayer—Los Angeles Temple." *Improvement Era* (Apr 1956) 59:225-27.

————. "'Education for Citizenship.'" *Church News* (13 Mar 1954) 2-3.

————. "The Enemy Within." *Instructor* (Feb 1956) 91:33-34.

————. "Essentials of a Better World." *Improvement Era* (Nov 1940) 43:656+; also in *Conference Report* (Oct 1940) 101-05.

————. "Faith and Freedom: Two Guiding Principles of the Pilgrims." *Instructor* (Nov 1956) 91:321-22.

————. "Favorable and Unfavorable Phases of Present-day Conditions." *Improvement Era* (Jun 1952) 55:406-08; also in *Conference Report* (Apr 1952) 11-16.

————. "The Founding of an American Republic." *Instructor* (Jul 1964) 99:249-51.

————. "Free Agency . . . A Divine Gift." *Improvement Era* (May 1950) 53:366-67, 378; also in *Conference Report* (Apr 1950) 31-37.

————. "The Gospel and the Individual." *Improvement Era* (Dec 1962) 65:900-03; also in *Conference Report* (Oct 1962) 5-8.

————. *Gospel Ideals*. Salt Lake City: Improvement Era, 1953.

————. "Honor, Honesty, Integrity." *Improvement Era* (Aug 1952) 55:565-66.

————. "Let Virtue Garnish Thy Thoughts." *Improvement Era* (Jun 1969) 72:28-31; also in *Conference Report* (Apr 1969) 93-97.

————. Letter to Ernest L. Wilkinson. N.d. Special Collections. Harold B. Lee Library, Brigham Young Univ, Provo, UT.

————. "The Light That Shines in Darkness." *Improvement Era* (Nov 1942) 45:690-91, 750; also in *Conference Report* (Oct 1942) 67-70.

————. *Man May Know for Himself.* Comp. Clare Middlemiss. Salt Lake City: Deseret Book, 1967.

————. *Pathways to Happiness.* Comp. Llewelyn R. McKay. Salt Lake City: Bookcraft, 1957.

————. "Principle of Choice Most Vital to World." *Church News* (2 Jan 1952) 2-4.

————. "Safeguard in Loyalty." *Church News* (29 May 1954) 2-3.

————. *Secrets of a Happy Life.* Comp. Llewelyn R. McKay. Salt Lake City: Bookcraft, 1967.

————. "Statement Concerning the Position of the Church on Communism." *Improvement Era* (Jun 1966) 69:477, 580; also in *Conference Report* (Apr 1966) 109-10, and *Conference Report* (Apr 1969) 93-97.

————. *Statements on Communism and the Constitution of the United States.* Salt Lake City: Deseret Book, 1964

————. *Stepping Stones to an Abundant Life.* Comp. Llewelyn R. McKay. Salt Lake City: Deseret Book, 1971.

————. *Treasures of Life.* Comp. Clare Middlemiss. Salt Lake City: Deseret Book, 1962.

————. "True Education: The Paramount Purpose of a Free People." *Instructor* (Sep 1952) 87:257-58.

————. "Vote Your Convictions." *Deseret News* (2 Nov 1964) A1.

Melville, J. Keith. *President John Taylor: A Latter-day Saint Legacy of Liberty.* Provo, UT: Extension Services, Brigham Young Univ, 1964.

Morrell, Jeanette McKay. *Highlights in the Life of President David O. McKay.* Salt Lake City: Deseret Book, 1966.

Nibley, Preston. "What of Joseph Smith's Prophecy That the Constitution Would Hang by a Thread." *Church News* (15 Dec 1948) 24.

The Personal Writings of Joseph Smith. Comp. Dean C. Jesse. Salt Lake City: Deseret Book, 1976.

Roberts, B. H. *The Life of John Taylor.* Salt Lake City: Bookcraft, 1963.

―――. *Mormonism: The Relation of the Church to Christian Sects, Origin and History of Mormonism, Doctrines of the Church, Church Organization, Present Status.* Salt Lake City: Deseret News, n.d.

Smith, George Albert. *Conference Report* (Oct 1911) 43-46.

―――. *Conference Report* (Apr 1914) 10-14.

―――. *Conference Report* (Oct 1917) 39-46.

―――. *Conference Report* (Oct 1921) 158-62.

―――. *Conference Report* (Oct 1922) 94-99.

―――. *Conference Report* (Oct 1924) 44-49.

―――. *Conference Report* (Oct 1928) 90-95.

―――. *Conference Report* (Oct 1936) 71-77.

―――. *Conference Report* (Apr 1940) 83-88.

―――. *Conference Report* (Apr 1948) 177-85.

―――. "Dedicatory Prayer . . . Idaho Falls Temple." *Improvement Era* (Oct 1945) 48:562-65.

―――. "Dedicatory Prayer: This Is the Place Monument." *Church News* (2 Aug 1947) 9, 12.

―――. "For Law and Liberty—and Salvation." *Improvement Era* (Nov 1950) 53:869-70.

―――. "From a Prophet to His People." *Improvement Era* (May 1949) 52:266+; also in *Conference Report* (Apr 1949) 165-71.

———. *Improvement Era* (Nov 1945) 48:712+; also in *Conference Report* (Oct 1945) 167-75.

———. "Liberty Under the Constitution." *Improvement Era* (Dec 1950) 53:963-65; also in *Conference Report* (Oct 1950) 4-9.

———. "Lincoln . . . and This Land." *Improvement Era* (Feb 1951) 54:77; also in *Conference Report* (Oct 1922) 94-99.

———. "Obedience to Law." *Improvement Era* (Jul 1949) 52:429, 477.

———. "Our Father's Work." *Improvement Era* (Nov 1949) 52:698+; also in *Conference Report* (Oct 1949) 4-9.

———. "Perpetuating Liberty." *Improvement Era* (Feb 1950) 53:93-94.

———. "Progress of the M.I.A.—Their Slogans." *Improvement Era* (Aug 1924) 27:899-904.

———. *Sharing the Gospel with Others.* Comp. Preston Nibley. Salt Lake City: Deseret Book, 1948.

———. "Welfare Program, A Wonderful Thing." *Improvement Era* (Nov 1949) 52:699; also in *Conference Report* (Oct 1949) 168.

———. "The Work of God." *Improvement Era* (May 1947) 50:266+; also in *Conference Report* (Apr 1947) 160-67.

Smith, Joseph. *Powers and Policy of the Government.* Nauvoo, IL: Taylor, 1844.

Smith, Joseph F. "An Address. The Church of Jesus Christ of Latter-day Saints to the World." *Improvement Era* (May 1907) 10:481-95.

———. "Magazine Slanders Confuted." *Improvement Era* (Jun 1911) 14:719-24.

———. "The Mexican Trouble—Loyalty to the Constitution." *Improvement Era* (Dec 1912) 16:91, 98-102; also in *Conference Report* (Oct 1912) 1-11.

———. "The 'Mormonism' of To-Day." *Arena* (May 1903) 29:449-56.

———. "Thrift and Economy." *Improvement Era* (May 1918) 21:631-37.

Smith, Joseph Fielding. "Blessed Is the Nation Whose God Is the Lord." *Improvement Era* (May 1943) 46:274-75, 312-13; also in *Conference Report* (Apr 1943) 11-16.

———. *Church History and Modern Revelation*. 2 vols. Salt Lake City: Deseret Book, 1953.

———. *Conference Report* (Apr 1935) 96-100.

———. *Doctrines of Salvation*. Comp. Bruce R. McConkie. 3 vols. Salt Lake City: Bookcraft, 1954-56.

———. "Founded in the Wisdom of God." *Improvement Era* (May 1950) 53:370+; also in *Conference Report* (Apr 1950) 153-59.

———. *The Progress of Man*. Salt Lake City: Genealogical Society of Utah, 1936.

———. *Seek Ye Earnestly*. Salt Lake City: Deseret Book, 1970.

———. *The Signs of the Times*. Independence, MO: Press of Zion's Printing and Publishing, 1947.

———. *Take Heed to Yourselves!* Salt Lake City: Deseret Book, 1966.

Smith, Joseph Fielding, Jr., and John J. Stewart. *The Life of Joseph Fielding Smith, Tenth President of The Church of Jesus Christ of Latter-day Saints*. Salt Lake City: Deseret Book, 1972.

Snow, Eliza R. "Eliza R. Snow." *Deseret News Weekly* (19 Jan 1870) 556-57.

Snow, Lorenzo. "Boys Are Welcomed Home By Patriotic Multitude." *Salt Lake Herald* (20 Aug 1899) 1.

———. "Mighty Demonstration of Joy and Rejoicing Greet the Heroes Everywhere." *Deseret Evening News* (19 Aug 1899) 1; also in *Deseret Semi-Weekly News* (22 Aug 1899) 1.

Taylor, John. *An Address to the Members of the Church of Jesus Christ of Latter-day Saints*. N.p.: n.p., 1882.

———. *Conference Report* (Apr 1880) 99-103.

———. *The Gospel Kingdom.* Comp. G. Homer Durham. Salt Lake City: Bookcraft, 1964.

———. "Introductory Address." *Mormon* (17 Feb 1855) 2.

———. *A Short Account of the Murders, Roberies, . . .* Martin Mormon Pamphlet Reprint Series, No. 23. Provo, UT: Martin, n.d.

Taylor, Samuel W., and Raymond W. Taylor. *The John Taylor Papers: Records of the Last Utah Pioneer.* 2 vols. Redwood City, CA: Taylor, 1984-85.

The Teachings of Ezra Taft Benson. Salt Lake City: Bookcraft, 1988.

The Teachings of Spencer W. Kimball. Ed. Edward L. Kimball. Salt Lake City: Bookcraft, 1982.

Teachings of the Prophet Joseph Smith. Comp. Joseph Fielding Smith. Salt Lake City: Deseret Book, 1976.

Thompson, Dennis L. "The Latter-day Saint Concept of an Inspired Constitution of the United States." Master's thesis. Tempe, AZ: Arizona State Univ, 1961.

Tyler, Daniel. *The Mormon Battalion.* Glorieta, NM: Rio Grande, 1881.

Vetterli, Richard. *Mormonism, Americanism, and Politics.* Salt Lake City: Ensign, 1961.

Wilford Woodruff's Journal. Ed. Scott G. Kenney. 9 vols. Midvale, UT: Signature, 1983-85.

Woodruff, Wilford. *Conference Report* (Apr 1898) 88-90.

———. "Discourse by President Wilford Woodruff." *Millennial Star* (23 Dec 1889) 51:801-02.

———. *Inaugural Address.* Salt Lake City: Barrett, 1896.

———. "Official Declaration." *Millennial Star* (20 Jan 1890) 52:33-35.

———. *Prayer Offered at the Dedication of the Temple of the Lord.* Salt Lake City: n.p., 1893.

———. "President Woodruff States the Facts." *Millennial Star* (16 Dec 1889) 51:788-89.

———. "Remarks." *Deseret News* (7 Oct 1857) 246.

The Words of Joseph Smith. Comp. and ed. Andrew F. Ehat and Lyndon W. Cook. Salt Lake City: Bookcraft, 1980.

Young, Brigham. "History of Brigham Young." *Millennial Star* (21 May 1864) 26:326-29.

———. "Oration by His Excellency Governor Young." *Deseret News* (9 Jul 1856) 4.

Subject Index

The subject and scripture indexes are referenced to chapter and quotation numbers rather than to page numbers. Quotations have been numbered consecutively within each chapter, and inclusive chapter and quotation numbers have been provided at the top of each page to help the reader locate specific quotations quickly. The index does not contain references to the Introduction or to the introductions for the chapters.

Oregon, 3.20

Organic act, 3.69

Orphans, 1.14, 2.37

—P—

Parents, 3.52, 7.13, 9.13, 9.28, 13.55
See also Fathers; Mothers

Passions, 2.33, 3.56

Patriotism, 1.14, 3.5, 3.46, 3.49, 3.80,
4.17, 11.6, 13.43, 13.99

Patriots, 1.14, 3.4, 3.7, 3.11, 3.25, 3.54,
3.61, 4.20, 7.13, 7.15, 9.41, 10.12,
13.46, 13.69, 13.122
See also Fathers of liberty; Fathers of
the nation; Forefathers; Founding
Fathers; Framers of the Constitution

Peace, 1.6, 1.24, 1.34, 1.39, 2.14, 3.26,
8.2, 8.6, 8.12, 8.20, 8.26, 11.19,
13.25, 13.91

Persecution, 1.19, 1.22, 1.38, 1.44, 1.47,
2.7, 2.14, 3.15, 3.22, 3.54, 4.8, 4.18,
13.9. 13.63

Pessimism, 11.17

Peter, 11.6

Petition for grievances, 13.38

Philosophies, false, 7.17, 11.13

Pilgrims, 8.15, 8.28, 12.5

Pioneer heritage, 11.12

Pioneers, 9.18, 11.4, 11.5, 11.19

Pledge of allegiance, 13.50

Plunder, 1.23

Police, 9.34

Politicians, 9.13, 9.44, 13.54, 13.78
See also Statesmen

Polygamy, 3.81, 6.3
See also Marriage, plural

Prayer, 1.14, 1.34, 2.40, 3.60, 6.5, 7.18,
8.18, 9.34, 9.37, 9.42, 13.1, 13.8,
13.14, 13.33, 13.34, 13.91
for government leaders, 1.5, 2.11, 3.41,
4.16, 4.20, 8.4, 8.6, 8.7, 8.16, 8.17,
8.22, 9.18, 9.25, 9.34
Intercessory, 9.24

Premortal life, 13.115

President of the United States, 1.30, 1.32,
1.35, 2.11, 3.8, 3.20, 3.41, 3.56,
4.15, 4.20, 8.7, 8.16, 8.17, 9.25,
10.3, 13.9, 13.25, 13.56, 13.111
cabinet of, 2.30, 4.20, 9.25
term of office, 2.9, 2.10, 2.11, 2.30
See also Executive branch

Press (media), 1.3, 13.57
freedom of, 13.38

Priestcraft, 1.9

Priesthood, 8.8, 9.19, 11.10, 13.10, 13.22,
13.63, 13.71, 13.91
restoration of, 13.98
See also Elders of Israel

Printing, 1.3, 10.13

Prison, 9.34

Prohibition law, 7.8

Promptings, 13.46
See also Inspiration

Property rights, 1.15, 9.10, 9.35, 13.38,
13.74

Prophecies, 1.23, 3.43, 3.44, 3.63, 3.79,
3.80, 7.16, 10.6, 10.12, 11.8, 11.14,
13.2, 13.17, 13.34, 13.71, 13.72,
13.121
See also Constitution, destruction of;
Constitution, on brink of ruin;
Constitution, overthrow of;
Constitution, saving; Elders of Israel; "Hanging by a thread"

Prophets, 2.10, 4.17, 7.2, 12.3, 13.11,
13.27, 13.46, 13.60, 13.71, 13.72,
13.82, 13.88, 13.110

*Prophets, Principles and National Sur-
vival* (book), 13.60

Prosperity, 3.18

Protection, guaranteed by the Constitution
and laws, 1.24, 1.30, 1.32

Protestant revolution, 10.5

Public office, 2.29, 13.16, 13.27
See also Elections; Politicians; names
of specific offices

Punishment, 1.30, 2.17, 8.12

Purity, 3.52, 3.60

—R—

Radio, 13.57

Scripture Index

The subject and scripture indexes are referenced to chapter and quotation numbers rather than to page numbers. Quotations have been numbered consecutively within each chapter, and inclusive chapter and quotation numbers have been provided at the top of each page to help the reader locate specific quotations quickly. The index does not contain references to the Introduction or to the introductions for the chapters.

OLD TESTAMENT

Exodus		**Isaiah**	
20:1-6	6.6	2:3	11.7, 11.8, 13.110
		60:17	2.30
Proverbs			
14:34	13.104	**Daniel**	
		2:34	13.100

NEW TESTAMENT

John		**Ephesians**	
8:32	9.40	6:16-17	11.19

BOOK OF MORMON

1 Nephi		**3 Nephi**	
13:16-19	13.100	21:4	13.119, 3.124
14:6	13.23	21:11, 14, 21	13.23
22	13.28		
		Ether	
		2:10	13.122
2 Nephi		2:12	13.122
1:5	9.25, 13.124	8:18-25	13.51
1:7	13.124	13:3	13.89
4:34	13.79		
Alma			
62:4	13.72		

DOCTRINE AND COVENANTS

58:21	1.1, 3.20, 3.70, 8.5	98:4-7	3.70
		98:5-6	1.2
58:26	13.63	98:5-8	13.100
58:27	13.63	98:5-10	13.22
84:114, 115, 117	13.23	98:6-7	10.17
		98:7	13.79
98:4-6	12.1	98:8-11	13.116

PEARL OF GREAT PRICE